D1427875

INSIDE

Ireland's Women's Prisons, Past and Present

CHRISTINA M. QUINLAN
Dublin City University

IRISH ACADEMIC PRESS
DUBLIN • PORTLAND, OR

First published in 2011 by Irish Academic Press

2 Brookside,
Dundrum Road,
Dublin 14, Ireland

920 NE 58th Avenue, Suite 300
Portland, Oregon,
97213-3786, USA

www.iap.ie

British Library Cataloguing in Publication Data
An entry can be found on request

ISBN 978 0 7165 3046 6 (cloth)
ISBN 978 0 7165 3047 3 (paper)

Library of Congress Cataloging-in-Publication Data
An entry can be found on request

Printed by Good News Digital Books, Ongar, Essex

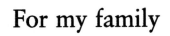

Contents

List of Tables, Figures and Photographs

Preface and Acknowledgements

This book emerged from a research project that in turn emerged from my voluntary work with women in prison in Mountjoy Prison. I started visiting the women's prison in 1998, the year before the Dóchas Centre opened. The Dóchas Centre is the women's prison at Mountjoy Prison in Dublin. It has from the start been a unique project, a progressive purpose-built women's prison. I didn't know when I started visiting the women's prison that the visits would grow into one of the major projects of my life. I didn't have any sense when I started out on the journey of where the journey would lead. I certainly never imagined that it would lead me to this point.

I know very many interesting women, and I met many of them in prison. Women who have experienced imprisonment in Ireland are a select group. They know, and only they know, what it is to be prisoner, a female prisoner, in the Irish penal system. These women are to be respected for dealing as they do with the difficult circumstances of their lives. They are to be admired for every day squaring up to the challenges that beset them. They have given me an unexpected, somewhat strange, and entirely fascinating experience. They have given me a substantial and very unique insight into women's experiences of imprisonment in Ireland. I had no sense when I started this project of the ways in which I would grow, change and develop through the simple work of gathering this story together and writing it down. The story of women's experiences of prison in Ireland is one that has been waiting a long time to be told. I am very glad that it has fallen to me to be the story-teller.

I'm grateful to so many people for helping me with this book. I am particularly grateful to the women imprisoned in Ireland who befriended me, helped me and encouraged me. I am grateful to John Lonergan, who retired from his position as governor of Mountjoy Prison in 2010, for all the help, support and encouragement he has given me; and likewise to Sean Aylward, secretary general of the Department of Justice and Law Reform. I would like to thank Kathleen McMahon, who resigned in 2010 from her position as governor of the Dóchas Centre, for making me welcome in the women's prison when it was a wing of St Patrick's Institution, and for making me part of the new women's prison, the Dóchas Centre. I remember with gratitude Governor Pat Laffan of Limerick Prison and the support he showed me, and am also grateful to Governor Éamon Mullane of Limerick Prison for all his help. I would particularly like to thank Dr Pat O'Byrne of DCU for being a volunteer befriender in the Dóchas Centre with me. I am grateful to all of the prison volunteers and befrienders who encouraged me and helped me in my engagement with the women's prison. I am grateful to all the staff of all of the prisons who helped me.

I am indebted to the School of Communications, DCU, for providing me with a grant which allowed me to undertake the research, and I would like to thank Dr Barbara O'Connor, Dr Pat Brereton and Professor Farrel Corcoran for all the valuable feedback they gave me. I am also grateful to Professor Pat Carlen, Senator Ivana Bacik (Reid Professor of Criminal Law, Criminology and Penology at Trinity College Dublin) and Professor Maria Luddy for all their time and the helpful feedback regarding my work. I am also grateful to Lisa Hyde of Irish Academic Press, who gave me tremendous support and encouragement.

I would like to express thanks also to my family and friends for their interest in this project, for allowing me the space to complete it, and for engaging me in their activities when and where they could.

My hope for this book is that it renders visible the experiences of women imprisoned in Ireland.

Foreword

This publication is the first substantial study of women's experiences of imprisonment in Ireland and a significant contribution to our story as a nation. It results from an ethnographic study carried out over a number of years and sheds light on women's experiences of imprisonment over the past 200 years.

The book explains how, in general terms, women imprisoned in Ireland are today, as they were historically, the most marginalised women in society. They are frequently the poorest women, from the poorest communities; addicted to drugs and/or alcohol, they are often pawns in the global trade of drug trafficking. Women currently imprisoned in Ireland tend to come and go regularly from prison. Many of them lead such marginalised lives that they view the women's prison as a refuge and they regularly seek shelter there. It is an extraordinary fact that today in Ireland, as it was in famine times, the poorest women in our society shelter in our prisons.

Our history we have to live with and learn from – but our present and future we can shape and this book provides accurate information to help us address what is an uncomfortable aspect of our society. To this end, I believe we can, and must, all learn lessons from the research detailed in this book. There are two specific aspects of the research that I found of particular interest – accommodation provided and media coverage.

The two women's prisons currently in operation in Ireland are described in detail; they are the Dóchas Centre, the women's prison within the Mountjoy Prison complex in Dublin, which has an official capacity for 105 women, and Limerick Prison with an official capacity for 20 women. The different regimes operating in the two women's prisons are very evident – Limerick Prison, the oldest operating prison in the country, has a traditional lock-up regime whereas the Dóchas Centre is the first purpose-built women's prison to be built in Ireland since the original female prison at Mountjoy Prison which opened in 1858. We must also remember and keep front-of-mind that women prisoners are held in the Central Mental Hospital in Dublin, the state's only forensic psychiatric hospital, in practice no more than three women at a time.

The model prison that is the Dóchas Centre emerged from years of negotiation, reflection and planning. It is interesting to note that two female Ministers for Justice contributed to the development of the prison, Nora Owen and Máire Geoghgan-Quinn; John Lonergan, the former Governor of Mountjoy Prison championed it and Kathleen McMahon, the first female prison Governor in Ireland managed it.

I first heard of how the Dóchas Centre was operating when a close friend told me of her own experiences of volunteering there, shortly after its official opening in 1999. They were the early days of what was a new and experimental way of dealing with the very difficult issue of women in prisons. It was well funded and there was a significant focus on providing suitable and life-enhancing activities – life-enhancing for the individual, their families and for the community. I recall my friend telling me how she spent 3 hours helping to look after a baby while the mother went to a cookery class, and returned with a sense of pride and delight. This accords more with what would be regarded, in progressive circles and countries such as Sweden, as the ideal of female imprisonment to be 'correctional' care as against what has been the traditional approach adopted of 'containment'. As President, I visited Mountjoy Prison on several occasions and saw the containment approach then in operation as the women were accommodated within the old women's prison; as High Commissioner for Human Rights, I visited the Dóchas Centre and was delighted to see a much better practice in operation.

The author, Christina Quinlan, outlines her concern that there are now plans to close the Dóchas Centre, one of the newest prisons in the country and a purpose built female prison. Kathleen McMahon resigned from her position as Governor in 2010. She resigned in protest at what she described as the undermining of the progressive regime there which was in part being accomplished she said by chronic overcrowding in the prison.

The Dóchas Centre has been an innovation in female imprisonment winning international recognition as a new standard in female imprisonment. It is an unexpected field in which Ireland has shown leadership responding to the United Nations long-standing concern for the humanization of criminal justice and the protection of human rights. I hope that this research will be widely read and assimilated by penal policy makers.

As I mentioned the media analysis conducted on the representations of the women's prisons and women prisoners in the press in Ireland is another very interesting aspect of the book. This analysis shows that although relatively substantial numbers of women are imprisoned every year in Ireland, around 1,000 women annually when the study was conducted, the press reports focus mainly on those women who commit the most substantial crimes, the most sensational crimes. The vast majority of women imprisoned in Ireland are imprisoned only for very short periods of time, a couple of weeks, a couple of days or even a couple of hours, for very minor crimes. But reporting of the sensational cases produces, as the book explains, a public perception of women in prison in Ireland that is completely at odds with reality. There is a suggestion in the book that it is the impact on penal policy makers of these media representations of Ireland's imprisoned women that may be largely responsible for the levels of security and control exercised in women's prison. In other words, the secure prison facilities provided for women in prison in Ireland are in part a product of media discourses on Ireland's criminal women.

As this book explains, in comparisons with the male prison population, generally large and stable in the sense that it is a relatively big population and they are serving relatively long sentences, the female prison population, generally small and unstable, is often constructed as more difficult, more marginalised, more troubled. This is a critical issue for women in prison in Ireland. It is a critical issue for them in terms of how they are represented and perceived and it is a critical issue for them in terms of how the women's prisons are managed.

The book is both sociological and criminological in its approach. It is a publication that is not always a comfortable read but it is an essential one for all involved and interested in our prison system – and what it says about us as a society. I would like to congratulate all involved in its publication and in particular Christina Quinlan.

Mary Robinson
Former President of Ireland and
President of the Mary Robinson Foundation
- Climate Justice
September 2010

Chapter One

Women in Prison in Ireland

One of the distinguishing features of women's imprisonment in Ireland currently, and historically, is the imprisonment of poor, marginalised women for crimes related to addictions. For example, on 17 June 2010, the following headline appeared in *The Irish Times*: 'Mentally ill woman forcibly ejected from prison against her will'. The story, by journalist Conor Lally, was relayed throughout that day in news bulletins on TV and radio.[1] It was the story of a woman, a Dubliner in her mid-20s, who was given early release from prison just a few weeks into a six-month sentence in the Dóchas Centre, the women's prison in the Mountjoy Prison complex in Dublin. When she refused to leave the prison, because she had no place to go, she was forcibly evicted by staff and left on the pavement outside. The woman, described in the newspaper article as homeless and mentally ill, had spent some of her childhood in care. She had a drug addiction and most of her criminal convictions related to crimes committed to support her drug habit. When left on the pavement outside the prison, she tried to scale the gates in order to get back inside. She was subsequently arrested for attempting to break into the prison and spent the night in a police station. The next day she was remanded back in custody in the Dóchas Centre. As this book testifies, this story provides a good example of the biographies of women imprisoned in Ireland, both currently and historically, and in its way provides a good example of the manner in which some women experience prison in Ireland.

This book explores the experiences of women imprisoned in Ireland over the past two hundred years; it follows the work of those who have studied women's experiences of imprisonment, a few in Ireland, many internationally. Their accounts have established that women generally commit little crime in society; that women constitute a minority of prison populations; that it is generally poverty that drives women into criminal activity and into prison; and that women's experiences of criminal justice and imprisonment are gendered. This study is sociological as well as criminological, exploring the phenomenon of identity and the manner in which identity is constructed. A key concern is the manner in which the individual's sense of self, his or her subjectivity, is constructed. In the contemporary debate as to whether women prisoners' identities are completely subjugated by prison or whether those prisoners are able to resist identity subjugation, analyses of the present-day experiences of women prisoners in Ireland suggests that, although subjugated as *prisoners*, they have developed ways to resist subjugation as *women*.

In recent years, studies of women in prison have begun to focus on the identities and subjectivities of imprisoned women. This book is a critical ethnography of women in prison in Ireland; it is an exploration of the manner in which the identities and subjectivities of Ireland's imprisoned women are discursively constructed and represented. Discourse is constitutive; it has the power to construct, to bring into being different realities. This study is concerned with analysing the manner in which, within sociocultural practice, female prisoner subjects are discursively positioned, how within different discourses their identities are constructed and represented. Fundamentally, the book is concerned with the way in which the self, the individual's sense of self, his or her subjectivity, is constructed. Subjectivities are not constructed in isolation but in relation to historical experience and the social and spatial as inhabited by the individual. Identities are constructed by means of a conjoining of the historical, the social and the spatial. The individual, within this triple dialectic, constructs her subjectivity. The discourses considered here are those of history, the media, criminal and penal institutions and penal experts. The book examines how, within these discourses, imprisoned women are subject positioned. Discourse means a broad constitutive system of meaning, or different ways of structuring areas of knowledge and social practice. This study considers how, through this discursive positioning of the female prisoner subject, social relations of power are reproduced.

Prisoners are defined by the fact that they are imprisoned; they inhabit or occupy prison space. It is their occupation of that space that, above all, identifies the women of this book as prisoners. The power to confer criminal identity rests with the courts. The individual who has been identified as criminal by the criminal justice system may be punished by the state with a prison sentence. While the criminal justice system confers criminal identity, it is the experience of imprisonment that confers prisoner identity. Thus, it is their occupation of prison space that produces female prisoners, that distinguishes the women featured in this study as prisoners. This book examines the discourses produced by the space that is Irish female prison space, and the manner in which that space impacts on the discursive production of the identities of Ireland's imprisoned women. In Ireland, women are currently imprisoned in one of three places. Most inhabit the Dóchas Centre, a purpose-built female prison with an official capacity for eighty-five women which opened in 1999 at a cost of £13 million (€16.5 million) and is situated within the Mountjoy Prison complex in Dublin. In addition, Limerick Prison, a male prison and the oldest prison in the country, currently has a capacity for twenty women. Women from the prison system are also held, no more than three at a time, in the Central Mental Hospital (CMH) in Dublin, the state's only forensic psychiatric facility.

The current profile of women in prison in Ireland is radically different from that of their male counterparts. Where there are about 3,750 men serving time in Irish prisons, many of them for serious offences, there are about 130 women, most imprisoned for nuisance-type offences. The population of the women's prisons is small and unstable, in the sense that the women generally come and go quickly from prison, for the most part serving very short sentences. In comparison with the male prison population, which is generally large and stable in the sense that they are serving relatively long sentences, the female prison population, generally small and unstable, is often constructed as more difficult, more marginalised, more troubled. This is a critical issue for women in prison in Ireland, in terms of how they are represented and perceived.

Issues concerning those feminist writers who study the female experience of the law and imprisonment are: the gendered nature of women's criminality and women's experiences in prison; the 'forgottenness' of female offending and women's imprisonment; and the vulnerabilities of women in prison. Carol Smart in 1976, pioneering these lines of enquiry, put forward a feminist analysis of female crime and criminality which highlighted the failure of earlier works on female criminality and female deviance to (a) consider the separate social worlds of men and women, (b) ask why female criminality differs from male criminality, and (c) ask why women are treated differently by criminal justice and penal systems.[2] Pat Carlen, who has written extensively on women in prison, has examined the relationship between poverty and crime, the differential treatment of women by penal systems, the invisibility of women prisoners, and the absence of coherent effective policies on women in the criminal justice and penal systems. This book focuses on profiling the women imprisoned in Ireland, on documenting their experiences of imprisonment, and on examining the manner in which their identities are shaped by those experiences.

Implicit in the concept of identity are issues of power and control – the degree of control we have over who we are and who we might become, and the power we have in shaping the self. Carlen and Worrall question the extent to which an individual is free to shape her own actions, identity and consciousness independently of the economic, ideological and political circumstances in which she finds herself.[3] In her work, Carlen, highlighting as mythical the benign prison and arguing for women's prisons to be 'otherwise and womanwise', reveals as middle-class ideologies the concepts of responsibility and accountability with which women in prison are charged while challenging the utility and validity of notions of agency and resistance among imprisoned women.[4] Bosworth's study of agency and power in women's prisons focuses on the effects of femininity on women in prison, on how women as agents negotiate power within prison, on how women negotiate the various discourses of prison and through these negotiations construct their identities.[5] Bosworth highlights the fact that few studies of prison have considered questions of identity or subjectivity, our sense of ourselves, or the way in which a person's gender, race or class influences their experience and understanding of prison and imprisonment. According to Bosworth, power in prison is constantly negotiated on the level of identity. She grounds her analysis in imprisoned women's own words and experiences in order to elaborate our understanding of imprisoned women's sense of themselves and their imprisonment. Worrall, commenting on the absence of self-identity among the imprisoned women she studied, said that the women appeared to be defined – and to define themselves – in relation to other people and how they believed other people viewed them.[6] Her exploration of the women's identities is grounded in the discourses defining their prison experiences and in their own responses to those discourses.

Very little has been published to date on the experiences of women imprisoned in Ireland. This book is an attempt to fill that gap. It has been written in order to record women's experiences of imprisonment in Ireland, in the same way that such experiences have been documented internationally.

Nell McCafferty, Ursula Barry, Alpha Connelly, Ciarán McCullagh, Ivana Bacik and Michael O'Connell have all written about the differential nature of female criminality in Ireland, the differential treatment of women before the courts in Ireland, and the correlation in Ireland between poverty and the crimes of women. In addition, several historians have documented Irish experiences of imprisonment.[7] Tim Carey published a book on Mountjoy Prison and its history with a couple of pages devoted to female prisoners and their experiences.[8] Sinead McCoole published two histories of Irish female revolutionaries and their experiences of Kilmainham Gaol.[9] There are occasional references to the experiences of imprisoned women in Pat Cooke's *History of Kilmainham Gaol*.[10] There is a chapter in Maria Luddy's book *Women and Philanthropy in Nineteenth-Century Ireland* dedicated to women in prison in Ireland,[11] and in 2001, Geraldine Curtin published her book on the women of Galway Gaol.[12]

Paul O'Mahony has written extensively about male prisoners and Irish prisons, and a four-page section of one of his books[13] is dedicated to Monaghan's work on women in prison in Ireland.[14] At the time of Monaghan's study (1989), there were forty-seven women in prison in Ireland; all were held in Mountjoy Prison as Limerick Prison was temporarily closed. Monaghan found that, among the sample chosen, the women were overwhelmingly from lower socio-economic backgrounds, the average age was twenty-six, the average number of convictions was eight, and their sentences were generally short. Some 71 per cent had been imprisoned for theft, with one woman serving a life sentence for murder. Almost three quarters had, at some stage, received psychiatric care, 53 per cent had abused illicit drugs, and over two-thirds had self-injured. The women had low self-esteem, describing themselves as unsure, unattractive, nervous, changeable and unimportant. O'Mahony, in his book, compares Monaghan's demographic, crimogenic and health data from her sample of thirty-four women with his own 1986 survey of 110 male prisoners, one-fifth of the male prisoner population of Mountjoy Prison at that time, when nationally there were almost 2,000 men in prison. In this unbalanced comparison, he found that many more female prisoners than male prisoners were from the lowest socio-economic grouping, that women prisoners exhibited most of the personal problems seen in the male prisoner sample, including 'hard drug use, suicidal behaviour and psychiatric caseness', but to a more serious extent.[15] He concluded that the concentration of disadvantage was more marked for the women than the men. This was because, in Ireland, very few women go to prison; those who do are generally among the poorest, the most disadvantaged, in Irish society.

Two healthcare reports have been published, one of which focused on Ireland's female prison population. Carmody and McEvoy's *Study of Irish Female Prisons* again found women in prison to be a very specific group: more likely to be poor, to be mothers and to have a family network, to have a history of psychiatric treatments, to have abused drugs from a young age and to be resistant to drug treatment; and less likely to be in a relationship.[16] The report attributed imprisoned women's tendency in prison to distress and self-injury to the exchange, through imprisonment, of the environment of the family home network for that of prison and prison cells. The second report was undertaken by the Centre for Health Promotion studies at the National University of Ireland (NUI) Galway. Although fifty-nine women prisoners (75 per cent of the female prison population at that time when women constituted 2 per cent of the Irish prison population) participated in the study, the report made no separate recommendations for the female prison population.[17] Again, in comparisons with the male prisoner population throughout the report, as with O'Mahony's comparison above, female prisoners were presented as more seriously marginalised, more seriously ill, and more seriously troubled.

Three PhDs have been completed dealing with women in prison in Ireland. In 1985 Francesca Lundström-Roche compared the 'ideal' and the 'real' of the prison experiences of women in prison in Ireland with the experiences of their Swedish counterparts.[18] She found Sweden's 'ideal' of female imprisonment to be 'correctional care', while Ireland's was 'containment'. Lundström-Roche studied the experiences of the prisoners and also those working in women's prisons, in both Sweden and Ireland. Interviewing sixteen Irish women prisoners and fifteen members of staff, she established a classificatory scheme of three groups among prison staff and three among imprisoned women. The prisoners' groups were: 'Losers', of which there were four among the Irish sample; 'Thieves and Robbers', of which there were eleven; and 'Exploiters', of which there was one. The staff groups were: 'Distanced', 'Undistanced' and 'Mature'. She then used this classificatory scheme to explore the prison experiences in both Sweden and Ireland. In Ireland she found the emphasis to be on security; both staff and women prisoners painted a grim, almost medieval picture of the prisons. The prisons were decaying, were gravely overcrowded and physically discomforting. In one element of the research, Lundström-Roche examined 'The Self'. Labelling this as 'Emotions' for women prisoners and 'The Job' for staff, she attempted, she wrote, to describe their innermost, private feelings and emotions. She describes experiences of infantilisation among the women, feelings of powerlessness, frustration and anger, and incidences of depression. She writes briefly of identity, in terms of loss of identity. This loss, she found, comes about when a woman, on committal to prison, leaves all her personal possessions at the reception area, is stripped of her clothes and jewellery and then dressed in what she terms the sexless, shapeless, uninviting garb of the prison. In terms of the experiences of women in prison in Ireland, Lundström-Roche's research was relatively constrained. Within the two nations studied, she explored the responses of both prison officers and female prisoners to their prison experiences.

In 2001, Celesta McCann James completed her thesis in which she explored the experiences of twenty women in Mountjoy Women's Prison.[19] At the time, the women in Mountjoy were still in the old female prison, a wing of St Patrick's Institution for Young Offenders. McCann James, in work comparable in ways to Bosworth's study of agency and resistance in women's prisons, examined the women's responses to forms of management in the

Irish female prison. She found that the women formed small seg-regated social groups within which they gained 'a sense of belong-ing and a framework by which they can control one another as they compete for limited resources and privileges in Mountjoy'. She found the social structures which control women in Irish society to be mirrored and intensified in the women's prison, and discovered that the women responded to their oppression within prison by organising 'a specific relational environment', the sub-groups. The women were found to align themselves with women they perceived as their peers. McCann James identified groups of 'drug addicts', 'mature women', 'school attenders', 'Travelling women', 'foreign women', 'kitchen crew' and 'loners'. These groups were found in the research to offer the women emotional and social substitutes for family and friends, while providing them with a competitive edge. McCann James also concluded that the prison's regime and management procedures reproduce and intensify women's powerlessness and inequality, while the subgroups further implement control mechanisms which parallel those used to oppress women in Irish society. The research conducted for this book picked up on McCann James's theme of control and responses to control within the Irish female prison. Where McCann James considered the manifestations and effects of oppression on a number of women imprisoned in Mountjoy Women's Prison in 1998, this book is concerned with documenting more broadly, historically and contemporarily women's experi-ences of imprisonment in Ireland.

In 2004, Barbara Mason in her research posited the Dóchas Centre as an experiment in women's imprisonment.[20] The study focused on the manner in which the women imprisoned in the Dóchas Centre coped with their new conditions, and how the prison officers reconciled the conflicting demands of the new regime with their more traditional role of discipline and control. Mason tracked the evolution of the experiment from what she found to be an initial period of 'great turmoil and uncertainty' created by the move, through a gradual period of adjustment, to a state of equilibrium. Following the turmoil, Mason documented the gradual development of the experiment during the 'settling down' period. Overall she concluded that staff and management did strive to meet the ideals as set out in the prison's vision state-ment, and that, despite many obstacles, such as breaches of security and resistance among some members of staff to the new ideals, the prison did eventually settle down into the new regime. These findings, according to Mason, contrasted with the outcomes of many other penal experiments, such as Holloway Prison in London, Cornton Vale in Scotland, and the new women's prisons in Canada.

In 2002, Ivana Bacik's 'Women and the Criminal Justice System' appeared as a chapter in Paul O'Mahony's *Criminal Justice in Ireland*.[21] In this work, Bacik, using annual police reports, demonstrates the low level of female crime in Ireland, particularly violent crime, and highlights, as the exception to this, women's relatively high participation in shoplifting offences. She establishes that women, even when convicted of a crime, are less likely than men to go to prison. She comments on the Dóchas Centre and its new facilities and draws attention to the reservations expressed by the Irish Penal Reform Trust (IPRT) regarding the emphasis on security in that prison. Finally, Bacik highlights as problematic, in terms of our ability in Ireland to address basic questions about women and crime, the lack of empirical research on women offenders here. In response to Bacik, this book provides substantial empirical research on Ireland's imprisoned women. In contrast to Lundström-Roche's thesis, this study is focused entirely on the experiences of women in prison in Ireland while, in comparison to McCann James's and Mason's theses, it explores more broadly the experiences of Ireland's women prisoners.

In relation to the contemporary debate as to whether women prisoners' identities are completely subjugated by the prison or whether those prisoners are able to resist identity subjugation, my thesis is that, although women prisoners are subjugated as *prisoners*, they have developed ways to resist subjugation as *women*. This conclusion is primarily supported by:

- An overall analysis of the two main discourses (social and penological) within which identities of imprisoned women are constituted;
- Literature reviews and empirical research whereby those two main social and penological discourses are shown to draw upon selected historical (e.g. Chapter 2) popular, media and professional representations (e.g. Chapter 3)

which, together, are partly constitutive of the discursive contexts wherein women prisoners in turn constitute their social and prison identities;

- Analysis of the strategies, social and spatial, in which women prisoners engage to protect their pre-prison identities (e.g. Chapters 4 and 6).

This study's appendix contains a synopsis of the research methodology employed in the research. There is an outline of the methods used and the fundamental sociological precepts within which the study is grounded, the critical ethnographic approach undertaken in the research and the feminist epistemological considerations that guide and support it.

The chapters are organised as follows. Chapter 1 contains a brief outline of the research that has been conducted; my own research is situated within that body of knowledge. Chapter 2 features an historical exploration of women's experiences of imprisonment. There is in this chapter an analysis of the historical discourses structuring the experiences and identities of women in prison in Ireland since the nineteenth century. The chapter documents the changes and developments in the Irish female prison over two centuries, while the philosophies and policies of the Irish female prison are considered. The institutions within which women were imprisoned are described, and the women imprisoned, the numbers held, the sentences received and the experiences of imprisonment are detailed. The data analysed is from published and archived memoirs, historiographies, prison records and reports. Chapter 3 presents a contemporary perspective on the women's experiences, featuring an analysis, within contemporary discourses, of the positioning of the women. The discourses considered are those of the media, of experts, and of the two women's prisons themselves. These discourses are examined in relation to the identities they ascribe to imprisoned women, while the manner in which the women are represented in the discourses is considered. The contemporary structures of the women's prisons are explored; the designs and the routines of the prisons are documented, as are the management and staffing, the educational and healthcare provision and the accommodations contained within. The data analysed is from observations, interviews, archives and newspaper accounts. Chapter 4 presents the women's own perspectives. It profiles those women currently imprisoned in Ireland, exploring the numbers held and the offences committed. The chapter documents the ways in which women themselves experience life inside, their engagement with the discourses of the prisons, and their sense of themselves as women and as prisoners. The analysis is primarily of data from interviews conducted with eighty-three of Ireland's imprisoned women. This is supported by analysis of data from observations conducted in the prisons, from documentary and other interview data, and from newspaper reports about the women and the female prisons. In Chapter 5, the scholars' perspectives are presented. Theoretical discourses of female criminality and the female prison are explored, as are the theories of lived space and female space and the theoretical discourses of prison and female prison space. The concern is with examining the manner in which, in the literature, discourses of space and female prison space are seen to shape and engender identities. Chapter 6 presents a photographic narrative of women's presentations of self within Irish prison space, a cultural inventory of Irish female prison space, and an analysis of the women's representations of self within that space. Through these analyses the effect on the women of their positioning in the various discourses explored in the previous chapters is demonstrated. The study is concluded in Chapter 7, which summarises the book and the contribution it makes to understanding women's imprisonment. The meaning, effect and implications of the experiences of Ireland's women prisoners are established. The main conclusions centre on the critical elements of women's experiences of imprisonment in Ireland and the manner in which these experiences shape the women, their identities, their subjectivities and their senses of self.

NOTES

1. C. Lally, 'Mentally ill woman forcibly ejected from prison against her will', *Irish Times* (17 June 2010), p.7.
2. C. Smart, *Women, Crime and Criminology: A Feminist Critique* (London: Routledge & Kegan Paul, 1976).
3. P. Carlen, and A. Worrall, *Gender, Crime and Justice* (Milton Keynes: Open University Press, 1987), p.1.
4. P. Carlen, *Sledgehammer: Women's Imprisonment at the Millennium* (Basingstoke: Palgrave Macmillan, 1998), p.171.
5. M. Bosworth, *Engendering Resistance: Agency and Power in the Women's Prisons* (Aldershot: Ashgate, 1999).
6. A. Worrall, 'Working with Female Offenders: Beyond 'Alternatives to Custody'?',

British Journal of Social Work, 19, 2 (1989), pp.77–93.

7. N. McCafferty, *In the Eyes of the Law* (Dublin: Ward River Press, 1981); U. Barry, *Lifting the Lid: Handbook of Facts and Information on Ireland* (Dublin: Attic Press, 1986); A. Connelly, *Gender and the Law in Ireland* (Dublin: Oak Tree Press, 1993); C. McCullagh, 'Getting the Criminals We Want: The Social Production of the Criminal Population', in P. Clancy, S. Drudy, K. Lynch and L. O'Dowd (eds), *Irish Society: Sociological Perspectives* (Dublin: Institute of Public Administration, 1995), pp.410–31; C. McCullagh, *Crime in Ireland: A Sociological Introduction* (Cork: Cork University Press, 1996); I. Bacik and M. O'Connell, *Crime and Poverty in Ireland* (Dublin: Roundhall, Sweet & Maxwell, 1998).

8. T. Carey, *Mountjoy: The Story of a Prison* (Cork: The Collins Press, 2000), pp.23–5, 137–40.

9. S. McCoole, *Guns and Chiffon* (Dublin: Dúchas, The Heritage Service, 1997); S. McCoole, *No Ordinary Women* (Dublin: O'Brien Press, 2003).

10. P. Cooke, *A History of Kilmainham Gaol* (Dublin: Stationery Office, 1995).

11. M. Luddy, *Women and Philanthropy in Nineteenth-Century Ireland* (Cambridge: Cambridge University Press, 1995), pp.149–75.

12. G. Curtin, *The Women of Galway Gaol* (Galway: Arlen House, 2001).

13. P. O'Mahony, *Crime and Punishment in Ireland* (Dublin: Round Hall Press, 1993), pp.198–203.

14. M. Monaghan, 'A Survey of Women in an Irish Prison', unpublished MPsychSc dissertation, University College Dublin, 1989.

15. The Irish female prison population at the time rarely exceeded forty; see O'Mahony, *Crime and Punishment in Ireland*, p.120.

16. P. Carmody and M. McEvoy, *A Study of Irish Female Prisoners* (Dublin: Stationery Office, 1996).

17. Centre for Health Promotion Studies, National University of Ireland, Galway, *Healthcare Study of the Prisoner Population* (Dublin: Stationery Office, 2000).

18. F. Lundström-Roche, 'The Affective Responses of Women Prisoners to Two Discrepant Penal Systems', *Criminal Justice and Behaviour*, 15, 4 (1989), pp.411–32.

19. C. McCann-James, 'Recycled Women: Oppression and the Social World of Women Prisoners in the Irish Republic', unpublished PhD thesis, National University of Ireland, Galway, 2001.

20. B. Mason, 'Imprisoned Freedom: A Sociological Study of a 21st-Century Prison for Women in Ireland', unpublished PhD thesis, London School of Economics, 2004.

21. I. Bacik, 'Women and the Criminal Justice System', in P. O'Mahony (ed.), *Criminal Justice in Ireland* (Dublin: Institute of Public Administration, 2002), pp.134–54.

Chapter Two

The Historical Perspective

This chapter examines the discourses of women's experiences of imprisonment over the nineteenth and twentieth centuries. It historically grounds the book; it charts the development of the Irish female prison, and it contains an exploration of the discourses describing, detailing and positioning the women over that time. The chapter is structured over two centuries in order to facilitate an exploration of the patterns and the changes, if any. The position of women in Irish society is outlined, and there is a consideration of the women's prisons, the philosophies, governance, structures and management of them, and also of the women imprisoned, the numbers held, the crimes for which they were imprisoned and the sentences imposed on them. The nature of the institutions within which the women were imprisoned is detailed. The women's experiences of those institutions are examined, as is the manner in which the women engaged with those institutions. The data analysed is from published and archived memoirs, historiographies, prison records and reports.

Institutions in our culture have taken the form of workhouses, hospitals, lunatic asylums, orphanages, monasteries, barracks, gaols, reformatory schools, industrial schools and borstals. In Ireland, as well as prisons, there were lock hospitals used to incarcerate women engaged in or accused of being engaged in prostitution, and Magdalen laundries, the carcereal appendage of the convent, used here for over a century to encourage conformation in non-conforming women.

In the last two centuries women convicted of crimes in Ireland were imprisoned in local and county gaols, and between 1718, the year of the Transportation Act, and 1853 they were transported first to America and then, after the American War of Independence, to

Australia and Van Diemen's Land (Tasmania). From the passing of the 1718 act until the outbreak of the American War of Independence, some 13,000 Irish criminals, unwanted at home, were transported to the American colonies as 'indentured servants'.[1] Dobash et al[2] detail how convict women were transported as sexual commodities. Transportation came to an official end in Ireland in 1853, but it ended earlier for women than for men; according to Carpenter,[3] the female convicts who had been transported to Western Australia had been 'so bad' the colony had refused to receive any more. The last ship left Ireland in 1856. In 1853 a new punishment – penal servitude – was instituted; where formerly criminals had been imprisoned for short periods of time, physically or symbolically punished, executed or transported, they were now to be imprisoned for long periods of time.

THE NINETEENTH CENTURY: WOMEN IN IRISH SOCIETY

In the 1800s Ireland was a colony of Great Britain. It was an agricultural country characterised by political unrest. For much of the century, most of the population lived at subsistence level. Throughout the first half the country endured food shortages and famine, the ultimate crisis coming with the Great Famine of 1845–50. The Great Famine had a substantial impact on Irish prisons, leading to an incarceration crisis. Between 1845 and 1849 the prison population rose from 16,696 to 41,989. The famine radically reduced the national population by almost two million. Many died from disease or starvation, while those who could emigrate did so. This population decline through emigration continued up to the end of the nineteenth century and into the twentieth. According to Luddy,[4] between 1851 and 1900, 1,941,618 men and 1,789,133 women emigrated.[5] As the population reduced, the Catholic Church grew in strength and the people, according to Inglis,[6] underwent a devotional revolution. One of the effects of this revolution was the development of a strict and rigidly enforced moral code.

Women in Irish society in the nineteenth century had a very narrow range of roles. Compared to men they lived very restricted lives; women were excluded from politics, while men also dominated the public sphere. Women did not have the right to vote, neither could they stand for election to political positions. Those women who were politically active, as Hayes and Urquhart[7] state, supported a range of single issues, among them equal educational opportunities, land reform, votes for women,[8] and the campaign to repeal the Contagious Diseases Acts. Women joined organisations like temperance societies and rescue missions, providing shelters for women caught up in drunkenness and prostitution. They visited and supported women in prison and provided shelter for them on their release. Philanthropy became a significant occupation for middle-class women in Ireland.[9] Women had few employment opportunities, were unskilled and had to cope with pregnancy and children. Working-class women emigrated from Ireland in large numbers and were employed abroad primarily as domestic servants, while those who stayed in Ireland earned money when and where they could. They worked at respectable occupations, in the home weaving and spinning, in factories and businesses, or working the land for their own and other families. Some women begged, some engaged in huckstering, and more in prostitution.

In her study of prostitution in nineteenth-century Ireland, Luddy[10/11] describes the 'common prostitute' of the 1800s as being poor and uneducated, aged twenty to thirty years. She writes of the casual nature of that occupation, outlining how many women would engage in prostitution as a temporary occupation, abandoning it when they could. She details the number of women arrested for prostitution between 1838 and 1899 in the Dublin metropolitan district: fewer than 3,000 in 1838, almost 5,000 in 1856 (the highest number, due to the effects of the Famine) and less than 500 in 1899. According to McLoughlin,[12] economic factors were, at that time, central to women's sexual expression. Women exchanged sexual favours within marriage for security; they were controlled in their communities by close observation and gossip; some were kept by the men with whom they had affairs and were generally admired for being financially astute. It was lower-class women, most of them pauper women, who engaged in prostitution. Women at the time were believed to have no sexual desire; they were compensated for this by a higher moral nature than men, and were thus responsible for men. Their sexuality was confined to expression within marriage, and sexual failings in women were regarded as more serious than in men.

One effect at that time of the narrowness of opportunity for

women, of the weight of their responsibilities and their consequent vulnerabilities, was their propensity, relative to men, to
seek shelter. Women in the nineteenth century were more likely
than men to avail of state or philanthropic institutional relief, to
shelter in workhouses and charitable homes.[13] Women, according
to McLoughlin,[14] tended to outnumber men by a 3:1 ratio in
workhouses: she details the Irish Poor Relief Act introduced in
1838 which instituted the workhouse as the only relief option for
the destitute. In all, 163 workhouses, 'utilitarian buildings without
comfort and ornamentation' each of which could accommodate
3,000 paupers, were built all over Ireland. The relative propensity
of women to seek shelter evidences their extreme marginality.
McLoughlin writes of the wretched and forsaken women of Dublin,
drifting in and out of the workhouse, of women sheltering in the
workhouse, of the workhouse being used as a family survival
strategy.[15] It is clear that in the nineteenth century in Ireland women
were more vulnerable than men; they had fewer resources and more
responsibilities, responsibilities they could not easily evade. They
had little means through which to provide for themselves and their
dependents. There were a couple of survival strategies available to
them; prostitution was one, escape through drunkenness another.
Many women from time to time, often too weak, too overburdened
or overwhelmed by their circumstances, sought shelter; thousands
of women throughout that century sheltered in prisons.

PRISONS: POLICIES, PHILOSOPHIES AND INSTITUTIONS

Historically, punishment in Ireland, as elsewhere, was a local phenomenon, and until the late 1700s, local bodies called grand
juries ran prisons. The administration of penality centralised
initially in Ireland in 1786 under the auspices of the inspector
general of prisons,[16] who was charged with inspecting all the prisons
in the country. Throughout the nineteenth century the grand
juries presented the country's prisons and the financial accounts of
the prisons to the inspectors general who in turn presented these in
annual reports to parliament. In 1808 the first annual *Inspector
General's Report on the State of the Prisons in Ireland* was presented
to the House of Commons. In 1822 two inspectors general were
appointed and given extra powers, and in 1825 these officials
divided Ireland into three districts for the purposes of prison

inspections: Dublin, North district and South district. In that year the prisons inspected were county gaols, district bridewells, smaller bridewells, manor prisons, general penitentiaries, lunatic asylums and convict prisons. There were sixteen prisons in the Dublin district, sixty-eight in the North district and seventy-one in the South district. The prison visiting circuit was about 3,000 miles.

Responsibility for all prisons and prison expenditure was drawn from the imperial exchequer.[17] In 1850 the Office of the Inspector of Prisons was established. The board of directors of the Irish Convict Prisons was set up in 1854 with Sir Walter Crofton, the prison reformer, as the first chair.[18] Under the General Prisons (Ireland) Act of 1877 the General Prisons Board was instituted.[19] It came into being in 1878 and was charged with the management of Ireland's convict and local prisons.

In the nineteenth century penal punishment was built on moral grounds and shaped by three fundamental changes: the increasing centralisation of prisons, the abolishment of transportation to the penal colonies in 1853, and the rehabilitative revolution in penality, the emerging philosophical ideas about the purposes of punishment propounded by reformers and Utilitarians, among them Jeremy Bentham, Elizabeth Fry, Sir Walter Crofton and Mary Carpenter. Prisoners were sentenced to prolonged periods of imprisonment during which they were to be encouraged to reflect on the errors of their ways, and they were to be brought to correction through admonishment, reflection and example. Imprisonment was to provide for the reformation and rehabilitation of criminals; it was designed to discipline them to work and industry. It was to be experienced as a punishment and was to function as a deterrent. While there is evidence in the reports of the inspectors general of an acknowledgement of the impact of prevailing social conditions on the circumstances of individual lives, persons were ultimately deemed to be responsible for themselves, their actions and their circumstances. Structural causes of widespread poverty in Ireland were overlooked. Frequently, behaviours engaged in for the purposes of survival were constructed as criminal, and criminalised individuals were generally imprisoned. Criminalised individuals could, it was believed, be restored to society through discipline and control. In the time spent in detention the individual was to be reformed and restored to society a functioning useful member.

For decades penal policy in Ireland was guided by the reports of the inspectors general, and these reports presented parliament with detailed financial accounts that were accompanied by very few statistics or details of those imprisoned. This indicates that the finances of the institutions were more important than the numbers, gender and/or experiences of those incarcerated. Throughout the nineteenth century, as detailed in the inspectors general reports,[20] thousands were committed to prison annually: in 1832, 16,056; in 1850, when the prisons were experiencing the worst effects of the Great Famine, 115,871 were imprisoned. In their report of 1847 the inspectors general wrote that 'shoals of vagrants' were drifting into prison from what were officially known at the time as 'pauperised districts'. They wrote that many, represented as criminals, engaged with criminality solely to secure the shelter of the prison. The gaols were 'crowded with multitudes' and 'classification was impossible'. Illustrating the manner in which the poor and destitute engaged with penal institutions, they wrote:[21]

> The calamitous visitation of the last few years, affecting the most opulent and the humblest poor alike, suspending employment and staying the hand of charity, has sorely tried the integrity of our people. Larcenies have multiplied, because ordinarily men will steal food rather than die. Many have notoriously appropriated articles of trifling value that they might obtain the shelter of a prison under the guise of commitment for a criminal offence.

Many of those sheltering in workhouses endeavoured to earn themselves a prison sentence. The inspectors general wrote: 'The pressure is exacerbated by paupers being sent to the prisons from workhouses for offences committed for the express purpose of getting themselves removed to a place where they will be better fed.' Prisoners were apparently better fed than paupers. By 1849 the inspectors general had remedied this situation by preparing a new 'lower scale' diet for general use in prisons, having established 'with the different medical officers' that 'no injury to the health of the prisoners' would result from the alteration.

All prisoners were classified into four broad categories: debtors, drunkards, vagrants and felons. Those classified as vagrants and drunkards were imprisoned regularly and for short periods of time, generally twenty-four or forty-eight hours. Throughout the nineteenth century individuals charged with vagrancy, begging and drunkenness were imprisoned in very large numbers; indeed, about half of all of those incarcerated every year were held for drunkenness. For example, in 1843 there were 18,848 criminal convicts, and 20,462 committals for drunkenness.[22] The gendered and class structure of that society, and of the programme of penal reform and reformation, is evident throughout the reports of the inspectors general, which document the zeal and activity of the upper and middle classes, 'the county men of Ireland' and 'the Protestant Ladies', in superintending the nation's prisons and prisoners. Those imprisoned were 'deemed to belong to a class and caste derived through hereditary and often progressive criminality'; among them there were said to be 'two great classes; those who were born into crime and those who have early fallen into wickedness and have been prematurely hardened'.[23]

The first annual *Inspector General's Report on the State of Irish Prisons, 1808* discussed the establishment of prisons, bridewells, penitentiaries and houses of correction throughout Ireland, in which 'the plan of reformation by means of labour combined with suitable discipline shall be effectively carried into execution'. The report noted 'the melancholy state of mind of prisoners', 'the disgusting state of the accommodation' and the 'nearly naked, squalid, sickly, half fed' appearance of the prisoners. It pointed to the tedium of imprisonment, the torpid idleness to which most prisoners were reduced. Change came relatively quickly, as a result of the work of prison reformers as well as the effects of the inspections of the prisons and the comments and recommendations of the inspectors. By 1824 the interior management of prisons was said to have greatly improved. In the annual report, a 'very striking change' was noted to have taken place; this was evident in the cleanliness of the yards, day rooms and cells, and in the comparative efficiency and zeal of the officers. By 1825 the interior management of the county gaols was reported to have undergone a very decided change for the better; 'many irregular and even immoral practices' were said to have been corrected with the 'improved character of the officers', and the establishment of schools, schoolmasters in male prisons and school matrons in female prisons. Frequently the matron of the prison assumed the role of school matron with her other duties.

In the 1825 report the inspectors general discussed the role and status of matrons in the women's prisons, highlighting the responsibilities accorded women in those roles and revealing the injustices and inequalities afforded them in terms of recognition, status and payment. 'We cannot but observe that the salaries granted to matrons are too low. The matron of a county gaol is in fact governess to the female prison, turnkey thereto, work mistress and school mistress, thus comprehending in her duties those which devolve upon four officers at least upon the male side of the prison.' In the same report, the inspectors general were fully supportive of the penitentiary system[24] with its panoptic plan and means of classification, but were critical of what they described as the focus of the 'friends of prison discipline' on the 'architectural advantages of prison' if and where the management of prisons, the internal management of the penitentiaries, was committed to the care of those 'unsuitable, unqualified or indisposed to give effect to the improved system'. The inspectors general were not always entirely supportive of the developments in penality. In 1852 they noted an absence of deterrents in the penal system, writing that there were no discomforts, no stigmas affixed through imprisonment. There was in the report a pondering of the difference between the experience of the workhouse and the factory with that of gaols. The gaols were said to be well lighted, warm and ventilated; clothing, bedding and food of the best quality were provided. Medical attendance was at hand for the most trifling of dispositions and a proportion of money earned was set aside for the prisoner until release. The industrial, they said, was being confounded with the punitive.

As the nineteenth century progressed and the work of penal reformers began to take effect, Ireland came to be regarded as having a model prison system; it was known as the Crofton (after Sir Walter Crofton) or Irish, system of prison management. The Crofton system operated through a programme of marks given to prisoners whereby they could develop a series of privileges. Prisoners were to be trained through dividing their time in prison into three distinct stages, each managed differently, and in prisons in different parts of the country, in order to accomplish different objectives. For the men the first stage was nine-months' separate imprisonment in Mountjoy Prison in Dublin; the second was associated labour on Spike Island in Cork; and the third was spent in what were known as intermediate prisons, such as Smithfield and Lusk in Dublin. After release, those prisoners who stayed in Ireland were kept under police supervision. The technology of the penitentiary system included separate silent accommodation; prisoners were held in solitude in order to facilitate reflection, and they were to earn their keep through work and industry. The inspectors general discussed at length both the separate system – the total separation (with constant employment) of prisoners from fellow prisoners – and the silent system, separate confinement of prisoners at night, with associated labour by day under rule of total silence.

Crime was believed to be a disease (1852 inspectors general report), and the only way to protect prisoners from infection or further infection was to segregate them. The accommodation of males and females in county gaols was, from 1852, to be completely separate. The architecture and design of the institutions controlled the individuals, as did the prisons rules and regulations, structures and routines. Prison discipline was deemed to be intimately connected with prison architecture, with the space that was prison space. In 1829 the inspectors general noted that the prison space comprised a prison yard, a stone floor and simple furniture, straw beds and the blankets of the cell, a vegetable diet or bread or potatoes. In a comment on the condition of the ordinary citizens at the time, they noted that 'it may sometimes happen that a poor man may be induced to prefer the supplies of a gaol to the want he is doomed to suffer in his own home.' They said that, given the above prison conditions, 'the cottage can only be inferior to the gaol ... if it presents a state of absolute suffering.' Clearly it frequently did, given the use that poor people commonly made of goals.

Throughout the nineteenth century, as Ireland became more urban, prisons became larger and more centrally located. Many new prisons were built, eight county prisons in the 1820s, among them Limerick Prison. Mountjoy Prison was opened in 1850, and Mountjoy Women's Prison, with 450 cells, in 1858. The inspectors general were replaced in 1854 by a three-man board, the Convict Prisons Board, with Sir Walter Crofton as its first chair. In 1877, under the General Prisons (Ireland) Act, the General Prisons Board was created, and the management of all of 'the county jails, debtors prisons, bridewells and convict prisons' was centralised and assumed by this board.[25]

THE WOMEN IMPRISONED

Women were imprisoned in the nineteenth century in Ireland in a variety of institutions: in the Central Criminal Lunatic Asylum in Dundrum which opened in 1850; in local and county jails, among them Grangegorman Women's Prison; and in Kilmainham Gaol and Mountjoy Prison.[26] According to Prior,[27/28] between 1850 and 1900 only 21 per cent of the 823 individuals committed to the Central Criminal Lunatic Asylum in Dundrum were women: fifty-five women were committed to Dundrum between 1850 and 1900 for killing a person, with most of the cases being that of infanticide; all of the women were poor, most were unmarried. Women guilty of infanticide were represented in the discourses of the institutions as being ill, mad rather than bad. Women's madness was at that time linked to their reproductive systems. Women were represented as being unpredictable, prone to madness, and in need of protection from themselves. Curtin in her study of Galway Gaol documents that lower-class women were imprisoned in local and county gaols often for short sentences imposed on them for crimes against morals.[29] These crimes involved prostitution and alcohol-related offences, minor assaults, petty theft, obscene behaviour, and drunkenness. The identities ascribed to the imprisoned women were signalled by their occupation; they were servants, hucksters, charwomen, labourers, prostitutes, beggars or tramps; or they were identified by their husbands' occupations. They were 'the blacksmith's wife' or 'the tinker's wife'. Their behaviour was deemed to be immoral rather than criminal but worthy of punishment by imprisonment just the same.

Women were imprisoned in Kilmainham Gaol in Dublin between 1796 and 1881 and in Portlaoise Prison until 1960. They were held in Limerick Prison, the oldest operating prison in Ireland, from 1821 and in Mountjoy Prison from 1858. Mountjoy Women's Prison was and still is the most significant women's prison in Ireland. Women were also held in local jails and bridewells in every town in the country. Luddy[30] outlines how Magdalen asylums began in Ireland, while Dobash et al[31] document the beginning of Jonas Hanway's and Robert Dingley's 1758 British establishment, a Magdalen house for the voluntary confinement of penitent prostitutes, designed to provide continuous seclusion, separate cell accommodation and enclosed cubicle chapels for women who were attempting to leave prostitution. Luddy[32] and Finnegan[33] detail the numbers of Magdalen asylums in Ireland attempting to reform prostitutes, at least eleven in Dublin by 1835 and more around the country. Luddy points out[34] that 'these asylums catered for a total of 10,674 women over the period 1800–99.'

Lock hospitals were used between 1864 and 1886 for the confinement of women deemed to be prostitutes and found to be infected with venereal disease. The word 'lock', which derives from the word 'loke' which meant a house of lepers, was used because of the difficulty in distinguishing venereal disease from leprosy.[35] The women were confined under The Contagious Diseases Acts 1864 and 1866.[36] These acts permitted the police to arbitrarily detain women on the streets, prostitutes, and, in the case of the 1866 Act, every woman believed to be a prostitute[37] for medical examination for venereal disease. If the woman was found to be infected, she could be confined in a lock hospital for up to nine months. If she refused to submit to medical examination she could be imprisoned for up to one month. The main lock hospital, Westmoreland Lock Hospital, opened in 1755 and relocated from Ransford Lane in Dublin to Townsend Street in the city in 1792.[38] From 1819 it dealt only with female patients, 26,500 women being treated from 1821 to 1853.[39]

The Contagious Diseases Acts operated only within areas containing military camps in England and Ireland: in Ireland, Cork, Cobh and the Curragh military camps. As Luddy points out,[40] the acts were designed to eradicate venereal disease but applied only to women; soldiers who infected large numbers of women were not treated for venereal disease in confinement, as were women. Finnegan[41] noted that an abolitionist objected to the legislation because it was designed, he said, 'to keep up a healthy supply of women for the gratification of the lusts of immoral men'. The acts remained in force until they were suspended in 1883 and finally repealed in 1886. While all of Ireland's institutions had a Christian ethos, this was particularly the case with female penal institutions. They were run by the state or by philanthropic or religious organisations and managed by women who were in turn supported in their work by lay or religious middle-class philanthropic women.

Women's experiences of imprisonment throughout the nineteenth century were shaped by the development of the penitentiary system, by the silent separate technology of that system, deemed by all those involved to be particularly effective in disciplining women. In the inspectors general report of 1840 the separate confinement system was said to be established in Grangegorman Female Prison and was reported to be 'very effective in classes sentenced to very short periods of imprisonment'. It was said that 'the prisoners' bitterest hours are those spent in the commencement of confinement, while after time the severity of the separation wears away and the interest in instruction in works and in the visits of officers and in every other instrument of moral reformation increases.'

Women's experiences of imprisonment in that century were shaped by the philosophies regarding imprisoned women of the Quaker prison reformer Mrs Elizabeth Fry, the Protestant Ladies' Associations, and the Mercy and Charity Sisters; by the separation in prison of male and female prisoners; and by the appointment to women's prisons of matrons and female officers. Mrs Fry was the person with the greatest influence in terms of shaping women's experiences of imprisonment in Ireland in the nineteenth century. She was immediately followed, in terms of influence, by the Hibernian Ladies' Association, an association of middle and upper class philanthropic Protestant women. This organisation was active in the women's prisons within the structure of the Ladies' Visiting Committees. The Sisters of Mercy laboured throughout the century in the women's prisons and in the provision of shelters and refuges for women leaving prisons. The work of the sisters never received the same level of commendation in the annual reports of the inspectors general as the labours of the Ladies' Visiting Committees. This may have been because the sisters were modest and self-effacing in terms of their work; it may also have been that their prison work was deemed to be fundamental to the nature of their vocations. Or it may have been a factor of the hierarchical nature of that society where the Protestant ladies, by virtue of their rank and position in society, were deemed to be entitled to shape women's experiences of imprisonment. Certainly the effusive reports from the inspectors general on the activities of the ladies evidence this, as they evidence the tendency of power in society to reinforce power, the tendency of hierarchies to self-reinforcement.

Despite their effusiveness regarding the work of the committees of ladies, the inspectors general were also assiduous in outlining in the reports the manner in which they assumed control of those committees. In 1828 they noted that they had, in order to 'add to both the efficacy and number of these associations', organised a meeting of ladies at the Richmond Bridewell under the patronage of the marchioness of Wellesley. Mrs Elizabeth Fry, at the insistence of the ladies present, took the chair, and under the guidance of the inspectors general, the ladies formed a central national institution. The inspectors general set out to 'regulate the proceedings of the ladies associations already formed', and instituted new associations in several towns. The two main points made at the first meeting, as recorded in the inspectors general annual prison report for that year (1828) were that female prisoners should be attended by female officers alone, and that the first class of imprisoned women should wear 'a good prison dress, with strict attention to uniformity', while the second class would be issued with 'a more appropriate courser dress'.

Mrs Fry, it was reported, felt that, above all, for a woman to be reformed she must be kept from the other sex. She was firmly committed to the ladies committees who, in her view,[42] effectively managed female prison officers. Mrs Fry said, 'I find a remarkable difference depending on whether female officers are superintended by ladies or not: I can tell almost as soon as I go into the prison whether they are or not, from the general appearance of both the women and their officers.' One of the reasons for this proffered by Mrs Fry was that the officers tended to be 'not very superior women', neither very high in principle or habit, and they were liable to be contaminated.[43]

> They soon become familiar with the prisoners and cease to excite the respect due to their office. Whereas the ladies go in once, twice or three times a week and the effect produced is decided. Their attendance keeps the female officers in their places, makes them attend to their duty, and has a constant influence on the minds of the prisoners themselves.

The inspectors general remarked that: 'A great and good effect is produced upon the minds of disgraced and degraded females, by the kindness and countenance of persons of rank and refinement of their own sex. The consequence is that it is in the female class, and under committees of ladies, extraordinary instances of prison reformation are to be sought.'[44]

One year later, 1829, the second report of the Hibernian Ladies' Society was published, and by this time the ladies had managed in many city gaols to affect Mrs Fry's recommendation that females, as much as possible, 'be confined in buildings wholly separated and distinct from the gaols of the male prisoners', and they were anxious to extend the system. Gender segregation in prisons was proposed by Elizabeth Fry in 1827 and enforced in Irish prisons from 1839.[45] The advantages of such a system were said to be: better means of inspection of the matron and the female assistants; more exclusive attendance by female officers; more convenience for the ladies disposed to visiting women in prison; and the facilitation of sufficient female classification. The higher classes were to be employed in the lighter and most eligible or profitable kinds of work while the lower classes were to be employed at washing or other more laborious employment. In the lower classes were to be placed vagrants, women of immodest character and women who had children in the goal, unless a separate room could be allotted to them. By 1835 the ladies' committees were recorded as a formal part of prison services, along with the school and the hospital. The Ladies' Society in their policy on the classification of female prisoners stated that: 'the principle of segregation is to be established not so much according to the offences of which they are respectfully committed as according to their general conduct, character and degree of criminality.' The women were not judged with regard to the offence(s) they had committed, but with respect to their presentation of self within prison.[46]

In the later decades of the nineteenth century, prison reformer Mary Carpenter[47] wrote that the management of convicted women was one of the prison system's most difficult problems. The organisation of women, both mentally and physically, was, she wrote,[48] much more sensitive that that of men, and the reformation of women, their restoration to a healthy condition when morally diseased and in an abnormal state, was far more difficult than that of the other sex. The reformation of the women was to be brought about through 'firm steady control against which it is evidently hopeless to rebel, combined with a strict and vigilant discipline administered with the most impartial justice'.[49]

Female prisoners were represented by Carpenter as having low intellectual powers, torpid from under-use.[50] She wrote that they had very strongly developed passions of the lower nature, and were extremely excitable, violent and given to frantic outbursts of passion. They were, she wrote, capable of a duplicity and disregard for the truth hardly conceivable in the better classes of society. All of these attributes, she continued, rendered any attempts to improve these women peculiarly difficult. The women needed, she believed, to be provided with an abundance of active useful work on which they could vent their restless excitable natures. Disciplinary regimes and boring repetitive work were to be used to calm and pacify them. Work would calm their spirits while giving them a sense of accomplishment. Attention was to be paid to their intellectual powers. They were to be taught to read so that their minds could be filled with interesting information, rather than pernicious thoughts. Women's affections were said to be particularly strong, and when perverted, instruments of much evil. If women were to be reformed, the 'afffectional' part of the woman's nature was to be targeted and won over to the side of virtue. Females were said to be 'more impressionable than males'. The female character was believed to be 'peculiarly open to good or evil influences'. No other 'class of criminals' were said to be 'so easily corrupted and further demoralised by ill-regulated intercourse', nor was there, it was said,[51] 'any class on whom moral government and instruction produced so rapid and so favourable a change'. It was necessary to be aware of the influence of the female character on the lower ranks of society, and with that in mind, to 'attend with every exertion to promote among them moral and religious improvement, industry and order'.[52] This construction and representation of the female prisoner was particularly powerful in nineteenth-century Ireland, and the prison experiences of women in Ireland were largely shaped by this construction and representation of the female prisoner.

There were several different opinions at that time as to which group of women in prison was the most difficult. Mary Carpenter recorded those engaged in prostitution as the most difficult: 'When what is holiest and best in woman has been perverted and diseased by unlawful intercourse with the other sex, there is engendered in her a hardness of heart, a corruption of the whole nature which would seem to make absolute reformation impossible.' Mrs Delia Liddiwell, the superintendent of Mountjoy Prison and formerly Marion Rawlins' deputy matron at Grangegorman,[53] on the other hand, believed that the most difficult female offenders to deal with were

> ... the young girls who have either been reared in or spent a long period in workhouses. When they are corrected, in even the mildest manner, for any breach of regulations, they seem to lose all control of reason, they break the windows of their cells, tear up their bedding, and in many cases (where they have been secured before they can do any other mischief) they have torn their clothing with their teeth. Their language while in this state is absolutely shocking.

There is strong evidence in this testimony of the performative in the manner in which the young girls presented themselves to that society; this is further evidenced by the following: Ms Liddiwell went on to say that these girls were intelligent, learned as fast if not faster than the other prisoners when in school, and were generally attentive. They seemed to Ms Liddiwell to be 'rather more animated by a most perverse tendency to mischief and a spirit of reckless insubordination than by a love for actual vice'. The inspectors general, in the mid-nineteenth century, had yet another population in mind in terms of the most difficult female prisoners to manage. They highlighted the problems of old and infirm women in the prison, 'women not fit for transportation, women who demand much attention from the staff, attentions the staff are not trained to give'.[54] The inspectors general argued that, contrary to prevailing societal constructions and representations of female criminality, the women's criminal dispositions were to be attributed in great measure to their extreme poverty. Within prison they said that the women did not engage in serious breaches of discipline, that their breaches were generally of a trivial nature – refusing to work, bursts of passion, and communicating with each other. It seems from the evidence that those working within female prisons, given their proximity to and consequent knowledge of female prisoners, did not share or agree with the judgements of those charged with the powers of criminal conviction. While the country's arbiters of criminal justice constructed and represented the activities of these women as criminal, the opinions of those working closest to them were that their criminal activities were in fact no more than manifestations of the women's extreme marginality.

CONDITIONS AND ACCOMMODATIONS

The accommodation and condition of women's imprisonment changed substantially throughout the nineteenth century. In the first report of the inspectors general on the state of Irish prisons it was noted that:

> There is a mixing of prisoners of under every kind of criminal charge, the untried and the convicted promiscuously herded together, from 10 to 12 persons in a cell 12 feet by 8. The hospital is ill contrived, ill ventilated and totally unsupplied. There is no bath and the privies are offensive and without sewers. There is a scanty allowance of blankets, particularly on the female side.[55]

The report of 1809 recorded male prisoners in Kilmainham Gaol were recorded as having iron bedsteads and beds filled with straw in which prisoners slept two to a bed, while female prisoners lay on straw on the flags in the cells and common halls. The report deplored the loss of one of the prison's two infirmaries; it had been let to a prisoner confined for debt. Between the first and third decades of the nineteenth century there was a dramatic improvement in prison conditions for both men and women. The report of 1825 found the depot at Cork to be a very significant prison for the accommodation of female convicts; it was said to be well conducted with female prisoners being instructed and kept constantly employed. The report also recorded that the female part of Newgate Prison in Dublin, 'which used to be too dangerous for visitors to pass through', had been transformed; 'idleness, dissipation and licentiousness' had been 'succeeded by industry and order'. The transformation was recorded as 'the effect of the labours of benevolent ladies who gave their attention to that prison'.

By 1825 the inspectors general were able to record that in fact 'no branch of prison discipline has advanced more than that of the female class'. Imprisoned women were apparently relatively easily disciplined and were said to develop when afforded any opportunity to do so. The inspectors general recorded in the 1835 report that imprisoned women did in fact 'prefer disorderly habits' and to be held within prisons where 'there is gaming, drinking and swearing going on'. The report recorded the erection of a wall in Kilkenny City Prison between the women's prison and the neighbouring brewery, without which, the report stated, the prison could not be said to be secure. The inspectors general went on to record that the well-run prisons, which supplied the women with 'what we may call comfortable decent bedding, fair food, and plenty of employment and instruction', were those that had the fewest returns. This may be attributable to the system of separation, which was said to be indispensable as an instrument of reformation, particularly for women of the class and character 'from which the inmates of prisons are usually supplied'. The 1835 report stated:

> To such and particularly to the most violent and abandoned, solitude and silence are insupportable, and those who in association are the loudest and the boldest are, when isolated, completely broken into submission and if not softened to repentance, as is often the case, are at least subdued into a wholesome fear of the recurrence of such seclusion.

The 1826 inspectors general report recorded the employments of men imprisoned in the Richmond Penitentiary as follows: shoemakers, ten; carpenters, six; weavers, fifty-six; tailors, three; labourers in the garden and elsewhere, thirteen. There were ninety prisoners in total. The employments of the women were recorded as: washing (ten), shoe-binding (thirteen), needlework (forty-one), knitting (fourteen). There were seventy-six prisoners in total. The 1851 report recorded the employment of males as masons, stone cutters, carpenters, tailors, shoemakers, weavers, smiths, painters, mat-makers and prison duties. Women were employed at needlework, knitting, spinning, washing, care of the sick and prison duties.

In 1836 the first prison designed for the confinement solely of female prisoners, the Richmond Female Penitentiary, was established, as the inspectors general wrote in the 1837 report, 'With the view of reclaiming, by the adoption of a course of improved moral training, the class of females who in large cities crowd the prisons, driven to the commission of crime by want or other circumstances'. As it was, the report stated, 'strictly laid down in the Prisons Act that it should not be lawful for any woman to be a keeper of a prison', a male governor was appointed to manage the institution with a female superintendent, head matron Mrs Marion Rawlins. Mrs Rawlins was appointed by Mrs Fry, having, the inspectors general wrote, 'proved her ability in the care of females in Cold Bath Fields Penitentiary', a UK prison. The hope was expressed that female prisons throughout the country would 'receive a stimulus from the example of the Grange Gorman Female Penitentiary'.[56] Grangegorman, originally Richmond General Penitentiary,[57] was assigned for female prisoners in 1836.[58] The inspectors general report of 1842 documented the Richmond Female Penitentiary as being divided into eighteen classes, each with its own matron exclusively attached to that class. Other posts filled by women at Mountjoy Prison included schoolmistress, laundry matron, class matron and assistant matron.[59] The prison had 256 cells and the inspectors reported that the women looked exceedingly clean and tidy, their dress and cells in perfect order and the women well behaved.

When the new women's penitentiary at Mountjoy Prison opened in 1858 it was managed through the Crofton or Irish system of prison management. Women imprisoned in Mountjoy served their sentences in three parts. Both Luddy[60] and Carey[61] detail how the Crofton system of stages of progressive classification was imposed upon female prisoners in Mountjoy. Like the men, the women began their sentence in the third class with a period of separation, although they were kept in isolation for four months while the men were isolated for nine months. At the end of the first four months the women entered the second class, when they were allowed to have their cell doors open so they could see out onto the corridor. For the women there were no alternative prisons or prison accommodation so they stayed at Mountjoy for the entire period of their sentences. When they were promoted to the first class they worked in the manufacturing of the prison – shirtmaking in the case of Mountjoy – in the prison laundry or at other tasks around the institution. As male prisoners progressed through their sentences to release, they moved from the convict prisons to intermediate prisons and from prison custody to police probation. Female prisoners, on the other hand, were not released on licence into the community but were moved from prison custody to convent custody; so instead of being released, they were moved from prison to a convent.

The Mountjoy Prison Female Convict Register details that most of the women were imprisoned for larceny and that, on release, were transferred to the custody of the Sisters of Mercy at Golden Bridge Refuge; a few were discharged from custody. There were other shelters. An establishment known as the Shelter for Females Discharged from Prison was established in Dublin in 1821 by two Quaker women following the suicide of two women released from prison;[62/163] more than fifty years later this was taken over by the Dublin Prison Gate Mission, while the Association for Bettering the Condition of the Female Prisoners in the City and County of Dublin opened in 1821 under the patronage of the archbishop of Dublin. There were other refuges for women around the country in the 1800s, the majority pursuing a policy of emigration for those they temporarily sheltered.[64]

In general, on leaving prison women were sent to private institutions, convents or philanthropic homes. Two such homes were established in Dublin for the purposes of providing an intermediary control experience for women prisoners: the Sisters of Mercy Convent at Golden Bridge and a Protestant refuge at Heytesbury Street established by 'some benevolent ladies'.[65] The refuges were to take the women from the prisons, further train them in domestic duties and discipline them into calmness, modesty, honesty and sociability. If the women did not behave, they could be returned to prison, but otherwise could be placed in jobs by the managers of the institutions or assisted to emigrate, being furnished with references that would help them get jobs abroad. All the evidence in all the reports documents that the women wanted very much to progress from prison custody to convent custody. This is perhaps an indication of the manner in which they presented themselves within prison, to prison staff and visitors, the Protestant Ladies and the Mercy Sisters. It seems likely that the women were sheltering in the prisons and the convents in the hope of escaping the lives they had led before being incarcerated. In the 1851 report the inspectors general documented the steps taken by government to discourage females from entering prison with their children in the hope of securing food and lodging in the prison and a free passage to the colonies through transportation. They wrote that the lord lieutenant had decreed that children over 2 years of age would no longer be permitted to accompany their parents from county gaols, that the increase in the number of female criminals could in part be attributed to 'this laxity'. So it seems that the women's performances were simply evidence of their extreme marginality and their desperation to escape the circumstances of their lives.

The women were said to 'earnestly and actively seek the shelter of convents', 'to endeavour to acquire, by strict adherence to the rules, the advantage of removal to the Refuges'.[66] They were fearful that, through some misdemeanour, they might be barred from the refuges and so 'be deprived from remaining for some time under the care of the Sisters'. The hope of admission to the refuge was said to work very effectually in disciplining the women, 'rendering their conduct uniform and correct'. The refuges were said to be 'a means of extending the moral good effected by discipline and instruction received in the penitentiary, a means of extending its effects beyond the prison and the period of imprisonment'.[67] The need the women had to seek shelter, and the lengths to which they were prepared to go in order to secure that shelter, in particular given the disciplinary nature of those institutions, evidences the wretched circumstances of their lives.

FEMALE CRIMINALITY IN THE NINETEENTH CENTURY
Women imprisoned in Ireland in the nineteenth century were generally the most marginal of that society. They were imprisoned in very large numbers, many of them regularly, in different institutions, for clothes-related offences and prostitution, and for offences related to their experiences of poverty and deprivation, loitering, vagrancy,[68] begging and child-related offences. The latter included concealment of birth, exposing children to unnecessary suffering, abandoning children and infanticide. In the 1852 report the inspectors general state that 'the wretchedness and filth of the inhabitations of the poor almost furnish an apology for turning children into the streets.' The nature of the offences for which these women were incarcerated, the state of the institutions in which they were kept and the lives and life experiences which generated their deviancies and deviant behaviours evidence the marginality of the women and their vulnerabilities within their impoverished existences and life experiences.

In the early decades of the nineteenth century women constituted nearly 25 per cent of the prison population. Carey details[69] that, in 1854, of the 60,000 prisoners in local jails, over 26,000 were women. Breaking this statistic down between the provinces, he found that Connaught and Ulster had the fewest women prisoners in comparison to men, while women accounted for the majority in Leinster. One of the main reasons for this was the large number of prostitutes associated with the garrisons of Dublin and Kildare. Table 2.1 details the numbers committed for trial over a number of decades in the nineteenth century, and the percentage that were women. Throughout the famine years classification of prisoners was impossible because of the numbers imprisoned and so there is no breakdown available of the overall figure and, consequently, no figure for the percentage of women among the numbers of those committed for trial.

Table 2.1
Numbers Committed for Trial, 1825–69

Years	Numbers Committed for Trial	%Women
1825	15,515	24%
1831	16,192	23%
1834	21,381	20%
1839	26,392	31%
1847	75,685	
1849	112,478	
1850	115,871	
1851	113,554	
1852	92,638	
1853	83,805	
1856	48,446	45%
1860	30,712	46%
1869	29,879	41%

As can be seen from the table, in 1856, when the worst effects of the Great Famine had abated, 48,446 were committed for trial, of which women constituted 45 per cent. In that year 4,243 women were imprisoned for drunkenness and 4,598 for vagrancy, 4,797 men were imprisoned for drunkenness and 3,001 for vagrancy. In 1869 women accounted for 41 per cent of the 29,879 committed for trial, in 1875 36 per cent, in 1885, 42 per cent. In 1885 there were eighty-two female convicts in custody and 754 male; 6,442 females were committed for drunkenness and 10,725 males. In 1895, 30,270 people were committed for trial, the lowest numbers since 1843.

For decades women accounted for less than 25 per cent of the annual prison population; then in the mid-1840s, as the country became stricken with famine, women very quickly came to constitute almost 50 per cent of the prison population. As prison numbers expanded rapidly at this time, the number of female inmates increased proportionately. Both men and women used prison as a survival strategy at this time, but women more so than men. Female criminality in the nineteenth century was predominantly an urban phenomenon. This is evident in the annual reports of the inspectors general and it may be explained in part by the relative freedom and anonymity afforded women by the city and in part by the extreme poverty of urban areas. In 1839 in Cork, nearly half of the population of those committed to prison were female, while over the same period in Donegal eighty women were imprisoned in comparison to 375 men; in County Galway the same year, 248 women were imprisoned in comparison to 912 men, while in Galway city forty women were imprisoned in comparison to ninety-one men.

As detailed earlier, Curtin,[70] in her study of the women of Galway Gaol, establishes that the women imprisoned were poor, with most serving short sentences for 'crimes against morals', crimes involving prostitution and alcohol, minor assaults, petty theft, obscene behaviour, drunkenness. In her work, Curtin relies on newspaper coverage in the 1800s for opportunities to hear the voices of potential prisoners. She comments on the satirical or unsympathetic tone of the papers, the reporting being structured, Curtin says, for entertainment rather than hard news value.[71]

According to the 1839 inspectors general report, broadly speaking both genders engaged in the same types of offences; for both men and women most of the criminal offences were larcenies and there was some violent crime. However, men committed a great deal more serious crime than women. In 1837 a total of 924 women were committed to prison in Kilmainham Gaol in Dublin. The crimes for which they were imprisoned were mainly simple larceny or larceny, one or two were imprisoned for attempted murder or assault, one for concealed birth, a couple for sheep stealing, four for forgery, four for vagrancy and five for misdemeanours. In the county and city of Dublin one was imprisoned for murder, one for manslaughter, one for concealed birth, three for sacrilege, 125 for larceny from a shop, 258 for larceny from a person and 388 for simple larceny. Other offences were assault, burglary, receiving stolen goods, vagrancy and misdemeanours. There were at the same time 1,875 men imprisoned in the county and city of Dublin. Among these, 228 were incarcerated for violent crimes including two for murder, three for attempted murder, ten for manslaughter and 204 for assault, 1,505 for stealing, including 783 for simple larceny, and fifty-nine on charges of conspiracy to raise the rate of wages. There were very few serious violent crimes such as murder. The National Archives contain the 'Irish Crimes Record, 1879–1893: The Return of Outrages Specially Reported to the Constabulary Office'. This record of serious crimes clearly demonstrates that all of these 'outrages', with very few exceptions, were committed by men. Women were more generally the victims of crime, including intimidation, manslaughter or murder.

The record of the population of the Richmond Female Penitentiary in 1839, as detailed in the inspectors general report for that year, provides an insight into the make-up of the crimes for which women were imprisoned. That population was recorded as follows: felons, 4,663, vagrants, 3,121, and drunkards, 3,974. The largest group (872) had been imprisoned for 'having in possession goods' (stolen), the next largest (322) for common assault, with the next highest number being held for receiving stolen goods. The other offences for which the women were imprisoned were property related and alcohol related, with one being held for deserting her child.

The 1850 report noted that 6,292 individuals had that year been committed to the Richmond Female Prison for twenty-four hours – vagrants, drunkards and beggars. As detailed above, this was a time when great numbers of women were sheltering in prison. There was, as highlighted earlier in this chapter, a policy in place 'which would allow no inducement in terms of shelter within the prison', and to discourage sheltering these committals were offered only 'the gruel dietary'. Beggars who had been committed for twenty-four hours were not supplied with any food 'unless their exhausted condition should absolutely require it … to counteract the disposition to seek admittance to a gaol merely for the sake of sustenance and shelter'. Their number was said to be 'fearfully great', while the prison was said to be 'open to contamination' due to a cholera epidemic that accompanied the Famine. Fears were expressed in the report that there would be a breakdown in order. Mrs Rawlins, matron of the female prison, called for a refuge 'on an extensive scale' for 'the unfortunate outcasts'.[72]

In the 1856 report it was noted that 'females though numerically decreased continue to increase their relative proportion to the males and bid fair soon to compose a full half of the aggregate of the criminal population.' In 1859, while the decrease in crime recorded every year since 1850 continued, there was said to be an increase in the committals of females for drunkenness. In addition, re-committal of females was said to be three times higher than for men, with 44 per cent of the female offenders said to be older women. In 1869 it was reported that 'abandoned women committed for loitering in the streets and similar offences against public order now constitute the great majority of the prisoners of that sex in custody.' It was also said that 'a small number of females, committed month after month and year after year, occupy the gaols of the country, some spending eight, nine and ten months of the year in prison and occasionally re-committed within a few days or perhaps hours after being discharged from a previous imprisonment.'

In 1880 the medical officer of Mountjoy Female Prison referred in his report to the inspectors general, published in turn in the report of the inspectors general to parliament, of 'a rather remarkable circumstance'. He wrote that the women who had in prison constituted what he referred to as the 'irresponsible class' had not been re-committed to prison. He referred to the distress occasioned him by these women who at times became excited to such a degree that they 'broke out into paroxysms of passion and violence which rendered it necessary to resort to measures of restraint to prevent them from injuring themselves'. He saw a gradual decrease of this class, he said, to the great advantage of the discipline of the prison, and also commented on the 'diminution in the re-commission of old broken down habitual criminals'. It seems that the desperately unfortunate women of that most extremely marginal generation who had lived their lives through the country's worst famine years, and who had all their lives sheltered in workhouses and prisons, were dying or had already died.

An analysis of the records of women committed to Kilmainham Gaol showed that convicts, who were imprisoned generally in the worst conditions in that institution, were imprisoned for clothes-related offences, prostitution and, to a lesser extent, child-related offences. A small minority were held for loitering, vagrancy or attempted suicide. The last woman imprisoned in Kilmainham Gaol (until the committal there of female political prisoners of the early twentieth century) was committed in 1881: 'her name was Eliza Keenan and she was imprisoned for knocking at a hall door without any proper excuse.'[73] In some years, one or two women were imprisoned in Kilmainham Gaol for the offence of concealed birth or infanticide. There are very few records of infanticide among the recorded offences of those imprisoned in Ireland and very few records of women having been imprisoned in Kilmainham Gaol for that offence. McLoughlin explains[74] that infanticide and the concealment of births did not come under any sustained official scrutiny in Ireland.

Among the prison registers in the National Archives recording the details of women imprisoned are the Mountjoy Prison Female Convict Register, 1868–1875, the Register of Vagrants, the Register of Old Offenders, the Register of Prisoners Committed under the Habitual Criminal Act 1869, the Register of Female Prisoners Committed for Further Examination and the Register of Female Prisoners, Grangegorman. The Register of Drunkards records that 6,344 women were committed for drunkenness to the Richmond Female Penitentiary in 1839. They were aged eighteen to seventy-four and were generally committed to prison for twenty-four hours, some for forty-eight hours. Among those detailed in the Mountjoy Prison Female Convict Register are Mary Riley, Mary Duff, Elizabeth Murphy and Mary Harrington. Mary Riley was sentenced to five years for manslaughter; her character, 'as far as could be learned', was recorded as 'bad', her conduct in her four months' separate confinement recorded as 'good'. Mary Duff was sentenced to five-years penal servitude for stealing goods and chattels. She was transferred from Kilkenny Gaol to Mountjoy Prison and was recorded as 'a bad character, living in a state of crime, badly instructed regards her religious duties'. Her conduct in her four-months' separate confinement was recorded as 'good'. She was reported once to the director for 'talking' and for this offence she lost marks, was reduced to second class and was for three days on a bread-and-water diet. Other punishments recorded in the register include admonishments: three-days close confinement, being reported to the director, and being forced to wear the canvas dress.[75] The register documents how women were forced to wear the canvas dress for 'raising their voices' and 'for crying loudly'. Elizabeth Murphy, 24 years old and from Kildare, was sentenced to seven-years' transportation for stealing handkerchiefs. Twenty-two-year-old Mary Harrington from Cork city was sentenced to seven-years' transportation for vagrancy.

Seven years, fourteen years and life were the standard transportation sentences for both men and women, and indeed for children over 12 years of age;[76] women were routinely sentenced to seven-years' transportation for crimes such as wearing stolen apparel, stealing potatoes or stealing ribbon. The women were recorded in the register as spinsters, servants and washerwomen. Those skilled among them were needle-workers and caterers; they were cape makers, stay makers, lace makers, dressmakers, confectioners and milliners.

Throughout the 1800s in Ireland, many women living lives of extreme marginality were imprisoned, most for petty offences, generally public order offences. One of the most striking features of Irish penality throughout that century is the pattern in the numbers imprisoned: from 16,000 in 1831, to 100,000 in 1850, to 40,000 in 1880. Another interesting feature is the relatively low level of female imprisonment every year except the Famine years, and the high levels of female imprisonment during those years. Worth considering also is the number of people committed to prison each year for vagrancy, begging and public drunkenness: in 1837 some 25,443 were imprisoned, 16,461 of them for drunkenness. The experience of imprisonment provided for women, and in particular the management and governance of women in prison by privileged volunteers, is also interesting, while another aspect that should be highlighted is the individual nature of the innovations introduced to Irish penality and the short-lived nature of the changes.

In the nineteenth century the visionaries were Sir Walter Crofton and Elizabeth Fry. Their innovations were admired and replicated internationally, because they seemed to work: the *Annual Report of the Directors of Convict Prisons, 1860* records that only seventy-seven of the 1,250 male convicts released on licence between March 1856 and March 1860 had their licences revoked; and by 1860 less than five per cent of the women who had passed through the refuges were re-committed to a convict prison. It is more likely that these accomplishments in terms of recidivism may be attributed to the ending of the Famine and the amelioration generally of conditions in the country (and that many of the individuals who had been imprisoned emigrated on release) rather than the effect of imprisonment or innovations in the penal system such as the separate silent system of the penitentiaries. In any case, the work of the innovators did not outlive them. As detailed in the reports of the General Prisons Board,[77] the male intermediary prisons closed down in the late nineteenth century – Spike Island in 1883 because of a breakdown in discipline, and Lusk in 1886 because it was deemed to be too expensive to run. In 1883 the men from Spike Island were moved into Mountjoy Women's Prison. The female prison was merged into the male prison, and the women were moved to Grangegorman Women's Prison. In 1891 the women's refuge Goldenbridge closed, and in 1897 Grangegorman Women's Prison was closed. The latter became the Richmond lunatic asylum, and the women were moved back to Mountjoy Prison. With the passing of the innovative reformers, responsibility for prisons and prisoners was left entirely to government officials. These officials administered prisons rather than prisoners, and they did this in an efficient, expedient manner.

THE TWENTIETH CENTURY: PRISONS, POLICIES, PHILOSOPHIES AND INSTITUTIONS

Very little was written in terms of official penal policy in Ireland over the twentieth century and this can perhaps be attributed to the fact that throughout the century, until the 1980s, the penal system was contracting, the numbers in prison were contracting and many prisons were closed down. In 1878 according to Carey, there were thirty-eight prisons and ninety-eight bridewells in Ireland,[78] and in 1914, he tells us that there was 'Mountjoy, the Maryborough convict prison (Portlaoise Prison), fourteen local prisons, one borstal (opened in Clonmel in 1906), one inebriate reformatory for "habitual drunkards" and five bridewells in operation'. In 1922 the outgoing British administration handed Mountjoy Prison over to the Irish Provisional Government. It was one of eleven prisons in southern Ireland encompassing a total of 2,361 prison places accommodating at the time less than 600 prisoners. In 1956, there were just three prisons in Ireland – Mountjoy and Limerick prisons for men and women, and Portlaoise Prison[79] – and four in 1958 according to O'Mahony,[80] who includes St Patrick's Institution, the young offenders facility which was then, and still is, accommodated in the original Mountjoy female prison, as a separate prison in his calculation.

In 1923 the Saorstát (Free State) was established and Kevin O'Higgins was the first minister for justice. The military authorities had taken over most of the prisons and were using them for internees. The 1922 report of the General Prisons Board recorded that only limited space could be allocated to civil prisoners, that the new police force, the Garda, had yet to be fully established, and consequently ordinary lawbreakers were able to evade arrest. In 1928 the General Prisons Board was dissolved[81] and the powers of the board transferred to the minister for justice. There were at that time seven local prisons, two convict prisons (Portlaoise and Mountjoy) and the borstal in Clonmel.[82] The board had closed all the bridewells.[83] In terms of policy,[84] the most critical document of the twentieth century is the 1947 *Rules for the Government of Prisons*. These rules are concerned with the administrative necessities of the prisons, and they are now, even though still used, very outdated.

From the start of the twentieth century the penal regime began to liberalise. In the 1940s a substantial number of concessions were introduced: associated recreation, prisoners being allowed to smoke and also allowed to wear their own clothes. The Prison Rules of 1947 replaced the nineteenth-century separate rules for convict and local prisons, and rules on penal servitude and hard labour were dropped. In the 1970s substantial changes were made in accommodations, structures and facilities. A relationship between these innovations in prison policy and an awakening public interest in the situation of adults in penal institutions was drawn by Osborough,[85] which he said was encouraged by the publication in 1970 of the Kennedy Report,[86] a damning indictment of the reformatory and industrial school system. New, more open institutions were introduced. There were developments in the spheres of education work and welfare, while the power of temporary release was granted. Education units were established and industrial training courses were introduced. Three major reports on prisons of the 1980s (two of them non-governmental, the McBride Report and that of the Catholic bishops) document the philosophies of Irish prisons, among them the notion that prisoners should be held in safe humane secure custody and that prison should be the punishment of last resort. The reports also document the inappropriate use of imprisonment, the shortcomings of prison as a deterrent, and the shortcomings of the accommodations and facilities of Irish prisons, most of which were, and still are, housed in nineteenth-century buildings.

Analyses of penal policy in Ireland are contained in four reports. The McBride Report,[87] commissioned by the Prisoners Rights Organisation, noted the relatively low numbers of women in prison (a daily average of twenty-four in 1974) and the relatively petty nature of the offences committed.[88] The second report, *The Prison System*, was produced by the Council for Social Welfare, a committee of the Catholic Bishops Conference, in 1983.[89] This report commented on the deplorable, inadequate, and overcrowded conditions of the female prison. In 1981, the daily average of twenty-three women prisoners in Ireland[90] were held in the ground floor wing of St Patrick's Institution, the young offenders facility housed in the original female prison at Mountjoy Prison.[91] The 1985 Whittaker Report was commissioned by the Irish government, and subsequently ignored by it.[92] The report highlighted as the core problem the overuse of imprisonment, the limited 'protective, deterrent, or corrective value of imprisonment, and the expense of it'.[93] It recommended a range of non-custodial penalties, among them confiscation of assets, required attendance at drug and alcohol treatment centres, and restraints on liberty operable within the community. It called for, as a matter of priority, the replacement of the 'existing sub-standard accommodation of imprisoned women' and recommended that most women offenders be accommodated in an open centre.[94]

In 1994 the first major document on prison policy in the history of the state was published, the Prison Service's five-year plan, *Management of Offenders*. This document detailed as one of the measures to be implemented in the following five years the provision of sixty places for women prisoners in a purpose-built facility. The document also promised a programme of Positive Sentence Management within which a range of services and facilities would be made available to offenders, 'to help them cope with their sentences, to preserve their physical and mental well-being, and to prepare them, as far as practicable, for early structured release under supervision ... if justified and earned' (1994: 40).

The report goes on to say that: 'the case of each offender usually presents a unique set of circumstances – upbringing, family relationships, nature and circumstances of the offence, willingness and capacity to make good – which may be expected to be reflected in his/her development programme and in the selection of a date for early release.'

A published discussion paper, *Tackling Crime*,[95] stated as a major impediment to the effectiveness in law enforcement the absence of an adequate number of prison places. Throughout most of the twentieth century penal policy in Ireland was designed to manage what was a shrinking prison population in a developing country. Towards the end of the century, a major change occurred in the prison population, with the development of a serious illegal drugs problem in Dublin initially, and Irish penal policy attempted to grapple with managing a growing and globalising prison population in a developed country.

THE PRISON POPULATION

The prison population began to diminish from the late 1800s and by the mid-1900s the numbers had fallen dramatically. This was particularly the case with regard to women's imprisonment. In 1912–13 the female prison at Mountjoy took 4,780 committals, mostly for petty crimes. At this time there were very high recidivism rates among imprisoned women, and nearly half of those committed that year would have previously been imprisoned more than twenty times. Carey[96] in his brief historical analysis of the imprisonment of women in Mountjoy Prison attributed high recidivism rates to the fact that women found it difficult to shake the habits of criminality once established, and to the particular difficulty imprisoned women experienced in trying to re-establish themselves in legitimate society after a term inside. According to Carey,[97] 'Many of the women were imprisoned so often they were effectively doing what penal historian Sean McConville described as "life by instalments".'[98] This highlights the 'little and often' syndrome of female imprisonment in Ireland, a feature that persists to the present day.

In 1914–15 some 7,773 women were committed to prison, 33 per cent of the total prison population. In the General Prisons Board's annual report for that year, the low numbers in prison were attributed to 'the depletion of the male population due to war, the greater prosperity in agriculture, higher wages and increased employment in industrial areas, and the granting of time for the payment of fines under the Criminal Justice Administration Act of 1914'. Carey attributes the decline in the prison population[99] 'first and foremost' to legislative changes that affected imprisonment: the 1907 Probation of Offenders Act, which replaced the 1887 Probation of First Offenders Act; the 1899 Fine or Imprisonment Act, which provided for the reduction of sentence on part payment of a fine; the 1907 Prisons Act which authorised partial remission of sentences for good conduct and industry; and the 1914 Criminal Justice Administration Act, which allowed extra time for the payment of fines. As Carey states, these pieces of legislation all combined to significantly reduce the prison population. The reduction in the early 1900s was also due to a shrinking national population, through death and emigration; a buoyant wartime economy in the second decade of the century; the enlistment of many men; and a focus by the state on the imprisonment of political prisoners. It was also attributable to a general development in living standards.

By 1930 the number of women in prison was down to 917, some 22 per cent of the prison population; the daily average prison population for this year was down 8 per cent on that of the preceding year. By 1935, the number reduced further to 666, or 17 per cent. In 1934, separate confinement during the first months of a penal servitude sentence was abolished. In the annual prison report of 1937, the minister for justice noted that 'the decline in the number of persons being sent to prison on conviction continues to be much more marked in the case of women.' The number of women received on conviction that year was 301, 44 per cent less than the annual average for the four preceding years. In 1946 there was a 7 per cent decrease in the prison population on the preceding year. The practice of allowing prisoners to receive parcels containing fruitcake, sweets and other small luxuries was introduced this year, and in 1947, 2,052 books were bought for prison libraries and 600 were received as gifts from members of the public. Smoking privileges were also granted to prisoners. In 1949 a 'Holy Year'[100] amnesty was granted. The annual prison report of that year details that 'the Minister for Justice, with the approval of the government, granted certain remissions ... to mark the beginning of Holy Year and as an indication of the government's complete harmony with the spirit of the Holy season.'

The habitus of the society, the nation and the state was Catholic. Catholic habitus embodied in the home, the school and the church produced specific Catholic, religious and ethical, ways of being.[101] Being a good Catholic facilitated the legitimate accumulation of economic, cultural, political and social capital. The church regulated social interaction and made decisions about education and work, about appointments and leadership, and political leaders and civil servants were socialised into this Catholic habitus. Through them the Catholic Church influenced the state; in fact it controlled it. In effect the state was Irish Catholic, and for most of the twentieth century, this was the case. There was a particular devotion to Mariology, and through this the ideal of Irish womanhood was represented in motherhood, home and family. Inglis[102] posits that Irish mothers had a pivotal role in Irish Catholicism, acting as the link between the institutional church and ordinary society, and developing vocations in their children. The ideal of Irish womanhood became manifest in a series of repressive legislation: in 1924 and 1927 legislation was introduced to restrict women's right to sit on juries; in 1927 women's right to sit all examinations in the Civil Service was curtailed; in 1932 the marriage bar was introduced where married women were obliged to resign from all Civil Service positions; in 1935 the government assumed the right to limit women's employment in any given industry; and in 1937 the Constitution defined women's role in the state exclusively in terms of the family, hearth and home.[103/104] An oppressive vision of the ideal of Irish womanhood, of which sexual purity was a primary characteristic, took hold.[105]

As the century progressed, the only route open for those women who wanted to control their own destinies was emigration, and huge numbers did just that. Emigration from Ireland over the last two centuries was a predominantly female phenomenon and such were the numbers emigrating in the mid-twentieth century that a Commission on Emigration was established.[106/107] Travers outlined the conclusion of the commission, that young people, more than two thirds of them women, were emigrating to 'escape the drabness of the average Irish village, with its frustrations, inhibitions and sterile outlook': and he wrote that even de Valera, then taoiseach, (prime minister) and later president, when faced with explaining why two thirds of the emigrants were women, was forced to concede that there were reasons other than employment. The women who stayed conformed, led the charge for conformity, or fell foul of the orthodoxies of the day.

By the middle decades of the twentieth century large recidivism rates among the diminishing population of imprisoned women were being highlighted in the annual prison reports.

- In 1950, 353 women were imprisoned, constituting 16 per cent of the prison population. Some 60 per cent had served more than five previous sentences, including 112 who had been committed to prison more than twenty times.
- In 1955, 71 per cent of female prisoners had served more than five prison sentences, including 130 who had served more than twenty.
- In 1960, 225 women were imprisoned, constituting 11 per cent of the entire prison population. Some 64 per cent had served more than five previous sentences, including 100 who had served more than twenty.
- In 1965, of 343 female prisoners, 45 per cent had previously served more than five prison sentences, including ninety who had served more than twenty.
- In 1970, of 273 female prisoners, 41 per cent had previously served more than five prison sentences, including thirty who had served more than twenty.
- In 1975, of 176 female prisoners, 30 per cent had previously served more than five sentences, including 5 per cent who had previously served more than twenty.
- In 1981 a total of 111 women were imprisoned, constituting 4.7 per cent of the entire prison population; by 1990 imprisoned women constituted less than 3 per cent of the prison population.

The sharply diminishing numbers in the late 1970s of strong recidivists is a repeat of a pattern established in the late nineteenth century. The diminishing numbers of women in prison over the twentieth century is a manifestation of the nation's economic and social development, and of the diminished need for women to shelter in prisons. It is a reflection of the emigration from Ireland of vast numbers of women and it evidences the low level generally of female criminality. It also reflects the control wielded in Irish society by the Catholic Church and the construction of the feminine within Irish Catholicism throughout the century.

In the nineteenth century every town in Ireland had its own prison, and the major towns had separate women's prisons. Throughout the twentieth century, due to falling numbers of imprisoned women, most of the women's facilities closed down: Galway's women's prison in 1930; Waterford and Dundalk in 1935; Cork in 1940; Sligo in 1950; and Portlaoise Prison stopped accommodating women in 1960. This left Mountjoy and Limerick Female Prison as the only women's prisons in Ireland. In 1960 there were on average twenty women in prison every day. The average number of women held daily in Mountjoy Female Prison in 1970 was fifteen, and in Limerick Prison three.[108] This phenomenon of low numbers of women in prison through these years was recorded internationally; Chesney-Lind[109] recorded a similar pattern in the US, as did Heidensohn[110] in the UK; indeed Carlen[111] noted that a Home Office report in 1970 estimated that by the end of the twentieth century fewer women, perhaps no women at all, would receive prison sentences. After the all-time low of 1970 the numbers of women in prison in Ireland began to rise again, to the current daily average of about 130 women in prison. As will be seen, the very few women who were imprisoned over the twentieth century were held in the most restricted conditions within Irish prisons.

THE WOMEN IMPRISONED

Generally the women imprisoned over the twentieth century were extremely marginal, deprived and impoverished women. They were imprisoned by the state when they displayed their circumstances through public drunkenness, prostitution, vagrancy, loitering or begging, or when through stealing they attempted to improve their circumstances. Middle-class women, when imprisoned, offended against not only the conventions of patriarchy but also those of their class. Criminality was considered to be a lower-class phenomenon.

The class structure of Irish society in the early years of the twentieth century is very evident in the collection of registers of the National Archives. Among them is the Mountjoy Prison

General Register of Convicted Prisoners (16.09.1912 to 14.07.1914). This register records the details of the convict women held in the prison for those years. It tells us that the women were small in stature, many around 4 feet tall. They were aged between sixteen and sixty, most had previous prison records, and many recorded no next-of-kin. Catholics for the most part, they had few occupations; some were recorded as prostitutes, some as laundresses, and some as charwomen. Among their recorded offences were soliciting (this generally warranted a prison sentence of fourteen days), being drunk (fourteen days), using profane language (seven days); and engaging in threatening or riotous behaviour (four days). Their prison sentences were generally accompanied by fines, 5 to 40 shillings.

The Mountjoy Prison Register of 1912–14 records the details of Mary Kelly; 4 foot 9 inches in height and 60 years of age, she had previously been committed to prison 109 times; she had no next of kin, no fixed address, no trade or occupation, had been imprisoned on this occasion for fourteen days and fined 20 shillings for the offence of using profane and obscene language. In the case of Esther Cosgrove, the record shows that she was 35 years old, 4 feet tall, and a charwoman from Charlemont Street. Her next of kin was her husband. She was imprisoned for one month for attempting suicide, received bail and was released. The register also detailed the case of Connie Jones, who had been imprisoned for two months for the offence of 'wandering' (likely to mean tramping). The register records twenty cases on each page, and on one page in September 1912, the twenty women detailed had been imprisoned for eight different offences; eight for using profane language, five for soliciting, two for an offence recorded in the register as 'indecent act', and one each for the following offences: obstruction, threatening behaviour, sheebeening (running an illegal public house), begging, and being drunk and disorderly. All were sentenced to days, up to fourteen days, in prison with fines of up to 40 shillings.

In addition to civilian prisoners, women were imprisoned in Ireland throughout the twentieth century for political activities. In the early decades politically active women were heavily involved in three substantial struggles – the labour struggle, the struggle for suffrage[112] and the struggle for an independent Irish republic. The women were suffragettes and republicans, trade unionists and activists. Cullen Owens[113] details that in the early twentieth century massive unemployment was a feature of Dublin life, one third of the city's population lived in over-crowded, unsanitary slums and Dublin's death rate was higher than any other city in Europe. At that time, James Larkin and James Connolly organised the workers in Dublin and this organisation culminated in the 1913 lockout, where employees on strike across the city were for eight months locked out by employers. There was massive civil unrest and men and women joined the Irish Citizen Army (ICA) to help protect the striking workers.

Among other issues, politically active women campaigned against a reprise of the Contagious Diseases Acts of the nineteenth century, in the shape of the 1918 Regulation 40 D DORA. This was similar to the Contagious Diseases Acts, and designed to protect soldiers against venereal disease. Under this act a woman could be arrested on suspicion of being infected with venereal disease, and a woman could be detained on the basis of a verbal charge made by a soldier.[114] Cullen Owens[115] details the emergence and development of the suffragette movement in Ireland, the formation in Dublin in 1876 by Anna Haslam of the first Irish suffragette society, and the inauguration in Dublin in 1908 by Hanna Sheehy Skeffington and her friends of a radical militant suffragette movement in Ireland, the Irish Women's Franchise League. Suffragette women and republican women were for the most part educated middle-class women with political agendas, although the radical and revolutionary elements of those agendas were generally constrained by the status of women in the Irish society of the time.

Republican women were imprisoned by the British in local jails and Kilmainham Gaol, again in the worst conditions. McCoole[116] writes that the women were held in the older west wing of Kilmainham, dating from the 1790s, which was in a poor state of repair with poor sanitary conditions. Following the 1916 Rising women were held in Mountjoy Prison and in various British prisons. They were also held in local jails and Kilmainham Gaol, and in the North Dublin Union,[117] a former workhouse used as a prison by the Free State Army during the Civil War.[118] The memoirs archived in Kilmainham Gaol document the following escape attempt from the North Dublin Union:

The really chief bit of excitement was when the decision was taken to make a tunnel as a means to escape to the outside world. Those engaged in this enterprise were at it for some days and it was very hush-hush, we only heard vague rumours of how things were progressing. However, the hopes of the workers were dashed to the ground when the plans of the tunnel were captured in a city office. They had met with some snags in the work of tunnelling and had sent out diagrams to the engineers outside for their advice.

Another memoir documents the following seduction: 'Vamped Sergeant C at Work House door and he promised to send in sweets. This promise he duly fulfilled. Oh! How we greeted those chocolates.'

These women are represented in literature and in their own memoirs as brave, gallant and self-sacrificing. They were political women. They were nationalists, and many were feminists. However, the roles allowed them in the republican movement were feminine and feminised. Cullen Owens[119] gives some sense of Irish society at that time: the extraordinary post-Famine wave of piety; the Catholic view that women's suffrage was incompatible with the Catholic ideal of the unity of domestic life; the profoundly anti-suffragette ethos of the day; and, despite the ideals of equality of the leaders of the 1916 Rising, the secondary supportive role offered from 1914 to 1916 by the Volunteers to Cumann na mBan. Following the 1916 Rising and the loss in the fighting or through imprisonment of many of the men, Cumann na mBan did take a more strategic role in Irish nationalism, but Margaret Ward outlines[120] how 'women's participation in the 1916 Rising established an image of the women's role within the nationalist movement which closely resembled that of an ideal housekeeper ...', and she says that with the beginning of the Civil War (in 1922–3) the minister for justice referred to women of the nationalist movement as 'hysterical young women who ought to be at home playing five-fingered exercises or helping their mothers with the brasses'.[121] Ward noted that the minister's patriarchal 'conception of the kind of sheltered lives women should be leading did not prevent him from jailing 400 of them'.

Despite the women's perceptions and portrayals of themselves as brave and gallant revolutionaries, women's involvement in revolutionary politics was considered at the time to be irreconcilable with their femininity and their familial roles, the critical identities ascribed to women in Ireland at that time. McCoole[122] records how many of the families of the women were ashamed of their experiences of imprisonment and that many, on being released from prison, never again spoke of those experiences. They were women who within a patriarchal society had deviated from their feminine roles.

The class structure of women's experiences of imprisonment is evident in the class division between republican prisoners and criminal women. The highest-ranking officials in Cumann na mBan were from educated middle and upper-class backgrounds and university-educated women were well represented among the ranks of imprisoned republican women.[123] The difference between poverty and privilege is highlighted throughout the diaries and memoirs of those republican women, and is illustrated in the fact that, as McCoole[124] details, the revolutionary women were moved from Mountjoy Prison to Kilmainham Gaol in 1923. The jail, having stopped receiving female convicts in 1881, was re-opened for the internment of republican women moved there after protesting their detention with common convicts in Mountjoy Prison. McCoole[125] records that the republican women were moved to Kilmainham Gaol in February 1923 'after a protest at their detention with common convicts in Mountjoy', that women convicts were brought from Mountjoy to Kilmainham to 'do the cooking and the general cleaning' … and that 'the Civil War prisoners were able to take a bath each morning with warm water provided by the convicts [women] who worked the furnace.'[126]

The class structure among the two groups of prisoners is evident too in the prison memoir of republican Hanna O'Connor, archived in Kilmainham Gaol. O'Connor's memoir is full of references to parcels from home, presents of food and slippers, cigarettes and scarves, letters from friends and comrades, and games of rounders, amateur dramatics, concerts and recitals. These depictions of prison with their mixtures of comfortable references to humour and heroism do not diminish the sacrifices of the women; they used hunger strikes frequently and efficiently and although no woman died, many suffered permanent ill health as a result. Hanna O'Connor's memoir records Maud Gonne's (Madame McBride) departure from Kilmainham Gaol on 27 April 1923.

> We have vivid recollections of the night she was released.
> When she was brought downstairs on a stretcher and the
> prisoners gathered round to give her a silent send-off. It
> seemed like a scene from a film with the lights burning dimly
> in the compound and dead silence prevailing. Truly it was a
> fit setting for her send off, but Madame McBride did not
> realise that her fellow prisoners were gathered round to pay
> her this tribute, as she was only half-conscious, and to some
> of us she seemed already dead.

In addition to female civil and political prisoners, women were
confined throughout the twentieth century up to the 1970s in convent Magdalen homes. These homes or asylums throughout the
twentieth century increasingly became homes for unmarried
mothers, where families concerned about public shame surren-
dered, consigned or condemned their daughters and sisters to the
care of the nuns who ran what had become the Magdalen laundries.
These experiences have been recorded in a number of documentary
and fictional accounts, all of which illustrate women's experiences within those institutions.[127] The women were deemed to
have 'fallen' and to be in need of punishment. The nuns running
the institutions, subject to the doctrines of their faith, to the stric-
tures of their orders, and to the powers of the bishops and priests
in their areas, controlled the women and infantilised them while
disciplining them for their sexualities. The women worked
as domestic help, they cooked, served and cleaned. They were
confined; they could not leave the convents. Their heads were
sometimes shorn and, as detailed in the documentaries and
fictional accounts, they were taunted, tortured, bullied and beaten
into submission to the regimes.

In the radio documentary 'The Magdalen Laundry',[128] the
narrator outlined how single women who became pregnant, or
those who just weren't wanted, were banished by their families to
the Mary Magdalen home laundry, 'banished to a legally indefensible detention which some of the women endured for the rest of
their lives'. The documentary outlines the modifications introduced in Ireland into the Magdalen asylum model, most notable
among them the involuntary nature of the confinement. One of
the contributors, Patricia Bourke Brogan,[129] a novice in the Mercy
Order in the 1960s, recalled:

I remember a long dark brown corridor, first of all a door was unlocked and I was led along the corridor and then another door was unlocked and each time a door was locked after me ... So I was imprisoned as well. It was a Sunday afternoon and the women were crowded into a room with a smell of stale perfume and cigarette smoke ... it was the look in their eyes really, this sort of trapped look. Their families had signed them in ... so first of all they were betrayed by their lovers, their men friends who didn't support them in the pregnancy, then their families, their brothers or sisters or parents who signed them in to this place, and they were there some of them for the rest of their lives.[130]

Some of the women would jump over the wall, or try to escape[131] in a laundry hamper, only to be brought back again. Patricia Thuillier, who was in the home in Castlepollard, spoke of her own experience in a Magdalen laundry: 'Someone always made a run for it, but they were caught and dragged back. I don't know of anyone who got away but the Guards were always being called ... I suppose it was like a prison.'[132]

The women lived, worked and died in complete anonymity sequestered within the Magdalen laundry. Milotte details the role of the laundries and other refuges for unmarried mothers in mid to late twentieth-century Ireland in the secret export of Irish babies for adoption, an activity he credits to de Valera,[133] born in America himself to an unmarried mother, as taoiseach first and then as minister for external affairs with responsibility for issuing the first 'adoption passports'. Milotte states that between the 1920s and 1970s over 100,000 babies were born in Ireland to unmarried parents, and he attributes the stigma that such an event occasioned to the hypocrisy of the times. He writes that there was scarcely a family in the 1940s, '50s or '60s in Ireland that didn't have a relative, friend or acquaintance who either got pregnant out of wedlock or fathered an 'illegitimate' child. Yet it was a taboo subject, never discussed in polite company and if mentioned at all then only in hushed tones of holy indignation. An appalling stigma was attached to 'illegitimacy', having a child out of wedlock was regarded as an 'unspeakably scandalous act'.[134] This sequestering in Ireland of single pregnant women continued until the 1970s. The Kennedy Report[135] observed that seventy girls, between 13 and 19 years of age, were being detained by the courts in convent Magdalen homes. The report highlighted the doubtful legal validity of the detentions and noted that girls with recurring sexual offences were unwelcome in reformatory schools and were typically sent to Magdalens.[136]

Over the twentieth century the crimes for which women were imprisoned, as in the nineteenth century, were related to their gender roles or their experiences of poverty and deprivation. David Kiely details some of the more sensational crimes and prison experiences of women imprisoned in Ireland over the twentieth century.[137] He writes of Annie Walsh from Limerick, the last woman executed in Ireland, hanged (as was her nephew) in Mountjoy Prison in 1923 for the murder of Annie's husband. Also Hannah O'Leary, reprieved from a death sentence and sentenced to life imprisonment in 1925 for her part in the murder and dismemberment of her brother Pat. She was released from Mountjoy Prison in 1942 on condition that she enter a convent, which she did and she lived there until she died in 1967. Then there's the case of Mary Agnes Daly who, found guilty of murder, was sentenced to death by hanging in 1948. Her death sentence was subsequently commuted to life imprisonment and she served seven years in Mountjoy Prison and ten years in a convent. Kiely also outlines the case of Mamie Cadden, the Hume Street abortionist, who was sentenced to death in 1956 for the death of Helen O'Reilly. Her sentence was commuted to life imprisonment and she was moved from Mountjoy Prison to the Central Mental Hospital, then Dundrum Central Criminal Lunatic Asylum, where she died in 1959.[138] Mamie Cadden had previously, in 1945, been sentenced to five-years' imprisonment for abortion when she had been implicated in the death of Edina Bird, a dancer at the Olympia Theatre in Dublin.[139] O'Brien,[140] in a lecture on the death penalty in Ireland to the Royal Irish Academy in 2004, said that the Garda reports on Annie Walshe amounted to 'little more than character assassination'. He also referred to the case of Jane O'Brien, who had been sentenced to be hanged; her sentence was commuted on appeal from the then archbishop of Dublin, Archbishop O'Byrne, who appealed for clemency because he felt that it would not be seemly to hang a woman during the Eucharistic Congress, which took place in Dublin in 1932.

In the late decades of the twentieth century the very small

number of republican women imprisoned in the Republic of Ireland were held in Limerick. A prison officer in Limerick Prison spoke in interview of some of them: Josephine Hayden: 'sentenced to four and a half years, served full time'; Rose Dugdale: 'served more than two years, only dealt with you when she had to'; Marion Coyle: 'served at least three years, background in the IRA, her boyfriend and uncle were shot by the Brits'; Marie Murray: 'sentenced to death for her part in the murder of off-duty Garda Reynolds, commuted to life in prison, she left Limerick Prison after seventeen years, did loads of degrees here and ran a marathon in the yard at Mountjoy Prison'. The officer said that all these women did hard time in dire circumstances, had very restricted visits, no televisions, no phone calls, no kettles.

The experiences of women in Mountjoy Prison at the end of the 1970s and the start of the 1980s was documented, in interview, by activist and writer Sue Richardson, who served time in Mountjoy from October 1979 to April 1981. The authorities had identified Sue as a political prisoner, a label she resisted. She successfully sued the state over the condition of her imprisonment, which was found to be unhygienic and dangerous to health and therefore unlawful and illegal, and she was released.[141] She spoke, in interview, of the monochrome environment that was Mountjoy Female Prison at that time. The women were in the basement of the B wing of St Patrick's Institution, which could accommodate twenty women at the time. She said that there was no colour at all and very little air. Lundström-Roche,[142] writing at that time, detailed that 'prison beige' was the dominant colour of the whole female prison at Mountjoy. Sue Richardson talked of the women with whom she had been imprisoned, drawing attention to the class structure and the gendered and poverty-generated nature of female criminality in Ireland:

> The women were there for very little, shop lifting, prostitution, snatching purses, very minor crimes most of them. I remember one woman who was there for six months for stealing an apple pie from a chipper; she got six months because of her previous. There were a couple of middle-class women, one was there for fraud; she served her sentence. Most of the women came from the north inner city [of

Dublin] from really poor families, and when they told you of their childhoods ... There were a few Travellers, and occasionally women from the country but very few of them. They were usually in for theft of some sort, but then most of us were in for theft of some description.[143]

Sue said that there were no dangerous women in the prison; they were all poor women who had engaged in criminal activity because they had no other way, and very few of them had any skills. Very evident in Sue's testimony is the controlled environment of the prison, and the controlled nature of the women's protests within the institution. She says that the women protested verbally, and spoke of the women's quick Dublin wit; otherwise there was very little protest. The environment was so controlled, an organised protest would have been out of the question. Any protest any individual engaged in within the prison resulted in that person being punished, either locked up or 'put in the black hole, a cell with no ventilation, no books'. Sometimes women would set fire to their cells or cut their wrists; some of the women had scars on their arms from their wrists to their elbows. Sue believed the cutting to be a form of resistance, as well as a cry for help: 'like saying I just can't take this any more but instead of saying this women would cut themselves'.

The different identities, indeed the clash of identities, between the women imprisoned and those imprisoning them was evident in Sue's testimony: she said that some of the officers had very low opinions of the women prisoners and treated them accordingly. Most of the officers were countrywomen, while most of the prisoners were from Dublin's north inner city. Culturally, she said, they were miles apart: 'the women prisoners were not within their ken.' The subservient status of the imprisoned women was reinforced constantly in the conventional modes of address within the institution where, according to Sue, some of the prison officers, 'when they wanted to get your attention, screeched at you and called you by your number, all of them called you by your surname, while you always had to address them as "Miss"'. This titled mode of address, from prisoners to prison officers, persists to this day within the women's prisons. Sue thought that the most striking thing about prison was the unbelievably petty rules. She believes that crime at that time (1979–80) was a form of rebellion for women against the roles they were given. She said that the criminal women of that time tended to be the less passive women in society, women who in desperate situations would not go to the church or to a charitable organisation like the St Vincent de Paul for help but would do something to help themselves. She believes that the rules, regulations and practices of the prison were designed to encourage such women into passivity. What is clear is that the women imprisoned in Mountjoy at that time were among the poorest, the most marginal women in the country. They had had very difficult life experiences, and were imprisoned in the starkest conditions, indeed conditions that were found by the High Court to be unfit and unlawful. The question remains: why, if in 1980 the conditions of her imprisonment were so unfit and unsuitable to warrant the release of Sue Richardson, were the same conditions deemed acceptable for all of the other women imprisoned with her, and indeed after her.

Throughout the twentieth century great numbers of women were imprisoned for drunkenness, as were one third of the 1,000 committals of women imprisoned in 1930. Large numbers were imprisoned for simple larceny, soliciting, assault and malicious injury to property being the next most notable offences. No more than three or four women were in prison in any year since the foundation of the state (1922), until recent years, for murder or manslaughter. Vagrancy and begging accounted for substantial numbers of imprisoned women until the 1970s, and from the 1990s begging again became a feature of the women's prison, primarily through the imprisonment of women immigrants from eastern Europe. Drug-related offences, possession, production, cultivation, import or export of drugs, or sale and supply only feature in the recorded offences from 1985. The tiny numbers of women imprisoned in Ireland in the mid to late twentieth century were kept in the worst conditions available in the prison system. Most of them were imprisoned regularly and for short periods; all were imprisoned in the most restricted and limited circumstances for offences generally of a petty, personal or sexual nature.

THE WOMEN'S PRISONS

The prison experiences of women in Ireland were, and still are, radically different from those of men. The range of prisons to which a man might be sent was not, and is still not, available to women. Unlike the men's experiences of imprisonment, there are no training units or Sheldon Abbeys (an open prison set in a stately home in County Wicklow) for the women. Where a range of prison industries were and are available to imprisoned men – among them bagmaking, matmaking, woodwork, cabinet making shoemaking, weaving, baking, carpentry and smithing, agriculture and horticulture, printing, tailoring, shoemaking, metal work, joinery, design and manufacture, upholstery, general engineering, metal fabrication, engraving, fabrics, leather work and industrial training – imprisoned women were offered laundry work, needlework, craftwork and knitting.

As explained, the female prison population contracted continuously throughout the twentieth century, until the last two decades, leading to a closure of women's prisons around the country. In 1956 the borstal in Clonmel, an institution for offenders aged 15 to 21, closed, as did other state industrial schools, and the female prison at Mountjoy, due to the falling numbers of imprisoned women, was converted into a facility for young offenders, St Patrick's Institution. This was explained in interview by Assistant Governor (as she was at the time) Catherine Comerford:

> In the 1950s and '60s the number of women started to reduce as the stealing issue went away. The women had social welfare and it was some support. They [the government] closed down Daingean and Letterfrack,[144] places like that [industrial schools], institutions for young boys, and they decided to move the boys into the female prison. They turned the female prison into a juvenile institution and we [the women's prison] got one floor of the B wing of St Patrick's Institution. The B wing couldn't accommodate more than twenty women [this was then the bigger of two women's prisons in the country, the other being Limerick Prison]. We didn't need to accommodate any more. When I joined in 1976 there were on average sixteen to twenty women in custody every day. In 1979 that number dropped to three. Quite an amount of women were coming in for prostitution[145] and shoplifting. There were one or two in for more serious crimes, embezzlement or fraud, membership of

an illegal organisation. It was mostly prostitution and shoplifting. That was 1979. Then in 1980, 1981, the drug situation exploded in the city and we went from an average of sixteen to twenty women to thirty to forty women in that small area. We had to put bunk beds in the cells.[146]

The two women's prisons were both accommodated on one wing of male institutions; the female prison at Mountjoy was accommodated on one wing of St Patrick's Institution, while the female prison in Limerick was accommodated, and still is, on one wing of the male prison at Limerick Prison. In 1985, the Whittaker Report noted that the two women's prisons, Mountjoy and Limerick, were in poor physical condition with inadequate medical, work, educational and recreation facilities and no provision whatsoever for training; the report details activities in all prisons in terms of work skills and training.[147] In Mountjoy Women's Prison the women were engaged in machine knitting, sewing and prison chores, while in Limerick they undertook prison chores.[148] Assistant Governor Comerford described the conditions within the women's prison at Mountjoy at that time:

> The numbers increased again in 1986. That was when the first prisoners were identified as having HIV and a place had to be found for them. That was a horrible couple of years. All the women who were HIV positive assumed they were going to die in twelve months and nothing we could say could ease their pain. People at that time were terrified of that disease. It was deadly and highly contagious. The staff were absolutely terrified. They wanted to wear suits, gloves and masks. It had a devastating effect on the prison. The women would cut their legs and fill their cups with blood, ring the bell and when we opened the door the contents of the cup would come flying at us. We were very scared. Some of the women got very ill, took overdoses and died. It was just too much for them. We were hearing every week of women dying.[149]

The Whittaker Report made recommendations for the women's prison in terms of adequate healthcare, facilities within the prison for childcare, back-up psychiatric care, drug and alcohol treatment programmes, a full welfare service programme, specialist counselling services, purposeful work activities, certified skills training and a full education programme.[150] It noted that advances made in male prisons in terms of education, work and training had not been made in the women's prisons.[151]

A sense of the nature of the women's experiences within that prison and the identities and subjectivities ascribed to women in prison at that time by the state and by society generally may be extrapolated from the 1985 report on prisons published by the Department of Justice.[152] The report commented on the very welcome addition to the female prison of a sewing room, 'as bright and cheerful as the knitting room', and described as a major development in the female prison the allocation of two female prison officers to groups of four offenders to act in a house-mother capacity: underpinning the idea of women as ill, as domestic and as familial, where male prisoners where guarded by officers and governors, female prisoners by house-mothers and matrons. To understand Irish society at that time it is helpful to consider the publication of *Irish Women: Agenda for Practical Action*,[153] which detailed the legal concerns of women in Ireland at that time: legislation on matrimonial property; the legal issue of illegitimacy; attempting to secure legislation on divorce or judicial separation; conjugal rights; the legalisation of family planning; and children's rights.

As the numbers of women in prison increased again, primarily because of the numbers being held on drug charges, the women in Mountjoy Prison were moved in 1990 to D wing, a wing of the young offenders' institution, a corridor of cells built on three levels which was refurbished for them. In relation to this facility, then director general of the Prison Service Sean Aylward said: 'I'm recollecting the conditions which I inherited in 1993, where the women were literally caged in one corner of the male juvenile prison.'[154]

The experiences of the women imprisoned in this facility were described as follows by then Assistant Governor Catherine Comerford:

> The women's prison subsequently moved to the D wing. The women were allowed a bath once a week, there were no showers. They were given a change of clothes, underwear and outer clothing once a week. They got one shampoo and one soap once a week. They had to ask me (I was chief officer at the time) or somebody else if they could have two sanitary

towels when they had their period. They came to you in the office and you took two sanitary towels, wrapped them up in paper, gave them to the woman and recorded it.[155] By 1980, with the explosion in the drugs problem, we had put showers in, the women could wear their own clothes, we had a laundry, we didn't need to send clothes out to be washed and ironed. They could wear jewellery, watches came later.[156]

Governor John Lonergan described that prison as follows:

They refurbished it[157] very much the way St Pat's was being refurbished, with a huge emphasis on gangways and wire. They did away with all the grass that was in the exercise yard and tarmacadamed all of it. They put big wire fences up all around and had a cage put up from the wing to the exercise yard, like they [the women in the prison] were monkeys or tigers or lions or something. The whole environment was wrong. Anyway it seemed that something needed to be done. [158]

In 1993 the second Commission on the Status of Women published an account of their visit to the Women's Prison in Mountjoy: there were at the time about thirty-five women in custody on any day, most of them imprisoned for drug-related offences. The report of the commission noted that the recommendations of the Whittaker Report[159] still needed to be implemented. In 1997 Taylor Black presented his four-part television documentary on Mountjoy Prison,[160] one part of which focused on the women's prison at Mountjoy. In the documentary, a female prison officer in the women's prison enumerated the female prison population at that time, the mid-1990s, as follows: thirty-eight females in the prison, forty-two females on TR (temporary release), 109 females at large (unlawfully free) and seven females on remand (in prison awaiting sentencing); a total of 196 women. From the very low numbers of women imprisoned in the 1970s, the female prison population had grown rapidly, leading to serious overcrowding. Part of the solution was to allow women out of prison on temporary release. In addition, the substantial numbers of women who were unlawfully at large no doubt also helped alleviate the overcrowding situation. Sean Aylward described the facilities of that prison as follows:

I can remember the sheer lack of activity. The basement area had an ironing board and a couple of washing machines and there were two or three women loading or unloading baskets and ironing and the rest of the girls were chatting. Then over in the educational facility, which was just a few prefabs, the range of activities was pathetic. There were a few teachers doing literacy work, a few women sewing Dubarry shoes (piecework) and a few women were sewing quilts, etc. Like the rest of the prison system there weren't enough places and when prisoner numbers would reach thirty or forty the chief [Kathleen McMahon, subsequently governor of the Dóchas Centre, now retired] would be on to me saying, 'for God's sake would you let some of them out.' The revolving door was in full swing and they [the women] were spinning in and out. The doctor's surgery was a converted cell. The little oratory was in a converted cell. Conditions were poor. Lighting was poor. The gym area had a low ceiling; it was just four cells knocked together.[161]

The women remained in that prison until 1999,[162] when they were moved into the new purpose-built facility, the Dóchas Centre.[163] Like the innovations of the nineteenth century, the Dóchas Centre is a product of a vision of a penal reformer, Governor John Lonergan, for women in prison. This vision was shared by some officials in the Prison Service, by many members of staff of the women's prison at Mountjoy, and by two successive female ministers for justice, Nora Owen and Máire Geoghegan-Quinn. The prison, as explained by the professionals working in and with the women's prison who were interviewed during the research undertaken for this book, took years to develop; as well as the building itself there is the entire social structure of the institution.[164]

The prison was officially opened by the minister for justice, John O'Donoghue, in September 1999. It cost £13 million (€16.5 million) to build and had then an official capacity for seventy-nine women, twice the number the old wing of St Patrick's Institution could accommodate. The prison was designed to be, to use the term of some members of prison staff, a 'family or home' style prison. Within the prison women are accommodated in seven separate houses, each with room for ten to twelve women, except Cedar House which can accommodate eighteen

2.1: The Dóchas Centre: the new women's prison at Mountjoy Prison which opened in 1999. The Healthcare Unit is on the right and the visiting area on the left.

women and Phoenix House which is the pre-release centre. In the houses, each woman has her own room, all the rooms are en-suite, and the women have keys to their rooms and degrees of freedom in terms of movement about the prison. Some are accommodated within the prison's Healthcare Unit, in the padded or strip cells – of which there are four, one strip cell (an ordinary cell from which all the furniture and fittings have been stripped) and three padded cells – when the prison is overcrowded.[165] Historian Peter Carey said[166] that, historically, 'the women were very hard to handle compared to the men. They were really really wild. Again it was their treatment of the women and their attitudes towards them that would have reinforced all this.' Despite the suggestion in the literature and in this chapter of high levels of mental illness among women prisoners, only three women prisoners at a time in Ireland can avail of psychiatric care in a psychiatric hospital, the only one available being the Central Mental Hospital, the most secure of Ireland's psychiatric facilities. There is a visiting psychiatric facility at the Dóchas Centre and a very limited visiting facility in Limerick Prison.

In a radically different penal establishment, the twelve women incarcerated in Limerick Prison[167] in January 2001 were held in a tiny wing of the prison, a small corridor of prison cells accommodated on three levels. In 2001 the women's prison at Limerick could only accommodate twelve women. The Council of Europe Committee had condemned the situation of the women held in Limerick Prison through the Committee for the Prevention of Torture and Inhuman or Degrading Treatment;[168] the women's conditions were also condemned by the director general of the Prison Service, by prison staff and by all who visited them. The then director general said: 'In Limerick Prison ... they [the imprisoned women] are in very confined quarters. We would close the place altogether except for the fact that there are women prisoners who want to be there in order to be close to their families. It's a terrible place.'[169] The officer at Limerick Prison, commenting on the accommodation of the women in C wing, the women's wing in the prison at that time, said that it would not be possible to 'manage a sentence' in C wing; it was 'simply just watch the days go by and mark it with meals'. He added that the conditions within which the women were being held were 'dreadful, a disgrace, indefensible', and that he was at a loss to know how the women had managed to survive in those conditions as long as they had.

The ground floor of the wing encompassed a big shabby draught-ridden room where the women worked on crafts, and a shed-like room, a food servery, where they received their meals. The food servery had a small free-standing food service unit with four serving trays and one free-standing domestic washing machine. There was no other furniture or decoration in the room. Their food was cooked elsewhere in the prison, brought to them on the wing and served to them in this food servery. The women ate the food while locked in their cells. The walls were not painted; the cement floor was not covered. The women's cells on the first floor, four in all, were very small and contained bunk beds to accommodate those who must share a cell. The second floor of the tiny wing contained the five cells of those who enjoyed single-occupancy cells. The cells had no in-cell sanitation. The women had a very shabby recreation room with a snooker table and a tiny 'schoolroom' with one computer; the schoolroom had to be vacated to accommodate professional visits to the women when necessary. The recreation yard was a small rectangular area enclosed by 40-foot-high metal walls. When male prisoners in adjacent yards played ball against these walls the walls reverberated to the sound of the balls bouncing off them. The noise from this was astounding. The recreation yard was covered over, so the women couldn't see the sky. Women in Limerick Prison do not engage in any paid work within the prison; neither do they participate in the school provided in the prison for the male prisoners.

TWO HUNDRED YEARS OF FEMALE IMPRISONMENT

The nature of female imprisonment in Ireland is evident in the protective, moral and religious character of much of that imprisonment, in the petty, personal or sexual nature of much of that imprisonment, and in the gendered nature of those experiences of imprisonment. The protective moral and religious nature of those experiences is evident from the 1900s to the present day and manifest in varied and ambivalent ways: evident for example in the policy of moving women from prison custody to the custody of convents, which persisted in Ireland into the late twentieth century; evident where male prisoners at the end of their prison sentences were released on licence into the community, while women prisoners were 'released' into the custody of a convent; evident historically in women's experiences of imprisonment in Ireland in lock hospitals under the Contagious Diseases Acts 1864 and 1866, in the imprisonment over the centuries of prostitutes and women deemed to be prostitutes, and in the incarceration, as detailed in this chapter, of women engaging in or suspected or accused of sexual misconduct in convent Magdalen homes.

The petty, personal or sexual nature of the offences of most women imprisoned in Ireland is evident in the extraordinary numbers held for public order offences; in the findings of the MacBride Report on the Irish Penal System,[170] which found that in 1979, with few exceptions, women were imprisoned for trifling offences such as drunkenness, larceny, soliciting and begging; and in the research conducted for this book into prison archives and records of the last two centuries. Both Department of Justice records[171] and the research into prison archives and records carried out for this book establish that from the 1930s to date, most of the women imprisoned in Ireland were incarcerated for drunkenness and loitering, for begging and vagrancy and from time to time and to a greater or lesser extent for soliciting; very small numbers (and although the numbers are rising, they are still very small) were imprisoned for serious offences such as manslaughter or murder.

Women's experiences of imprisonment in Ireland were and are patriarchal. This is evident right through the history of those experiences: in imprisoned women's experiences of transportation, Dobash et al[172] documented how conditions for female convicts sentenced to transportation were much worse than those for men, that, in effect, convict women were transported to the colonies as sexual commodities. It is evident in Ireland's model prison system, the Crofton points system, within which imprisoned men moved to progressively less secure prisons while women were forced to remain in the same prison for their entire sentence. It can be seen in the release-on-licence experience of men, contrasted with the release into the custody of a convent for women. It is apparent in Ireland's peculiarly female carcereal archipelago, which, as well as prisons, encompassed lock hospitals and Magdalen asylums. It is evident in the conditions in which women in prison in Ireland were kept, generally the worst available within the prison system. It was, and can still be, seen in the work opportunities available within prison for women; while men can engage in a range of agricultural, horticultural, technical, craft and manufacturing pursuits, any woman afforded work opportunities is offered cleaning, catering, laundry work and sewing. It is apparent in the *architecture parlante*[173] of the contemporary female penal institutions: in the male-ordered, male-structured and male-oriented Limerick Prison and Central Mental Hospital where women are held, in each of these institutions, is one small area; and it is evident in the 'family and home design' of the new women's prison at Mountjoy, the Dóchas Centre. The nature of the institutions within which women are currently imprisoned in Ireland evidences contemporary public and political discourses of identity, and women in prison in Ireland, women who are at present held in marginal sections of male institutions or in the only female institution, the new women's prison which is structured around an ideology of family and home.

This chapter, with its exploration of the subjectivities historically ascribed to women in prison in Ireland, goes some way to accomplishing the aim of this book, to explore historically, socially and spatially women's experiences of imprisonment in Ireland. The chapter details the women's prison experiences historically, establishing the subjectivities ascribed to the women, subjectivities of poverty, petty infantilised criminalities, criminalities related to lack of opportunity, to poverty, to patriarchal conceptions of femininity and to pathologised perceptions of female sexuality, all of which were manifestations of the status of women within Irish society, manifestations of the lack of opportunity for women in that society and of the ideal of the female role in that society, the mother at the centre of the family and home.

NOTES

1. T. Carey, *Mountjoy: The Story of a Prison* (Cork: The Collins Press, 2000), p.2.
2. R.P. Dobash, R.E. Dobash and S. Gutteridge, *The Imprisonment of Women* (New York: Blackwell, 1986), p.33.
3. M. Carpenter, *Reformatory Prison Discipline: As Developed by the Rt. Hon. Sir Walter Crofton, in the Irish Convict Prisons* (London: Longman, 1872), p.71.
4. M. Luddy, *Women and Philanthropy in Nineteenth-Century Ireland* (Cambridge: Cambridge University Press, 1995), p.13.
5. See also M. Luddy, *Women in Irish History from Famine to Feminism, 1850–2000* (London: Routledge, 2010).
6. T. Inglis, *Lessons in Irish Sexuality* (Dublin: University College Dublin Press, 1998), p.7.
7. A. Hayes and D. Urquhart (eds), *The Irish Women's History Reader* (London: Routledge, 2001), p.28.
8. R. Cullen Owens, 'Votes for Women', in A. Hayes and D. Urquhart (eds), *The Irish Women's History Reader* (London: Routledge, 2001), p.37.
9. M. Luddy, '"Abandoned Women and Bad Characters": Prostitution in Nineteenth-Century Ireland', *Women's History Review*, 6, 4 (1997), pp.485–503.
10. Luddy, *Women and Philanthropy in Nineteenth-Century Ireland*.
11. M. Luddy, *Prostitution and Irish Society, 1800–1940* (Cambridge: Cambridge University Press, 2008).
12. D. McLoughlin, 'Women and Sexuality in Nineteenth-Century Ireland', in A. Hayes and D. Urquhart (eds), *The Irish Women's History Reader* (London: Routledge, 2001), p.81.
13. Luddy, *Women and Philanthropy in Nineteenth-Century Ireland*, p.15.
14. McLoughlin, 'Women and Sexuality in Nineteenth Century Ireland'.
15. Ibid.
16. J. McGowan, *Nineteenth-Century Developments in Irish Prison Administration* (Dublin: Institute of Public Administration, 1977).
17. Ibid.
18. N. Osborough, *Borstal in Ireland: Custodial Provision for the Young Adult Offender, 1906–1974* (Dublin: Institute of Public Administration, 1975).
19. The independent Irish state was established in 1922. In 1928 the General Prisons Board ceased to exist and responsibility for the nation's prisons was assumed by the minister for justice of the government of the new independent state.
20. Annual inspectors' general reports on Irish prisons, relevant years (National Library, Kildare Street, Dublin).
21. *Annual Inspectors' General Report on Irish Prisons, 1847* (National Library, Kildare Street, Dublin).
22. *Annual Inspectors' General Report on Irish Prisons, 1846* (National Library, Kildare Street, Dublin).
23. *Annual Inspectors' General Report on Irish Prisons, 1852* (National Library, Kildare Street, Dublin).
24. The report of the inspectors general of 1834 discusses the penitentiary principles from the US from *Mr Crawford's Report on the American Penitentiaries* (sanctioned by parliament). This report documented the establishment in Pennsylvania of a system of solitary confinement, with labour for a long sentence, without labour for a short sentence, in the

prisons of Philadelphia, Walnut Street Penitentiary, and in New York, in the state prisons of Auburn and Sing Sing. The technologies of the prisons encompassed punishment and reformation, instruction in letters and trades, general employment and solitary sleeping cells.

25. See Irish Prison Service, www.irishprisons.ie/about_us-history.htm (accessed 20 June 2010)
26. Designed by Colonel Joshua Jebb, it opened in 1850.
27. P. Prior, 'Mad, Not bad: Crime, Mental Disorder and Gender in Nineteenth-Century Ireland', *History of Psychiatry*, 8, 4 (1997), pp.501–16.
28. P. Prior, *Madness and Murder: Gender, Crime and Mental Disorder in Nineteenth-Century Ireland* (Dublin: Irish Academic Press, 2008).
29. G. Curtin, *The Women of Galway Gaol* (Galway: Arlen House, Ireland, 2001).
30. Luddy, "'Abandoned Women and Bad Characters'", p.87.
31. Dobash et al., *The Imprisonment of Women*, p.37.
32. Luddy, "'Abandoned Women and Bad Characters'".
33. F. Finnegan, *Do Penance or Perish: A Study of Magdalen Asylums in Ireland* (Piltown, Co. Kilkenny: Congrave Press, 2001).
34. Luddy, "'Abandoned Women and Bad Characters'", p.91.
35. Luddy, *Women and Philanthropy in Nineteenth-Century Ireland*, p.105.
36. Finnegan, *Do Penance or Perish*.
37. Curtin, *The Women of Galway Gaol*.
38. The archive of the Westmoreland Street Lock Hospital is now held by the Royal College of Physicians, Kildare Street, Dublin. The archive contains the records of the hospital from its foundation in the 1780s to the end of the nineteenth century. When the hospital closed in the 1950s the records for the twentieth century were destroyed. Librarian Robert Mills suggested (in a telephone conversation with the author) that the destruction of the records was 'probably related to confidentiality concerns'.
39. Luddy, *Women and Philanthropy in Nineteenth-Century Ireland*, pp.105–6.
40. Ibid., p.109.
41. Finnegan, *Do Penance or Perish*, p.206.
42. *Annual Inspectors' General Report on Irish Prisons, 1833* (National Library, Kildare Street, Dublin).
43. Ibid.
44. Ibid.
45. Luddy, *Women and Philanthropy in Nineteenth-Century Ireland*, p.159.
46. See E. Goffman, *The Presentation of Self in Everyday Life* (London: Penguin, 1990).
47. Carpenter, *Reformatory Prison Discipline*.
48. Ibid., p.67.
49. Ibid., p.69.
50. Ibid.
51. *Annual Inspectors' General Report on Irish Prisons, 1837–8* (National Library, Kildare Street, Dublin).
52. *Annual Inspectors' General Report on Irish Prisons, 1829* (National Library, Kildare Street, Dublin).
53. See R. Lohan, 'Matrons in Mountjoy Female Prison, 1858–83', in B. Whelan (ed.), *Women and Paid Work in Ireland, 1500–1930* (Dublin: Four Courts Press, 2000), pp.86–102.
54. *Annual Inspectors' General Report on Irish Prisons, 1851* (National Library, Kildare Street, Dublin).
55. *Annual Inspectors' General Report on Irish Prisons, 1808* (National Library, Kildare Street, Dublin).
56. *Annual Inspectors' General Report on Irish Prisons, 1837* (The National Library, Kildare Street, Dublin).
57. Luddy, *Women and Philanthropy in Nineteenth-Century Ireland*, p.159.
58. It subsequently became a psychiatric hospital and is now a campus of DIT (Dublin Institute of Technology).
59. Luddy, *Women and Philanthropy in Nineteenth-Century Ireland*, p.160.

60. Ibid., p.161.
61. Carey, *Mountjoy: The Story of a Prison*, pp.81–7.
62. Luddy, *Women and Philanthropy in Nineteenth-Century Ireland*, p.167.
63. Carey, *Mountjoy: The Story of a Prison*, p.25.
64. Luddy, *Women and Philanthropy in Nineteenth-Century Ireland*, pp.169–72.
65. Carpenter, *Reformatory Prison Discipline*, p.77.
66. *Annual Inspectors' General Report on Irish Prisons, 1859* (National Library, Kildare Street, Dublin).
67. *Annual Inspectors' General Report on Irish Prisons, 1838* (National Library, Kildare Street, Dublin).
68. All begging was to be recorded as vagrancy from 1848.
69. Carey, *Mountjoy: The Story of a Prison*, p.139.
70. Curtin, *The Women of Galway Gaol*.
71. Ibid., p.3.
72. *Annual Inspectors' General Report on Irish Prisons, 1850* (National Library, Kildare Street, Dublin).
73. S. McCoole and N. O'Sullivan, *Hard Lessons: The Child Prisoners of Kilmainham Gaol* (Dublin: Stationery Office, 2002), p.8.
74. McLoughlin, 'Women and Sexuality in Nineteenth-Century Ireland', p.83.
75. If there wasn't enough room in the ruled register to record all the incidences of misconduct and the punishments conferred on the offending woman, the person charged with the recording cut some ruled paper from a copy register, recorded the details on it and glued it, meticulously, into position in the register.
76. McCoole and O'Sullivan, *Hard Lessons*, p.7.
77. Relevant years.
78. Carey, *Mountjoy: The Story of a Prison*, p.125.
79. Ibid., p.206.
80. P. O'Mahony, *Crime and Punishment in Ireland* (Dublin: Round Hall Press, 1993), p.88.
81. General Prisons Board (Transfer of Functions) Order 1928; see www.irishprisons.ie/about_us-history.htm (accessed 7 August 2010)
82. *Annual Inspectors' General Report on Irish Prisons, 1828* (National Library, Kildare Street, Dublin).
83. Ibid.
84. The twentieth-century legislative framework for the management of prisons and prisoners is as follows: The Prisons (Ireland) Act 1907; The Children's Act 1908; The Criminal Justice Administration Act 1914; The Visiting Committee Act 1925; The Criminal Justice Acts 1925, 1951, 1960 (Miscellaneous Provisions) 1997; The Prisons Acts 1972, 1974, 1977, 1980; The Transfer of Sentenced Prisoner Acts of 1995 and 1997 (see Byrne et al., 1981, for a complete list of statues and statutory instruments).
85. Osborough, *Borstal in Ireland*.
86. *Reformatory and Industrial Schools System Report*, chaired by District Justice Eileen Kennedy (the Kennedy Report) (Dublin: Stationery Office, 1970).
87. *Crime and Punishment: The Irish Penal System Commission Report* (Dublin: Ward River Press, 1982).
88. Ibid., p.93.
89. Catholic Bishops Conference, *A Report on the Prison System* (1983).
90. Ibid., p.11.
91. The original female convict prison at Mountjoy in Dublin opened in 1858.
92. *Report of the Committee of Inquiry into the Penal System*, chaired by T.K. Whitaker (the Whitaker Report) (Dublin: Stationery Office, 1985).
93. Ibid., p.11.
94. Ibid., p.14.
95. Department of Justice, *Tackling Crime: A Discussion Paper* (Dublin: Stationery Office, 1997).
96. Carey, *Mountjoy: The Story of a Prison*, pp.137–40.
97. Ibid.

98. Ibid., p.138.
99. Ibid., p.130.
100. In Roman Catholic tradition a Holy Year, or Jubilee, important religious event.
101. T. Inglis, *Lessons in Irish Sexuality* (Dublin: University College Dublin Press, 1998).
102. Ibid.
103. C. Beaumont, 'Gender, Citizenship and the State in Ireland, 1922–1990', in D. Alderson, F. Becket, S. Brewster and V. Crossman (eds), *Ireland in Proximity: History, Gender, Space* (London: Routledge, 1999).
104. Y. Scannell, 'The Constitution and the Role of Women', in B. Farrell (ed.), *De Valera's Constitution and Ours* (Dublin: Gill & Macmillan, 1988), pp.123–36.
105. M. Valiulis, 'Neither Feminist nor Flapper: The Ecclesiastical Construction of the Ideal Irish Woman', in A Hayes and D. Urquhart, *The Irish Women's History Reader* (London: Routledge, 2001), pp.152–9.
106. P. Travers, 'Emigration and Gender: The Case of Ireland, 1922–1960', in M. O'Dowd and S. Wichert (eds), *Chattal, Servant or Citizen: Women's Status in the Church, State and Society* (Belfast: The Institute of Irish Studies, Queen's University, 1991), pp.187–200.
107. P. Travers, 'There was Nothing for Me There: Irish Female Emigration, 1922–71', in P. O'Sullivan (ed.), *Irish Women and Irish Migration* (London: Leicester University Press, 1991), pp.502–22.
108. I. O'Donnell, E. O'Sullivan and D. Healy, *Crime and Punishment in Ireland, 1922 to 2003: A Statistical Sourcebook* (Dublin: Institute of Public Administration, 2005).
109. M. Chesney-Lind, 'Patriarchy, Prisons and Jails: A Critical Look at Trends in Women's Incarceration', *The Prison Journal*, 71, 1 (1991), pp.51–67.
110. F. Heidensohn, *Women and Crime* (London: Macmillan, 1985).
111. P. Carlen, *Criminal Women* (Cambridge: Polity, 1985).
112. The Representation of the People Act was passed in 1918, giving the vote to women of 30 years of age and older, and to men over the age of 21, http://www.parliament. uk/documents/upload/1918-rep-people-act.pdf (accessed 7 August 2010).
113. R. Cullen Owens, *Smashing Times: A History of the Irish Women's Suffrage Movement, 1889–1922* (Dublin: Attic Press, 1984), pp.36–8.
114. Ibid.
115. R. Cullen Owens, 'Votes for Women', in A. Hayes and D. Urquhart (eds), *The Irish Women's History Reader* (London: Routledge, 2001).
116. S. McCoole, *Guns and Chiffon* (Dublin: Stationery Office, 1997).
117. For details of Countess Markievicz's experiences of solitary confinement in Kilmainham Gaol following the 1916 Rising and proclamation of the Republic, her experience of a life sentence in Aylesbury Gaol in England when her death sentence was commuted to life imprisonment, and her experience of hunger strike in the North Dublin Union in 1923 during the Civil War, see McGowan, *Nineteenth-Century Developments in Irish Prison Administration*.
118. See McCoole, *Guns and Chiffon*. See also S. McCoole, *No Ordinary Women* (Dublin: O'Brien Press, 2003).
119. Cullen Owens, *Smashing Times*.
120. M. Ward (ed.), *In Their Own Voice: Women and Irish Nationalism* (Cork: Attic Press, 1995).
121. Ibid., p.61.
122. McCoole, *No Ordinary Women*.
123. Ibid., p.46.
124. McCoole, *Guns and Chiffon*, p.42.
125. Ibid.
126. Ibid., p.43.
127. 'The Magdalen Laundry', radio documentary, RTÉ, 1992; 'Dear Daughter', television documentary, Irish Film Board, 1996; 'Sex in a Cold Climate', television documentary, Channel 4, 1998; *Sinners*, film, BBC Northern Ireland and Parallel Film Productions, 2002.
128. 'The Magdalen Laundry', RTÉ Radio 1, 14 November 1992.

129. See also P. Burke Brogan, *Eclipsed* (Co. Clare: Salmon Publishing, 1994).

130. Taken from 'The Magdalen Laundry', radio documentary.

131. See also Curtin, *The Women of Galway Gaol*.

132. M. Milotte, *Banished Babies: The Secret History of Ireland's Baby Export Business* (Dublin: New Island Books, 1997), pp.136–52.

133. Ibid., p.25.

134. Ibid., p.18.

135. *Reformatory and Industrial Schools System Report* (Kennedy Report).

136. M. Raftery and E. O'Sullivan, *Suffer the Little Children: The Inside Story of Ireland's Industrial Schools* (Dublin: New Island, 1999).

137. D. Kiely, *Bloody Women: Ireland's Female Killers* (Dublin: Gill & Macmillan, 1999).

138. R. Kavanagh, *Mamie Cadden, Backstreet Abortionist* (Cork: Mercier Press, 2005).

139. T. Prone, *Irish Murders: The Shocking True Stories* (Dublin: Poolbeg Press, 1992), pp.11–30.

140. G. O'Brien, from a lecture on the death penalty in Ireland (given in the Royal Irish Academy, Dublin, 2004).

141. The State (Richardson) v. Governor of Mountjoy Prison, High Court, 28 March 1980 (see R. Byrne, G. Hogan and P. McDermott, *A Study in Irish Prison Law* (Dublin: Co-Op Books, 1981), pp.3, 9).

142. F. Lundström-Roche, 'Women in Prison: Ideals and Reals', unpublished doctoral dissertation, Department of Sociology, University of Stockholm, 1985.

143. Sue Richardson, in interview with the author.

144. In fact, Letterfrack closed in 1973 and Daingean in 1974.

145. In the *Annual Report of the Irish Prison Service, 1945*, the numbers of females under 21 years of age committed on conviction for soliciting and allied offences was twenty-six. This fact was commented upon in a note from the minister. It was commented upon again in 1948, when there were eighteen females committed for soliciting.

146. Catherine Comerford, then assistant governor of the Dóchas Centre, in interview with the author.

147. *Report of the Committee of Inquiry into the Penal System* (the Whitaker Report), Table 3, p.252.

148. At the same time men were engaged in the following: joinery, metalwork, upholstery, leatherwork, tailoring, shoe repair, catering, baking, community building work, assembly work, woodwork, physical training, clothing manufacture, industrial training in engineering manufacture, craft work, printing, Braille and 'talking-book' production, equipment repair, woolcraft, screen printing, computer-based training, industrial training in electronics, drawing, car driving, heavy goods vehicle driving, apprenticeships, farming, ground works, building renovation, gardening, horticulture, animal husbandry and marquetry.

149. Catherine Comerford, then assistant governor of the Dóchas Centre, in interview with the author.

150. *Report of the Committee of Inquiry into the Penal System* (the Whitaker Report), p.76.

151. Ibid., p.77.

152. *Annual Report of the Irish Prison Service, 1985*.

153. Working Party on Women's Affairs and Family Law Reform, *Irish Women: Agenda for Practical Action* (Dublin: Stationery Office, 1985), pp.22–3.

154. Sean Aylward, then director general of the Irish Prison Service, in interview with the author.

155. One of the teachers in the school in the Dóchas Centre (in interview with the author) remembered that the women 'had to produce dirty sanitary towels to get a clean one'.

156. Catherine Comerford, then assistant governor of the Dóchas Centre, in interview with the author.

157. The Irish Prison Service refurbished D wing in 1990 moving the women into it.

158. John Lonergan, then governor of Mountjoy Prison, in interview with the author.

159. *Report of the Committee of Inquiry into the Penal System* (the Whitaker Report.

160. 'The Joy', broadcast on RTÉ television, January/February 1997 (Poolbeg Productions, Laragh, Co. Wicklow).
161. Sean Aylward, then director general of the Irish Prison Service, in interview with the author.
162. The experiences this accommodation afforded the women during this time have been documented by Alan Roberts in his novel *The Rasherhouse* (Cork: The Collins Press, 1997).
163. Dóchas is the Irish word for hope. The prison was named by Tara O'Callaghan, a former prisoner, now deceased.
164. C. Quinlan, 'A Journey into the Women's Prison', *Women's Studies Review*, vol. 9: 'Women's Activism and Voluntary Activity' (2004), pp.59–79.
165. European Committee for the Prevention of Inhuman or Degrading Treatment or Punishment (CPT), *Report to the Government of Ireland on the visit to Ireland*, 36 (2003), p.22 highlighted the practice in the Dóchas Centre when the prison was overcrowded of accommodating imprisoned women in padded cells.
166. The CPT requested information on measures taken to ensure that all prisoners at the Dóchas Centre are provided with appropriate accommodation.
167. In interview with the author.
168. Limerick Prison is the oldest operating prison in Ireland.
169. Council of Europe, *Report to the Irish Government on the Visit to Ireland Carried out by the European Committee for the Prevention of Torture and Inhuman or Degrading Treatment or Punishment (CPT) from 31 August to 9 September 1998* (Strasbourg: Council of Europe, 17 December 1999), CPT/Inf (99)15[EN], p.10.
170. Sean Aylward, then director general of the Irish Prison Service, in interview with the author.
171. Prisoners' Rights Organisation, *Crime and Punishment: The Irish Penal System Commission Report* (the McBride Report) (Dublin: Stationery Office, 1982), pp.50–1.
172. Irish Prison Service annual prison reports, relevant years, http://www.irishprisons. ie/publications-annual_reports.htm (accessed 7 August 2010).
173. Dobash et al., *The Imprisonment of Women*, p.33.
174. D. Garland, *Punishment and Modern Society: A Study in Social Theory* (Chicago: University of Chicago Press, 1990), p.259.

Chapter Three

The Contemporary Perspective

This chapter explores the manner in which within the contemporary discourses imprisoned women are subject positioned, the manner in which their identities are constructed and represented. The discourses explored here are those of the print media, the criminal justice system, the Irish Prison Service, and the structures of the Irish female prison. These discourses represent the various gazes ascribing identities to the women. The data analysed is from observations within the women's prisons and of senior management meetings within the Dóchas Centre, from interviews conducted with thirty experts and from an analysis of press coverage of women in prison and the women's prisons.[1] The focus of this chapter is on the experiences of women imprisoned in Ireland from 2000 to 2005.

EXPERT GAZES

Since panopticon (the title given by Jeremy Bentham to a sketch he made in 1791 of a penitentiary), the gaze has been central to prisoners' experiences of imprisonment. The technology of the gaze with the modern prison, as will be detailed in Chapter 5, has developed from a Benthamite panopticism to a Foucauldian panopticism. Within Foucauldian panopticism, a subtle calculus of power acts on human subjects to produce docile bodies and this power is said to be present in the various institutions designed to control. It is wielded within these institutions by experts and professionals, Foucault's permanent petty tribunals. Dominant individuals hegemonically articulate the norms of society and they communicate them. These norms are then enforced. This, as Foucault detailed, is the order of things.[2] The norm and indeed the abnormal is constantly articulated and communicated within society. For those unable or incapable of attaining or maintaining the norm, support is provided. This support, as we saw in Chapter 2, frequently takes the form of shelter. For those wilfully, or even simply obviously, falling short of the norm, stigmatising labels such as deviant and criminal are rapidly affixed, forcefully encouraging conformity. When all else fails, corrective programmes are available – rehabilitation and cures in clinics and hospitals, and punishment and rehabilitation in prisons.

The power to order things and to produce docile bodies is deeply embedded in society. It is embedded in notions of what is right and what is proper in terms of human behaviour,[3] in terms of how we live and what it is that we live by. In Ireland, the order of things is patriarchal. The patriarchal order has been shaped in large part by the religious, predominantly Catholic, habitus of Irish society. This habitus was deeply rooted and, for a long time, unchallenged. The changes in our society, when they did come, came from the many challenges presented at the end of the twentieth century to this order of things. Foremost among these were three major cultural shifts. The first was Ireland's membership of the European Union, through which the country became less isolated and increasingly globally engaged, socially, politically and economically. The second was a fundamental undermining of Catholic authority and influence, which was from the end of the twentieth century continuously challenged. Finally, and possibly most significantly, there was the second wave of the feminist movement and the changes the movement accomplished. In 1971 the Irish Women's Liberation Movement six-point manifesto (*Chains or Change*) was published. In 1972 the *Report of the Commission on the Status of Women* was published highlighting a gendered definition of women's citizenship which it described as a harmful cultural stereotype. Ireland joined the EEC in 1973. The marriage bar, introduced in 1932 excluding married women from public service employment, was removed in 1973. In 1974 legislation on equal pay was introduced and followed in 1977 by legislation on employment equality. The automatic right to women of jury service, denied in the 1927 Juries Act, was restored in 1976 and in 1990, Mary Robinson, a leader in the women's movement, was elected president of Ireland, the first of two female presidents to date.

There is no doubt that the habitus of Irish society was changing. Despite the evident changes, however, the patriarchal habitus did continue to order things, and to be reflected in the order of things. Although a woman had been elected president, she was extraordinary. This was illustrated in an award-winning photograph published in *The Irish Times* and reprinted in John Horgan's biography of Mary Robinson.[4] The photograph, titled 'A Woman in a Man's World', depicts President Robinson inspecting a military guard of honour. On the same page of the biography there is a photograph of the president concluding her inaugural speech. There are twenty-six people depicted in the photograph, apart from the president; all but two of them are men. The two women depicted are barely evident. Very evident among the men are the cultural trappings of power: wigs of the legal profession, upper-class morning coats, militaristic uniforms, and the familiar (male) iconic faces of Irish politics. In the photograph, Mary Robinson is very obviously a woman in a man's world.

The changes in Irish society and the challenges to patriarchy prompted the development of an apparently more egalitarian society and a rapidly developing economy. Despite the changes, there are as yet few women in powerful positions in Ireland. This is said to be a manifestation of a socialisation process which transmits traditional assumptions about women's roles, the prioritisation of a home and family-based role for women. As Scraton said, power is institutionalised in a masculine and indeed masculinist form.[5] The issues in terms of the effect of these traditionalist assumptions regarding appropriate roles for women are as follows: the continued relegation of women to the private sphere; adherence to the prioritisation of caring familial roles; and the perpetuation of gender inequality in terms of status, power and employment.

In Ireland the state is the people. The mandate to govern in Ireland is given to the government by the people within a fair and democratic system. The people, through democratic elections, rule, or at least decide who rules and in large part how they rule. In this way, the government and the individuals who comprise government are subject to the people. The powerful hold their positions through the will of the people. This reliance of power on the will of the people explains the reactive nature of government and thus the reactive nature of the Irish criminal justice and penal systems. This reactive nature is demonstrated in Chapter 5 of this work, where O'Donnell and O'Sullivan trace the development of criminal justice policies to the murders of Jerry McCabe and Veronica Guerin.[6] The force of the moral panic generated by the murders was seen in turn to generate an equally forceful criminal justice response.

The reactive capacity of the state is implicated in discursive constructions of criminal deviance, and in cultural conceptions of the state's penal institutions and the criminal justice system. Crime in Ireland, as explained in Chapter 5, is perceived as being violent, and drug and property related. The gazes of the state were seen to readily fall on such criminality. In Ireland, criminals, given this construction of criminality, tend to be poorer people. Criminalised individuals, generally poorer less educated people, when imprisoned by the judiciary, generally affluent, well-educated people, are, through imprisonment, stigmatised and dangerised. In this way such subjectivities are constructed and represented within power relations.

Prisoners' subjectivities are in large part discursively produced. The project of constructing prisoner subjectivities is accomplished for the most part through expert discourses. Penal gazes through expert discourses ascribe identities to and inscribe identities upon imprisoned women. In general, for prisoners, the powerful shaping discourses are multiple and frequently distant, and they often develop and perpetuate stereotypical and ideologically informed perceptions of prisoners based on myths, half-truths and generalisations. Goffman, drawing on Meade's work, wrote of managing spoiled identities,[7] of identity as a performance of belonging.[8] He spoke of the many different identities an individual assumes in the course of a lifetime in order to be what s/he is expected to be. For Butler, identity is always performatively constituted; she wrote of identity being developed through performance, identity as imitation, fabrication, and manipulation.[9] She suggests that this acting, this performance, is a manifestation of power.[10] Using the theories of both Goffman and Butler, this book explores the manner in which the subjectivities of imprisoned women are discursively constructed, and how the discursive or narrated subject becomes the performed subject.

THE PRESS

Many prisoners, in addition to being subject to the political gaze, are also faced with an intense and pervasive media gaze. Media representations of criminal women and women in prison are seen in this work to be particularly problematic. Most problematic are the ideological representations of some of these women, the stereotypical representations of others, and the mythical characterisation or narrativisation of more. In the following pages, the discursive production of imprisoned women in the press in Ireland is considered.

The print media in Ireland has a primary role in shaping the social construct that is women in Ireland, in shaping the constructs feminine and femininity, in producing, circulating and perpetuating images and standards of normative femininity. The press has a major role in the development of penal policy through its influence on public opinion and on ministerial and government departmental opinion. These opinions, influenced as they are by the press, shape in turn the penal policy which controls and orders the prison experiences of these women. The media in Ireland, as detailed by McCullagh,[11] O'Connell[12] and O'Donnell and O'Sullivan,[13] can stir the public mood, and indeed often generates it. The various techniques employed by the media shape public perceptions of individuals, groups and institutions in society. Among the techniques used by the media, as detailed by Morrissey, are the narratives that are told; the stock stories used, the story formats; the myths and legends evoked; the discursive acceptance or rejection of protagonists; the construction of subject positions; and the promulgation of normative roles.[14]

In the media analysis conducted, 672 newspapers were examined in the period September 2000 to October 2001. The broadsheets were *The Irish Times*, the *Sunday Tribune*, the *Sunday Independent* and the *Sunday Business Post*. Together these newspapers published nineteen articles, eleven photographs and one cartoon which depicted an imprisoned woman and a man she had been linked with. Over the entire period of the study, a time when 1,000 women were committed to prison in Ireland, the broadsheets wrote about eight women, all of whom had been convicted of extreme offences. Four tabloid newspapers were included in the study, one daily and three Sunday newspapers. The daily newspaper the *Evening Herald* had more articles about women in prison than any other newspaper, twenty-one articles ranging in length from sixteen to 800 words; it also published twenty-two photographs. All of this reporting focused on just twelve women. The *Sunday World* had proportionately more articles than any newspaper and it carried the most photographs, forty-nine in all, many very large and in colour, and many of them front page. Catherine Nevin was the most prominent female prisoner. Seven of the articles published in the *Sunday World* were about Catherine Nevin and there were several photographs of her, most very large and in colour. Among the articles was one entitled 'Catherine Nevin's fellow husband murderer, Traveller Bridie Doran'. Among the other women reported upon were Nora Wall, a Catholic nun jailed for life on being convicted of the rape of a child, a conviction quashed four days into the life sentence; Carol Anne Dunne, a patient in the Central Mental Hospital, referred to in the paper as 'the Devil Killer'; Melody McGovern, 'the 'Joy Escapee' whose appearance in the paper gave it an opportunity to link her with her sister Sonia who was narrativised as 'a busty TV lap dancer'; and Margaret Connors, narrativised as 'the dog-fight bookie Mum'.

The press selected, from the hundreds of stories of women imprisoned, twenty-two stories to report, eight in the broadsheets and fourteen in the tabloids. The analysis showed that the stories selected were generally the most extreme. The discourse that emerged was one of danger. Within the moral structure of the discourse, imprisoned women were subject positioned as dangerous, posing a threat or a risk to society. This resonates with Beck's work on 'risk society'[15] and with the work of Lianos and Douglas,[16] who all highlighted the discourse of risk in contemporary society. Lianos and Douglas also wrote of the capacity of the prison to 'dangerise' prisoners. This resonates with the theory of a perceptual exaggeration in society of the pathology of the incarcerated (see Chapter 5). It also resonates with Foucault's[17] statement that society signals 'wild beast' identities of prisoners to prison guards who in turn signal these identities to prisoners; and then when prisoners have learned these wild beast identities well behind bars, prison guards send them back to society. This communication process between society, the institution that is the prison and prisoners is a signalling triangle; at the core of the triangle is the media.

Cohen and Young[18] outlined three socially constructed discourses of crime: official, media and public discourses, arguing that public discourses of crime are massively dependent on media and official discourses. Morrissey, in her work on official discourses, detailed a symbiotic relationship between the media and mainstream legal institutions, evident she said in the generally faithful reporting of the criminal narratives of criminalised individuals of the criminal courts.[19] The media is dependent on markets and so produces discourses and narratives consonant for and in its markets. According to Cohen and Young, the media reflects an image of society as it has already been pre-constituted by the powerful, and it is in this way that the media is of major ideological significance for the maintenance of the status quo in society.[20]

Despite very low levels of criminality and the petty nature of female criminality, imprisoned women are subject positioned within media discourse as substantial dangerous criminals. By way of generating a comparison between male and female offending, an analysis was conducted of court reporting of criminal cases, published in *The Irish Times*, over one month (March 2001). Over that time, the paper reported on the cases of ninety-eight men appearing in court on criminal charges. The men were charged with murder (eighteen), attempted murder, attempted murder and rape, manslaughter, assault and rape, sexual abuse, sexual assault, human trafficking, armed raids, armed robbery, smuggling, and dangerous driving causing death. There were drugs charges, charges of false accounting, terrorist-related charges and child pornography charges. Two men were having their assets frozen by the Criminal Assets Bureau, one man was charged with defamation for naming a female business associate in a sex advertisement he had created, and John Gilligan was in court that month charged with, among drugs and firearms charges, the murder of journalist Veronica Guerin. In that month, *The Irish Times* reported on five women appearing in court on criminal charges: two were charged with drug trafficking (one of whom was from South Africa), one with forgery, one was fined for running brothels, and one was given fourteen days to close a crèche she was running which was infringing childcare regulations. Also striking, in terms of a public discourse of female criminality, are the crime biographies published in Ireland over the last two decades. The titles of the books on male criminals and criminality

– *Gangland*,[21] *The General*,[22] *King Scum*[23] and *Evil Empire*[24] – give a sense of the power and force of Ireland's prominent male criminals. The titles of the accounts of Ireland's prominent female criminals highlight the personal and/or sexual nature of much of female criminality in Ireland, among them *Lynn: A Story of Prostitution*,[25] *Ladies of the Kasbah: The Story of Ireland's Most Infamous Brothel and the Women who Worked There*,[26] *Sex in the City: The Prostitution Racket in Ireland*,[27] and among the three books published to date on Catherine Nevin, *The Black Widow: The Catherine Nevin Story*.[28] In addition to this, the director general of the Prison Service said that at the time of interview (2001) there were 390 men in prison in Ireland convicted or accused of sex offences, one in seven of the male offenders in custody. These men, he said, were from the whole spectrum of Irish society, and 61 per cent were charged with or convicted of child abuse. He concluded that neither that social spectrum nor that type of offence was reflected in the female prison population. The publication in 2007 of *The Scissor Sisters*,[29] the story of 'the torso in the canal' murder for which two sisters, Charlotte and Linda Mulhall, and their mother, received convictions, demonstrates the shift towards more violent crime among women in Ireland. This is evidenced in the rise in the first decade of the twenty-first century in the numbers of women serving sentences for manslaughter and murder in Ireland. Among them is Sharon Collins, who, in July 2008, was found guilty of soliciting Egyptian poker dealer Essam Eid to kill her partner, P.J. Howard and his two sons so she could inherit Howard's estate.[30]

The analysis of the press coverage showed the discourse of danger to be pervasive and communicated throughout. It is useful to remember that O'Connell found that due to the nature of media crime coverage in Ireland, the Irish public believed itself to be experiencing, despite relatively low crime rates, a law and order crisis.[31] Within the discourse of danger, there were three main narratives: badness, madness and desperation. Primarily the narratives were of killer women, evil and cruel women. There were some narratives of psychiatric, suicidal and anorexic women. To a lesser extent were the stories of women who were tragic and lonely, simple-minded and backward. Catherine Nevin featured most prominently. She was narrativised as 'Catherine Nevin', 'Nevin', 'Killer Catherine Nevin', 'Killer Nevin', 'Evil

Nevin', 'Murderess Nevin', or the 'Black Widow'. Catherine Nevin became notorious through the media coverage of her crime, her trial, and her imprisonment. She was frequently linked to other imprisoned women who were also depicted in the press as notorious. In one of the main narratives Catherine Nevin was the 'Black Widow' who was engaged in violent conflict with 'drugs queen' Regina Felloni, the convicted drug-addicted daughter of drug lord Tony Felloni.[32] In another narrative Catherine Nevin was reported to have been 'devastated since the release of her jail bodyguard – a Traveller husband-killer who became her best friend'.[33] As the 'Black Widow' she was again reported to be 'devastated' when 'her only prison pals', 'two cocaine smuggling Brazilian drug mules' were to be deported.[34]

Throughout, Catherine Nevin was narrativised as notorious. The other women, the two Brazilian women, Regina Felloni, and the Traveller, Bridie Doran, who were all convicted of serious offences, featured in these press articles only in relation to Nevin. Linking the women with Nevin made the stories more extreme, more substantial, and more fraught with danger. The journalists and the story editors clearly believed that the linking of the stories made them more interesting to readers. Ultimately the linking made the newspapers more marketable. One year after her conviction, almost half of all the published articles in the sample studied were about Catherine Nevin and half of all published photographs were of her. Nevin was a middle-class, middle-aged businesswoman who, in 1999, was convicted of conspiracy to murder her husband and subsequently sentenced to prison under life sentence. It could be said that she has in recent years provided Irish society with a moral panic and a public spectacle of Irish female criminality. In her criminal persona she contravened the norms of Irish society in terms of both her gender and her class roles, and the extraordinary interest in her evidences the class structure of Irish female criminality – the perception in Irish society that criminality is a lower-class phenomenon – and the predominantly petty nature of female criminality in Ireland, to which the Catherine Nevin case is an exception.

Throughout the sample articles, the sexual narrative was very limited. There were in total only four stories of an explicitly sexual nature. The most substantial of these related to the decision of the Director of Public Prosecutions not to prosecute a senior care officer of the Central Mental Hospital who had been accused by nine female patients of sexual assault. In that article the women were represented as vulnerable, but that this vulnerability was guarded by the state through the reporting of the decision not to prosecute. This seemed to imply that that situation had been taken care of, that there was no further cause for concern. The benevolent state had dealt with the situation; having found the weakness in the system, had removed it and could now be counted on to resume the proper care of these women.[35] Another sexual narrative was created by the *Sunday World* around the story of Melody McGovern, who had escaped from the Dóchas Centre by walking out of the prison with a group of visitors.[36]The newspaper used Melody's escape story as an opportunity to discuss, using sexual imagery, her sister's lap-dancing career. The third article was in the *Evening Herald*, a short piece about a 38-year-old woman charged with sexually assaulting an 8-year-old girl.[37] And there was also the article about Nora Wall, the Catholic nun whose life sentence for rape was quashed four days into the sentence.

There was in the reporting a discourse of desperation. This was created through the narratives of lonely women, suicidal women, tragic women and backward women. The *Evening Herald* carried a substantial story about Deirdre Rose, a 20-year-old pregnant wife and mother, imprisoned for life for murder, and subsequently released after serving eighteen months.[38] According to the article's headline, 'pregnant killer Deirdre', who was said to be 'suicidal, anorexic and backward', had spent a 'lonely 21st birthday in Mountjoy'. The *Evening Herald* reported on the suicide in prison of Lynda Byrne,[39] and also carried a story about a teenage girl who 'had been jailed for her own protection after threatening suicide'.[40] This girl was back in court again the following month, when she was once more sent to Mountjoy Prison 'as a last resort'.[41] There was also in the reporting some evidence of a narrative of motherhood. As the stories were generally of the more extreme cases of imprisoned women, the mothers who featured in the articles were generally represented as extremely deviant. Among the mothers were the 'dog-fight bookie Mum' and the 'killer Mum', the 'pregnant killer', and the 'evil Mum-to-be', the latter three appellations all referring to Deirdre Rose.

Throughout there was little positive reporting, and it was at times less than factual, beyond the actual crimes with which the women were charged or convicted. As detailed in Chapter 5, the media, selecting from the vast array of information available, provide us with guiding myths which shape our sense of our world. Cohen and Young explain that in terms of accuracy in reportage, there is much evidence that the media consistently get things wrong and report less than factual accounts of issues or events.[42] This was found to be the case in this analysis. When the findings of the media analysis were compared with the findings from the ethnographic research conducted in the prison, stories of friendships within prison were shown to be fabricated and/or exaggerated. Stories of parties and revelries were personalised and intrusive, and frequently inaccurate or fabricated. Indeed, the reporting was almost invariably exaggerated, inaccurate or untrue. The female prison was characterised in the press as being focused on family values. It was represented as a well-ordered holiday camp with occasional hill-walking trips in the Wicklow Mountains, or as a private school with graduation day barbeques where steaks, giant burgers, ribs and side salads were served. The friendships among the women – generally fabrications either on the part of the journalists or the journalist's informers – were depicted as shallow, opportunistic relationships entered into for protection or through greed or avarice.

The prison itself was positioned within a discourse of danger, a place governed by secretive underworld codes, where a woman would need a bodyguard, where the only real safety lay in isolation. Women prisoners were represented as having to be manipulative, conniving and ingratiating to survive. Frequent staff shortages and a consequent lack of supervision were reported to have facilitated the development of a drug culture which had flourished and prevailed unchecked. The impression given was that the fundamental issue for imprisoned women was learning how to survive. Still, the women were represented as being 'admitted' to the prison, as one is admitted to hospital, while the state was represented as an institution observing a constitutional obligation to protect, often protecting people from themselves.

The representation in the Irish press of women imprisoned here is the main public representation of these women and it was found in analysis to be generally partial, hostile and exaggerated. The implication of this in terms of public perceptions of imprisoned women is profoundly troublesome, particularly in light of the general nature of female criminality in Ireland, established as being predominantly of a petty, personal or sexual nature. The selection by the press of twenty women to narrativise, from a potential population of 1,000 women, produced a skewed perspective on imprisoned women. In this limited representation, the narratives were stock stories, the characters mythical. Morrissey outlined the process by which the media does this.[43] The characters are, she said, subjectified through the principles of story-telling; the story-telling the media engages in is limited to a number of stock tales or narratives arising from popular stories or myths. One of the most common of these is the morality play, which places the forces of good on one side and the forces of evil on the other. The media, in mediating the event within the imperatives of limited time and space, according to Morrissey, reduce and simplify often complex stories to easily understood and easily judged tales, and within this process, individual subjectivities can become stereotyped, victimised or even mythified.

As with Smith's finding of the 'unnatural' representation in the media of women killers Myra Hindley (the White Devil) and Rose West (the Black Widow),[44] and Morrissey's study of, among others, the 'vampire lesbian killer' Tracey Wiggington,[45] we in Ireland have our own Black Widow, Catherine Nevin, our own Devil Killer, Carol Anne Dunne, and our own Scissor Sisters, Linda and Charlotte Mulhall. With the focus in the press on the serious violent crimes committed by very few women, the narratives presented and the discourse produced mythologise female criminality in Ireland. The subject positioning of imprisoned women within violent, dangerous narratives has substantial implications. For the women the implications arise from the interpellation of them as dangerous. Morrissey uses this Althussarian[46] term which she defines as the process through which individuals are compelled to identify with the representations which their culture supplies.[47] This means that the press, by subject positioning the women as dangerous, encourages them through this process of interpellation to identify themselves with the subject positions provided. The imprisoned women recognise themselves in these interpellations and, as they do, so too do those imprisoning them.

PRISON STAFF

This section examines the manner in which imprisoned women are subject positioned within the discourses of the staff and professionals working in and with the women's prisons. As will be seen, McKinnon's assertion that power is institutionalised in a masculine and indeed masculinist form is most applicable to Ireland's prisons. Responsibility for prisons in Ireland rests with the minister for justice, equality and law reform, currently Dermot Ahern. The minister at the time of the completion of the research for this book was Michael McDowell, a former attorney general. The minister delegates responsibility for the prisons to the Irish Prison Service, whose director general at the time was Sean Aylward, a career civil servant who has worked in the Department of Justice for most of his career. He is now secretary of the department, while Brian Purcell is currently the director general.

Women in senior prison officer positions included chief officers, assistant governors and one deputy governor, Kathleen McMahon. In 2002 Kathleen McMahon was promoted from her position as deputy governor of the Dóchas Centre to governor of that prison, the first woman in the history of the state to be appointed to that position. She resigned from this post in 2010. Kathleen's immediate supervisor, her mentor and guide, was John Lonergan, governor of Mountjoy Prison, who entered the Prison Service in 1968. John Lonergan was governor of Mountjoy Prison from 1992 to 2010 and also between 1984 and 1988; in the intervening years he was governor of Portlaoise Prison. He retired from the Prison Service in 2010. In all of the expert interviews conducted for this research, John Lonergan, and his vision for women in prison, was credited with the realisation of the Dóchas Centre, with the building itself, with the ethos of the prison, and with the innovations in the regime there. John Lonergan has been the pioneer in terms of women's imprisonment in Ireland in the late twentieth century. His personal and professional philosophy, in line with the philosophies of the reformers of the nineteenth century, is Christian.

Prison is a specialised space, a punitive space, designed for custody and control. Prisons attempt the construction of separate worlds with separate space and separate use of space; the control that is the control in prison space, expressed in confinement and routine, has been considered by theorists, among them Sim,[48] Foucault,[49] and Garland and Young.[50] Irigaray's notion of space as a container, an envelope of identity is useful in relation to prisons and the capacity of prisons to ascribe identities, and it is particularly useful to think of prison as an envelope of identity when considering the experiences of individuals criminalised by the criminal justice system and the judiciary; individuals who are, through the experience of imprisonment, stigmatised and dangerised.[51]

The following paragraph gives some sense of women's experiences of imprisonment in Ireland, and of the manner in which, through these experiences, the women's identities are constructed, their subjectivities shaped. In Ireland, women are imprisoned in a closed world, in which they must contend with the censuring of correspondence, letters and phone calls, and with the monitored weekly half-hour visits with family and friends. They must contend with control and the invasive nature of that control: the surveillance, the compulsory searches, the relentless observation and the continuous monitoring. They must come to terms with the lack of privacy and with the 'jollying along', the head patting, the false promises ('prison promises') and the patronage. They must deal with the spatial arrangements within the prison, a prison divided or demarcated into prisoner space, staff space and visitor space. These experiences represent the routines of the women's prisons. The routinisation of prison life facilitates what Butler (1993) calls the reiterative practice through which discourse produces the effect that it names. The demarcation of prisoner space is part of the prison's citation of identity, and it is related to Goffman's theory of how one's identity shapes one's access to space.[52] Goffman held that a person's world is divided up spatially by his personal identity as it is by his social identity, that our identities dictate where we may go, where we will be permitted or accepted and where we are threatened by our identities. The citational process of the naming of the women 'prisoners' ascribes that identity to them, and with that, particular senses of space and particular experiences of space.

In their prison space the women must deal with the constant waiting – waiting to be unlocked, for lock-up, for a visit, a phone call, food, for shop orders. They must engage with the prison regime in order to make any request – for extra soap, more sanitary towels or tampons, a different deodorant, new underwear or a new nightdress. They must deal with prison hierarchies, the titles and the obsequies, the 'yes Miss' 'no Miss' hierarchical dialogues. Sue Richardson commented upon this means of subjugating prisoners in her testimony on her experience of imprisonment in 1979; it is still a part of prison life. Finally, prisoners' subjectivities are shaped by the fact that they must contend with the prisoner culture produced by the closed world of punishment that is the prison, with the gossip, the bullying, the threat or fact of aggression or violence, the sharing of space, the negotiation of space, and with the power differentials of the different personalities among the prison population. If it is, as de Certeau suggests, that the inscription of the neighbourhood inscribes itself on the subject as a mark of indelible belonging[53] and if this is applied to imprisoned women's experiences of the neighbourhood of the prison, then it seems likely that the space that is prison space, and experiences of imprisonment within that space, are fundamental to the construction of the identities of imprisoned women.

The professional information pyramid operating within the women's prisons involves information being fed from discipline and civilian staff working with the women to the management of the prison and from these people on to the Prison Service. This information is framed by staff generally concerned with issues of security and control, staff trained to focus on such issues. This focus must be generated by the central management of the Prison Service, as it is the demands of the state that drive the information pyramid. The discourse of danger within which imprisoned women are subject positioned in the press fits very well with this discourse of security in the Prison Service and the women's prisons. In terms of prison design and management, the women are dangerised, which is evidenced by the emphasis on security and control.[54] Lianos and Douglas[55] suggest that, in the context of a dangerised world, deviance is an instrument for the perpetuation of social division. It seems to have this effect in Ireland, where many authors have found that experiences of imprisonment are largely confined to poorer, socially and economically disadvantaged sectors of Irish society.

The prison staff interviewed for the research generally constructed their roles with the imprisoned women in terms of security and control; their role with the women is a disciplining one. They encourage, inveigle and ultimately coerce the women into engaging with the structures they provide for them in order to produce and maintain the supportive and/or controlled environments for which the prisons were designed. Many authors detail the control exercised over women in prison. For Jose-Kampner this control is manifest in the architecture, the regime, the rules and regulations, the discipline, the linguistics of the prison;[56] for Sparks and Bottoms it is manifest in the signs and symbols of the prison, its rituals, its education and healthcare, its organised physical coercion.[57]

Within all the prisons the regime of prison officers is quasi-militaristic; prison officer culture is male, in some prisons bordering on machismo. Prison officers are trained at Beladd, the prison officers training unit at Portlaoise; they received nine-weeks' training. Currently prison officers participate in a two-year training programme, most of which is undertaken on placement in prisons. Representatives of management of the Prison Officers' Association (POA) described in interview the militaristic nature of that training; much of the focus is on prison officers' uniforms, the maintenance and upkeep of the uniform and appropriate standards of presentation for both the uniform and the uniformed officer, and there is an emphasis on physical fitness. All prisoners are guarded and managed by staff who have undergone this militaristic training and the prisoners are subject positioned as prisoners within militaristic discourses throughout that training. The terms of employment for civilian staff working in prisons demand that they too undergo prison officer training at Beladd before they take up posts within Irish prisons. For example, all of the nurses working in the Dóchas Centre, all qualified nurses, all of them female, were obliged to undertake this training, training which might be seen as a means of co-opting civilian staff into the culture of the prisons. As Morris details, prison is a man's world, in and out of the system.[58] Civilian staff in the prison are supported by the physical strength and discipline of the discipline staff: the prisons, the schools within the prisons and the healthcare provision within the prisons operate, despite some prison managers' focus on care and therapy, within a model of male coercive control. For Eaton control is manifest in women's prisons in the presence of men who reiterate a model of coercive control with which female inmates are already familiar.[59] This is a model with which, as will be seen, women imprisoned in Ireland are very familiar.

In the new women's prison, while the focus of management and staff is on security and control, concepts of respect for the inmates are anchored for the prison's managers in notions of care and therapy. One of the governors favours titles such as matron rather than governor and care staff rather than prison officer(s), suggesting that the female prisons need care, compassion and therapy, rather than security. Many authors, Carlen among them, have critiqued therapy, describing it as 'moral management', and discussed a 'new theology of therapy' and 'perpetual therapy', its subversion of the individual, its legitimisation of unanimous decisions, and its pressure towards conformity and the elements of control manifest in its implements: drugs, straitjackets and cellular confinement, referents for power. Heidensohn suggested that the special approach to treating women in prison is based on the notion that those few offending seriously and frequently enough to warrant imprisonment must be physically and/or mentally in need of therapy, so, she says, the female prison system is therapeutically oriented.[60] The Dóchas Centre was described by one of the professionals interviewed for this study as 'an annex of the Central Mental Hospital'. Within the prison, women inmates are respected as the ill are respected; they are jollied along, encouraged, gently persuaded, teased, and ultimately coerced into engaging with the prison system.

Control in the Dóchas Centre is in part exercised in the emphasis of regime there on the development and nurturing of very close relationships between staff and inmates, such close relationships having long been a feature of women's imprisonment in Mountjoy. Prison staff have a great deal of knowledge about the women and their families and these relationships are among the most prized resources of the prison. One of the nurses, in interview, said that when she started to work in the Dóchas Centre she was in awe of the level of knowledge the officers had of the women and their families. Foucault contends that power is based on detailed knowledge, that we are controlled by discourses used to observe and define us;[61] he draws on the work of Nietzsche when he contends that what is behind all knowledge – savoir – and behind all attainment of knowledge – connaissance – is a struggle for power.[62] There is in the close relationships fostered in the Dóchas Centre an appropriation in a sense of the lives of the women by the staff. The intimate knowledge prison staff have of the inmates establishes for them and their colleagues their dedication to these women, while for the inmates it encourages a surrender of themselves, of their independence and of any privacy they might have to the staff of the prison and the prison's professional discourses.

The women have no control, no autonomy. They must ask a member of staff for everything they need and must wait to be given everything by a member of staff. Some of the women will curry and cajole, pleading elaborate cases. They will move and/or amuse the staff and management with their stories and with the manner in which they present them, perform them, and the benevolent staff and management, amused and/or moved by the pleas of the begging women, will respond and may reward the begging with a gift from the prison's gift economy. Both Mauss[63] and Douglas[64] have written about the gift. Mauss[65] writes of the continuous flow in all directions of presents given, accepted, reciprocated, obligatorily and out of self-interest, for services rendered and through challenges and pledges. These prison gifts are very different. They are more akin to Douglas's concept of the gift;[66] she holds that there are no free gifts, that gift cycles engage persons in permanent commitments which articulate the dominant institutions. Gifts within the remit of the staff of the prisons include cigarettes, sweets, crisps, chocolate and biscuits, include extra toiletries, visits in the Dóchas Centre from one yard to the other, time spent in a friend's room, extra phone calls or longer phone calls. Gifts within the remit of management include money, clothes and shoes, trainers and tracksuits, accommodation in progressively less secure accommodation within the prison, as well as temporary release, days out or weekends at home. With these gifts women are rewarded for conformity, for engaging with the system.

One of the officers in Limerick Prison said that the women imprisoned there 'have no discipline', that 'dealing with male prisoners is a hundred times easier'. Pollack highlighted the informal agreement among prison officers that imprisoned women are more difficult to deal with than men.[67] The officer went on to say that the prison was 'kept busy with women imprisoned for not paying fines, for not paying back loans to credit unions, for not having a TV licence, for not paying parking fines', adding that the biggest problem in Limerick Prison was the fact that the women had nothing to do, no work opportunities. While there might be a class on (in the school), he added, maybe only one or two of the women would attend. He said it was a bad mix, with too much time on one's hands and problems outside the prison. 'The women demand constantly and they have childish ways of trying to manipulate,' he said. It may be that these childish ways are related to the gift culture of the prisons which reward, arbitrarily, particular behaviours. It may be that they are related to these women's ways of being in the prison and in the world, ways of being which are products of the patriarchal culture and the performance of the feminine demanded by and rewarded in that culture.

Imprisoned women are viewed and managed differently by long-serving discipline staff and by new discipline staff. In addition to this, in the Dóchas Centre the women are viewed and managed differently by prison officer staff there than by prison officers from Mountjoy Prison conscripted to duty in the Dóchas Centre when the centre is understaffed. There is in fact a struggle between the traditional macho prison officer culture and the new supportive prison officer culture of the Dóchas Centre. One of the most visible signs of the clash of cultures is the wearing of uniforms. Generally, Dóchas Centre prison officers wear civilian clothing, some wear a combination of uniform and civilian clothing, while a few wear full uniform. Prison officers in Limerick Prison wear the uniform, as do those from Mountjoy Prison drafted in to work in the Dóchas Centre. The officers in Mountjoy call themselves 'the jailors'. They don't like working in the Dóchas Centre because, they say, it 'is not a real prison'.

The representatives of management of the POA interviewed said that the needs of imprisoned women – 'physical, psychological and everything else' – are different to the needs of imprisoned men. They said that women in prison need the support of staff, that they draw strength from prison staff and from each other. Women in prison communicate more with prison staff, they added, while men 'put on a macho image and get on with doing their time'. The women were said to talk and talk, while the men would not talk freely or open up, were more contained. They told of how, when a female prisoner is ill, the other women are around her, encouraging her, bringing her around, whereas if a male prisoner is ill the men leave him alone to get over it.

The POA representatives told me that, at Beladd, prison officers are trained to be suspicious of prisoners, not to get too close to them, told that the further they stay away from prisoners the better they are doing their job. Then, the POA representatives said, prison officers may be sent to the Dóchas Centre where women prisoners engage with prison officers in a way that men never do. The officers are told that 'all the rules that apply in the male prison don't apply over here', they said, adding that 'prison officers are not trained to respond to the needs of women prisoners, there is no structure in place to indicate to them how they might appropriately respond, and no structure in place to affirm an appropriate response if one was made.'

Women prisoners were said in the interviews not to constitute a significantly large group within Irish prisons. The Irish legal system is found (in Chapter 5) to be informed by stereotypical assumptions and myths regarding male and female roles which are said to disproportionately disadvantage women. Fennel describes the Irish legal system as partisan in nature, informed by stereotypical assumptions and myths with regard to male and female roles, which she says, operate to disproportionately disadvantage women.[68] The testimony of a number of the interviewees for this research supports this finding. They said that the judiciary in Ireland sees women differently to how they see men; the then director general of the Prison Service, Sean Aylward, in interview suggested that because criminal men have dominated the criminal justice system over the years, there has been 'a certain cultural confusion' among the judiciary when dealing with women.

A number of interviewees, governors of prisons and the representative from the Probation Service (an agency within the Department of Justice and Law Reform) felt that one of the biggest concerns in criminal justice in Ireland was the way in which females are dealt with. They said that men get many more chances than women, that men would not receive custodial sentences for the trivial offences for which women might get six or nine months. The probation and welfare officer said that this was due to 'the patriarchal nature of the bench' and the effect of 'middle to upper class male judges' passing judgements on women in difficult circumstances, 'all middle class men in the powerful positions and making decisions about disadvantaged women'. One of the interviewees said that when a woman goes to court, her case may not be dealt with; 'she'll be held on remand for another four or five months.' Prisoners can be held indefinitely on remand in

Ireland. Worrall outlines how lengthy remands are imposed upon women in order to give the judiciary time to amass reports on the female offenders and then punish women more.[69] Many authors explored the concepts of chivalry, male paternalism and the 'gender contract' to explain the more lenient treatment of women by the criminal justice system (see Chapter 5). They found that women who play the stereotypical female role will be treated more leniently, but, as Carlen highlighted, women who do not or who cannot play that role are usually more severely punished.[70]

With the opening of the Dóchas Centre a new prison regime was developed, at its centre a cross-disciplinary management forum designed to facilitate information sharing and team building, leading to a more efficiently operating prison. The forum was found on analysis to be focused on issues of security and control, the prison's culture of institutionalisation, a culture which the forum determined was to be challenged as much as possible, and on normalisation, that the environment of the prison should be 'normalised' as much as possible. Foucault refers to the 'normalising gaze' of the prison with its great instruments of power, surveillance and normalisation.[71] Sim in his analysis of the experiences of female prisoners of medical power in prisons found the female experience of normalisation to be quite distinct from the male experience.[72] He wrote that returning women to their normal roles warranted a degree of intervention and surveillance which was much more intense than the experience of men. A great deal of concern was expressed at the meetings of the cross-disciplinary management forum regarding the women being imprisoned. Many members of the group expressed concern about the use of women's imprisonment for punishing petty crime. They talked about the high numbers of women inappropriately committed because of their psychological make-up, and of the courts using the women's prison to unload social problems. They said that women are sent to prison because there is no place else for them to go and that the crimes for which women are imprisoned are generally very trivial – that a woman might get six months for taking two deodorants, for taking six packets of razor blades, for non-payment of a fine, for not paying the proper bus fare, for not having a TV licence. They said that homeless women and/or women who are a nuisance on the street would be imprisoned. They were concerned about the frequently inappropriate use of imprisonment and the needless criminalisation of some women. John Lonergan said that prison was the main agency picking up mentally ill and homeless women.

The group was concerned with the problem of homelessness among the women; the drug problem in the prison was the focus of a lot of the group's attention, as was the concept of drug-free houses within the prison and the practical implications of the use of drug-free houses for prison management. The lack of any counselling service, particularly drug counselling, was also an issue, as was the loss at the time of the prison psychology service; the psychologist had resigned and the members of the group felt that replacing her was not a priority for the Prison Service. One of the interviewees illustrated the state-driven surveillant role of the psychology service within the Irish Prison Service: 'The main reason psychologists exist within Irish prisons is to attempt to stop re-offending.' As Carlen stated (1986), within prison the state pays the medics and psychiatrists who examine imprisoned women. The women don't consult the medics; the state consults the medics about the women.

The group was concerned about accommodation available to women leaving the prison,[73] about the hostels available to the women in Dublin – Haven House, Regina Chaeli, and Morning Star – and the standard of that accommodation. Through the discussions at the forum, the class structure of experiences of imprisonment emerged: women from certain geographic locations were sent to prison, those from certain postal districts in Dublin, namely Dublin 1, 7, 9 and now 24, from the inner city, Ballyfermot, Finglas, Clondalkin, and Tallaght, a few from Bray and a few Travellers, and women from certain other urban centres, Cork, Athlone and Limerick. The women were described generally as having poor prospects, as being drug dependent, in poor general health, with perhaps multiple pregnancies, with 'the virus', or from very deprived backgrounds; they were strong recidivists, young malnourished drug addicts. A newer, very young member of the prison officer staff at the Dóchas Centre said that when she started to work there she was shocked by people coming back to prison after serving a sentence. 'I thought, Jesus, you do a spell and that's it, never again, you'd be reformed, you'd be the best person ever, and that just isn't the case and that's what shocked me. I suppose I didn't know much about drugs and the hold drugs get on people.'

The women were represented as people with serious mental illnesses, who would be more appropriately cared for in the acute psychiatric services. Very few were involved in serious crime. There were no major drug barons in the female prison, no mass murderers; most were petty criminals with severe social problems coming from backgrounds of physical, sexual and emotional abuse, from three or four generations of poverty.

There was a focus and preoccupation among the participants at these meetings with activities in the prison, with planning, organising and running activities and with encouraging and monitoring participation in them;[74] the group was particularly interested in the ability and propensity of the women to commit to activities, with disciplining women to commit to activities and then disciplining them into honouring those commitments. Group members represented themselves as managing the women; they were in control of them, their agenda was to accommodate the women safely, providing, in consultation with the women, activities for them and engaging them in those activities. They structured their roles with the imprisoned women, as did all the members of staff, around their disciplines and their concepts of care provided within an ethos of security and control.

The interviewees spoke of the experiences the women had of home and family. They were concerned that there was no place for the women at home; that at home they had no security, no sense of trust. They said that the women within their families were subjected to all kinds of suffering and abuse. Yet these experts represented the women almost entirely in terms of their familial obligations. Walby,[75] Bartky,[76] Radke and Stam[77] and Bourdieu[78] explored the depth, pervasiveness and interconnectedness of different aspects of women's subordination in contemporary society, through women's everyday experiences, of the family, of confinement to the private sphere, of housework and wage labour, of the threat and fear of male violence, and of men's flight from responsibilities, from fatherhood. Walby wrote of patriarchal sexual relations, of sexual violence, of compulsory heterosexuality and of the sexual double standard all as aspects of women's subordination within patriarchy.

The interviewees spoke at length of the women in terms of their families and their familial obligations. They represented imprisoned women as carrying the full burden of the family and

3.1: The Dóchas Centre: a view of the Big Yard

the home. They said that these women had huge responsibilities in their lives and very little support. One interviewee said:

> The women in the prison are the most marginalised. They are caught in a trap of drugs and prison, a vicious circle. They come from three or four generations of poverty. They have no education. There is no place for them at home. The only place is the street and their streets, their whole environments, are full of drugs. They come from very deprived backgrounds. They have no security at home. A lot of them have been sexually abused. A lot of them just seem to accept that as their lot in life.

Another said: 'The women are responsible for the family, and life has been very tough for them. They've been abused by the men in their lives. They are in very unhealthy relationships. They have come out of very dysfunctional families and they are going back into them, complicated chaotic families.' Another: 'The majority of the women who come in here are poor, their parents are probably split up, maybe another man has moved into the house. There's a lot of abuse, a lot of drugs. The women from a young age have been well exploited.'

Compared with men, women were said to be the main caregivers and so needed much more intensive work. The evidence for this perhaps explains the frequent claims that women in prison are more demanding than men. It seems it is the overwhelming responsibilities of women that cause them to make more demands than men on prison staff. One interviewee said:

> Women worry about having a roof over the family's heads, about money coming in from the social welfare, about ill family members. Their homes have to be taken care of, their children, their old parents, their aunt and uncles, grandparents. Their dogs have to be taken care of. Imprisoned men don't worry like that, they sit back. The men would have a lot of queries, for instance, will you ring my solicitor, can you see the Chief or the Governor about this or that, could I be moved to another wing or another prison, I'd like to do a drug awareness programme, I'd like to do pre-HIV test counselling, and lastly, and not too many requests like this, would you ring a family member for me.

The interviewees generally expressed their belief that men in prison are able to cut themselves off more, that men remove themselves easier from a family situation, that the separation from children and family 'hits women more than men', that 'when men come into prison they leave their problems at home, women bring them with them.' A male governor interviewed said that 'men who are involved in crime would not show the same care or concern for their families at home ... men don't seem to have the same level of responsibility especially with young families.'

One of the chaplains interviewed said that it was important for the women to have children but the women couldn't parent, that the women wanted to be good parents but didn't know what that was because they hadn't received it themselves. It was also important, the chaplain added, for the women to have a man but that they were in and out of relationships, they had nothing stable. Another interviewee said that the women had 'grown up around prison; their mothers are raising their kids and that was their mothers' experience as well, everyone gets to be a mother but it's to the grandchildren.' The women were represented as somehow failing in these roles, as falling short of the ideal of motherhood. Walby takes a different perspective; she writes of women's problematic experiences of the family relative to ideological representations of the family 'as a consensual unit with a fair division of duties'.[79] Despite difficult experiences of the family, the women embraced motherhood. They are immersed in a heterosexual culture within which it is appropriate for a woman to be in a relationship with a man, and even though these women suffer greatly in these relationships, heterosexual familial ideology is so powerful in their cultures that the women actively pursue these frequently overwhelmingly responsibilities and damaging relationships.

PRISON STRUCTURES

Prison structures shape the way in which women, from day to day, experience prison. In Ireland, the structures of the prisons are primarily the manner in which the women are received into prison, prison healthcare, prison educational provision, and the women's accommodation. The following pages describe these structures and the manner in which imprisoned women experience them.

In the Dóchas Centre the women are held, apropos the vision statement, 'in a caring safe environment'.[80] In Limerick Prison women are imprisoned in a basic lock-up regime within which they are constantly monitored; they are held, apropos the mission statement of Limerick Prison, 'in humane, safe and secure custody'.[81] The women's accommodation in Limerick Prison was changed twice within the first five years of this century, the prisoners moving each time into what the Prison Service described as new and/or improved accommodation. In the Dóchas Centre, with the progressive atmosphere of a new prison, new structures were instigated around the new order: in the new purpose-built school; in the modern Healthcare Unit; in the introduction of the multi-disciplinary bi-monthly meetings for staff and management; in the civilian dress of the discipline staff of the prison; and in the 'family or home-like' structure of the prison. There are no such new structures in Limerick Prison.

RECEPTION

Entry to the Dóchas Centre is gained through an electronically controlled sliding door. Through the first door entry is gained into the small outer reception area, known in the prison as Control. The director of the Irish Penal Reform Trust in interview said of this door: 'I think the door is symbolic of the new female prison, the beginning is the door and the end is the padded cell. That tells me that nothing deep has changed, there are good superficial changes but the ethos is still about control.'

The visitor gives their details and the purpose of their visit to the officers behind the glass window at Control and will then be asked to wait in the tiny reception room opposite the glass window, a small room with six or eight comfortable chairs and a low coffee table, until the person they are visiting is located and directed to come to Control. The visitor then moves through the second electronically operated door (only one of these doors can be open at a time) into the main reception area. In this area there is a door leading into Control, a door leading into the visitors' area, a door leading to the administration offices of the prison, and a door leading into the prisoners' reception area.

In the prisoners' reception area there are two search rooms, one toilet, two showers, a bathroom, a reception desk and a laundry area. In this area, prisoners coming into the prison are strip searched, encouraged to shower and wash their hair, their belongings are searched and stored, and here they are held until a nurse comes from the Healthcare Unit to bring them into the prison. This process has been examined by a number of authors, among them Eaton,[82] O'Dwyer and Carlen,[83] and Lundström-Roche.[84] They all write about the capacity of this process to strip individual identity while simultaneously ascribing prisoner identity. This is the ritual within which every woman's sense of self is subsumed into the identity 'prisoner'. The strip-searching ritual is, to use Garfinkel's term, a degradation ceremony;[85] it is, as Garfinkel suggested, about identity degradation. Garfinkel states that through the ritual the individual becomes 'reconstituted'.[86] In relation to women's experiences of imprisonment, it is through the strip-searching ritual that individual identity is removed, prisoner identity ascribed, and a female prisoner is brought into being. The ritual of strip-searching is experienced by all of the women all of the time. Every time they come and go from the prison this stripping in front of discipline staff or stripping by discipline staff takes place. There is no discretion in the stripping. All of the women are subject to it, regardless of their crime or prison status, their drug status, their age or their physical and psychological states of being. The prison officer staff of the reception area said that the women are searched top first, then bottom. The officers say that the women are never naked, and there are no internal body searches.

The women in Limerick Prison, at the time of the primary research collection, were held in C class; they moved into this 'new' accommodation in 2001. A deputy governor at the prison said that the move by the women to the redecorated and in-part refurbished male wing of the prison was 'what you might call our second phase of development ... our third phase will be the examination of a totally new facility for females approaching the facility that is the Dóchas Centre, room accommodation rather than cell accommodation, a structured arrangement of treatment and sentence management.' Unfortunately the 'third phase' resulted in a totally different development whereby the women were moved into accommodation similar to the accommodation the women in Mountjoy Prison left behind in St Patrick's Institution in 1999 – cellular accommodation with in-cell sanitation. There are some photographs of the accommodation of this 'new' women's prison in Chapter 6.

The approach to the female corridor in the prison was along the inner wall of the prison to a metal door.[87] When the bell on the door rang, an officer unlocked the door, and then unlocked an indoor gate into the women's prison. Inside the gate was the reception area. This was equipped with two showers, two toilets and two wash hand basins, all shrouded by one very big cream-coloured plastic curtain. When women are committed to Limerick Prison the prison officers there told me that they are body-searched, a pat down over clothes, not strip-searched. They are required to shower and encouraged to wash their hair. Before showering they hand out their clothing to be searched by the officers and afterwards are given what clothing they require and escorted to their cells where they are given whatever they need from the supply of toiletries and bedclothes available.

In 2001 the women committed to the prison were taken along the ground floor corridor, which contained a schoolroom (formerly a five-man cell), a computer room with two computers and a printer, and two strip/isolation cells. An officer commented that they couldn't manage without a strip cell, that there are violent women in the prison and that they calm down in the strip cell. He added that normally a woman is held there for no more than a couple of hours. He said that the strip cell acts as a deterrent. The women, he said, sometimes come into prison with syringes hidden in body cavities, and that women with full-blown AIDS have spat at staff and squirted AIDS-infected blood at them.

The accommodation of the female wing consisted of a corridor on the first floor, on which there was an office where the officers congregated and a very small governor's office, which accommodated the governor's parade or any professional visits to the wing. There was a small food servery, which doubled as a 'domestic science' room, and there were sixteen cells, some equipped with bunk beds for double occupancy. The model of sanitation on the ground floor was repeated in two locations on the accommodation corridor, two showers, two toilets and two wash hand basins, shrouded in one big cream plastic curtain.

Throughout this committal experience the women's degraded identities are conveyed to them. With every step, the discourses of the prisons communicate to the women their new prisoner identities; their ordered existences, the militaristic nature of that order, the compulsion to obey, the physical coercion, the grim, bleak surroundings, the punishment technologies, prison walls, locked doors and punishment cells. The process exemplifies both the constitutive power of discourse and Butler's theory of the constitutive power of reiterative and citational practice.[88] The constitutive power of these prison discourses brings into being female prisoners. The female prisoner is constituted thorough the discursive practices of the prison, its language and its materiality.

In Limerick Prison, when the women, in 2003, moved to the accommodation they currently occupy, they found the standard to be much the same; however, it was new – and the particular shades of pastel paint and the patterns of the chintzy quilt covers and curtains were new whereas the wing (corridor) they left was old. Heidensohn[89] noted that in sexually segregated prison systems, female regimes differ only in detail from male regimes, and that despite gallons of pastel paint and flowery curtains over windows the effects of the old institutions remained; both Bowker[90] and Chesney-Lind[91] remarked that women were afterthoughts in prisons built primarily to hold men.

In the second move in Limerick Prison the cells were provided with in-cell sanitation, utterly inappropriate and completely insensitive of women's needs, and actually torturous given that the women occupy double occupancy, cells. The toilets are unhygienic, given their proximity to the work surfaces of the women's cells, and the fact that the women eat all their meals in their cells. This accommodation has a sealed tomb quality; sounds echo hollowly around it. Initially, the women were slightly panicked by the new wing. This was evident in the very specific comments several of them made, for example 'they shouldn't be allowed to do that' or 'they shouldn't be allowed to keep the women in that place.'

3.2: One of two duplicate corridors in Limerick Prison (current accommodation)

HEALTHCARE

In the Dóchas Centre when a prisoner is ready to move from the reception area into the prison, a nurse escorts her to the Healthcare Unit. The role of the nurse in the committal process is significant, signalling as it does a therapeutic aspect to the process and to the experience of imprisonment. It masks to a degree the compulsion that pervades the entire experience. The nurse encourages, and in a way manipulates, compliance with the regime. The Healthcare Unit is a three-storey building at the centre of the prison. Its size and position, both physically and symbolically, signal some curative capacity on the part of the prison, as well as the prison's discursive positioning of imprisoned women as ill. The ground floor of the unit is entirely secured, reflecting again the discourse of danger within which the women are positioned. It is comprised of a dental surgery, a nurses' station, a psychologist's room, a treatment room, a surgery and a pharmacy. The chaplaincy is also on the ground floor of the unit, outside the secure area. When the prison is overcrowded, this is contained by prison management in the Healthcare Unit. The second report of the European Committee for the Prevention of Torture and Inhuman or Degrading Treatment or Punishment (CPT) requested that measures be taken to ensure that all women imprisoned are provided with appropriate accommodation.[92]

First thing every morning the women come to the Healthcare Unit for drugs, mostly physeptone (phy'), used in drug detoxification programmes. They come straight from bed, in dressing gowns and nightwear. One of the nurses said that, on that particular day, thirty-five of the women in the prison were on phy', just under half of the prison population of that day. The militaristic surveillant nature of the institution was evident in the manner in which nurses dispensed drugs, under prison officer escort. The women's first-thing-in-the-morning expedition for drugs represents one of the main trajectories prisoners initiate from their rooms. The signs of the prison conveyed by this particular trajectory are the routineness of the expedition and the disciplined nature of the drugs' distribution.

Throughout the day and night, prisoners are committed to the prison. One afternoon, the following activities occurred. At 2 p.m. a new committal arrived and a nurse went to meet her. This new prisoner was then registered in the Healthcare Unit; all this took about fifteen minutes. The nurses were occupied throughout the afternoon with meeting individual prisoners and updating records. At 4 p.m. the women were queuing again for medication, once again all dispensed under prison officer surveillance and within their control; this took about forty-five minutes. It was a busy period but slightly less busy than it had been that morning. At 4.45 p.m. it was tea time. Sausage rolls, beans and bread and butter were served in the dining room (a centralised facility). After tea, it was back to the Healthcare Unit. The new prisoner who had been committed after lunch had been released already and another woman had arrived. The new arrival had been committed for assaulting a Garda. It was this woman's first time in prison. She had expected to go home after her court appearance but instead was committed to prison. She had two children at home and was very upset and concerned for them. One of the nurses expressed anger that this could happen to a family in contemporary Irish society: 'The women come from areas where it is taken for granted that this can be done to them. They don't even have a sense of outrage about it. It seems so unfair; their kids are just thrown about. If it happened at other addresses in Dublin it wouldn't be tolerated.' The women are locked into their rooms and/or locked into their houses by 7.30 p.m. At 8 p.m. the medication round begins. This time, because the women are locked up, the nurses, with a prison officer escort, take the medication to the women.

The second (top) floor of the Healthcare Unit is comprised of accommodation units for both women newly admitted to the prison and those living in the Healthcare Unit. Women live in the Healthcare Unit if the prison is overcrowded or when they are ill, physically or psychiatrically or both.[93] On the top floor one day during the observation, one woman was locked in a dark room, the darkness being her choice. When the door opened a strong unclean odour emanated from the room. The nurse commented: 'a social phobic who cannot self manage'. The next woman was also locked up; the nurse gave her tablets and morphine: 'she sniffs paint.' A very young girl, about 16 years old, was locked in a strip cell: 'must have been misbehaving, she's in prison for stealing golf balls off a golf course.' There were three women in the padded cells, all accommodated there because the prison was overcrowded. The padded cells in the Dóchas Centre are a major part of what Garland refers to as *architecture parlante*,[94] the symbolically significant architecture of the new women's prison. They are arguably the most powerful of the prison's signifiers, suggesting to the imprisoned women, and the community of the prison and beyond, the women's dangerised identities.

One of the nurses explained that a governor could send women to the pad for punishment or if they are threatening to harm themselves. The nurse showed and explained the refractory gown and blankets. These are made of hard, cold synthetic fibre like fibreglass. They are given instead of blankets and night-clothes to women being held in the pads on punishment or for observation. The nurse explained that the women couldn't tear these garments to make ligatures, that they might use ribbons from nighties and belts from dressing gowns, or tear nighties into strips to make ligatures. She added that sometimes women try to choke themselves with their own hands. She explained that they can't do this; as soon as they lose consciousness they begin to breathe again. With the refractory gown and blankets, the women, she said, can't come to any harm in the pad, provided they haven't a cigarette lighter concealed inside themselves.

3.3: Padded cell with refractory gowns and blankets: Dóchas Centre

An officer explained how a woman would be taken under restraint to the padded cells. Through that explanation the extremely punitive nature of this process of control, the dominating and potentially sexually charged nature of the process, became apparent. The officer explained how, very slowly using 'control and restraint', a woman is taken to the pads. In the process she is overpowered and restrained; one officer seizes her head while another seizes each of her arms. They walk slowly towards the pad, staying very close to the woman. The prisoner is always gowned in the pad by the officers, in other words stripped naked and dressed in the refractory gown if held for security or punishment. Carlen[95] writes of the vulnerability of women prisoners when naked, exposed to the lust, derision, or just cold casual inspection of their gaolers, whether they be male or female, homosexual or heterosexual.

The documented reasons (in the appropriate record book at Control in the Dóchas Centre) for using the padded cells were as follows: at the woman's own request; the woman was suicidal; the woman broke up or burned her cell; she was drunk on committal and was sent to the pad for observation; the woman was fighting; was setting fire to plastic; was sniffing air freshener; sniffing a solvent; was agitated; hysterical; depressed; she was cutting herself; she assaulted an officer at court; she's there on doctor's orders; there for her own safety; she had self-inflicted burns; she had barricaded herself in her cell; she had been attempting to escape; she was there for being disruptive; for threatening staff; she had attacked an officer; she was being very aggressive; she was sent there on return from the Central Mental Hospital; she had been in breach of temporary release (TR); she had been unlawfully at large; she was taken there on return from hospital; at a psychiatrist's request; she was on special obs, (special observation). In the year 2000 there was a monthly average of fifteen committals to the pads; the highest number was twenty-eight, committed in June, and the lowest number was six, committed in December. There was at this time a daily average of about ninety women imprisoned in the Dóchas Centre.

The nurses said that some women would ask to go to the pads. This seems to illustrate Carlen's contention that imprisoned women feel 'horribly at home' within psychiatry.[96] It is likely also that some of the women's representations of themselves as depressed might relate to Liebling's[97] gendered use of words, that women use the word depression and men the word bored to describe the same sensation; Liebling also found that where men could externalise problems – blaming the prison, the pressures they were under, the failures of others – women internalised them. There were in the Dóchas Centre, over the month of January 2001, more than 600 incidences of women being placed on special observation.[98] The reasons given were as follows: the woman was pregnant; was depressed; couldn't sleep; had received bad news; had family problems; was suicidal; was distressed; on return from a court visit; on return from hospital; the woman was cutting herself; she appeared strange; she was physically ill; was facing more charges; she'd had a past suicide attempt; on medical/psychiatric recommendation; had had a possible miscarriage; had been sentenced; would not communicate; was staying in her room; was staying in bed; she'd had a death in her family; was fighting; had refused TR; was on return from Christmas TR; was argumentative; her boyfriend broke off their relationship; this was her first time in prison; this was her first serious charge. It appears from this evidence that any negative behaviour on the part of the women is pathologised and they were very quickly placed on observation. Some were taken to the pads to be stripped and held there for observation.

Many authors have explored negative and self-injurious behaviour among imprisoned women. Carlen[99] suggested that, while prison staff have a tendency to pathologise resistance to prison regimes, it is perhaps imprisonment itself that causes depressed or bizarre behaviour. Sim highlighted the fact that acknowledgement of the rationality of negative responses of those imprisoned to their circumstances has only relatively recently emerged.[100] Sim described how the internalised anger and powerlessness of imprisoned women manifests itself in self-injurious behaviour, self-injury, arm slashing, head banging against walls, attempted suicide and suicide. He quotes Carlen as saying that women's prisons are closed, frightening and damaging places;[101] that sources of violence include both physical and pharmaceutical control; that imprisoned women have no effective way of countering prison controls or abuses; and that in the absence of legitimate grievance strategies, some prisoners 'can only stave off their prison-induced fears of death, madness and institutionalisation and general loss of identity by engaging in survival strategies that may seem inexplicable'.

One of the nurses interviewed said that the women serving long sentences were generally not drug addicts and that they took up very little of the nurses' time. She added that women who are in for a long time make some arrangements for their domestic situation and are consequently more settled, more stable in prison. Other women, she said, are in prison for such a short time their home problems impinge on them. These women the staff of the Healthcare Unit see on a regular basis, many of them several times a day. 'The women might have headaches, toothaches or period pains, they may have fallen and hurt themselves, they may have been in a fight and been hurt, or they may get a panic attack, or they might be upset about something.'

The nurse said that there was a high staff prisoner ratio in the women's prison because the healthcare needs of women in custody far outweigh those of men in custody, because of the women's poor general health. This is related to the extreme marginality of many of the women imprisoned. As detailed in Chapter 1, the population of the women's prisons is small and unstable, in the sense that the women often come and go very quickly from the prison, for the most part serving very short sentences. In comparisons with the large stable male prison population, women prisoners are often constructed as more difficult, more marginalised, more troubled.

Older, more mature, better-resourced women tend to serve long sentences; they enjoy reasonably good health and reasonable standards of education. In the Dóchas Centre these women are designated 'trustees' by prison management. By designating some women prisoner's trustees, the managers have 'othered' the rest of the population. Through this othering process, the rest of the imprisoned women become 'other' than the trustees, less than them. Lianos and Douglas[102] discuss what they call the primitive fear of otherness in relation to the concept of dangerisation. Trustees are not monitored as much as non-trustees. They settle into their niche within the control environment of the prison, learning quickly to wait for their needs to be met by a professional staff primarily focused on the often critical needs of the impoverished, malnourished, uneducated, ill and generally addicted women, and on the needs of the homeless women who, deemed public nuisances, are imprisoned and needlessly criminalised by the Irish criminal justice system.

In Limerick Prison, the discursive subject positioning of women was evident in the language of the healthcare provision, in the gendered nature of that provision, and in its spatial experience. One doctor working from a small surgery located in the men's prison provided healthcare. The prison had no nurses, but it had six male medical orderlies, prison officers mostly from nursing backgrounds. It had one visiting psychiatrist, who came to the prison one morning a week. The prison doctor in interview said that they could have 230 prisoners in Limerick Prison, including the women[103] and 'very high rates of psychiatric illness'. He said that out of twelve women in the prison at that time, he would see two to four every day. On the subject of self-injury among the women prisoners, he said that there would be 'incidences of cutting and self mutilation, tentative enough injuries, never a risk to life', and that such incidences would occur every few weeks, 'if a visit went badly or a privilege was denied, if there was an emotional upset'. He added that the women's coping mechanisms were not what they should be: 'Looking after fifteen female prisoners was probably the same as looking after fifty male prisoners; the women are more vocal, more inclined to express themselves, more inclined to be verbally abusive, women prisoners unhappy with their medication will pretty much make it obvious, men are more accepting.'

The doctor readily spoke of the inadequate standard of accommodation in Limerick Women's Prison, of the lack of facilities, the poor small exercise yard, the 'gym of sorts', the fact that the prison was too confined and limited in terms of things to do, the fact that the women in Limerick Prison were generally unhappy with their basic facilities, their toilet facilities, the 'slopping out', the inadequate showers, and that there was a general unhappiness with the food. It seemed likely that the poor condition of the women's prison prompted the inmates' negative responses rather than any instability in the women held there. This instability was evident in the doctor's testimony of very high rates of psychiatric illness, self injury, emotional upsets and in his testimony of the women's inadequate coping mechanisms.

EDUCATION

Imprisonment raises many issues in terms of education. The punitive nature of prison space and its agenda of security and control contests the agenda of education, growth, development, self expression, self-actualisation, independent thinking and creativity. Frequently within prison space, security considerations override all other considerations, educational, social or personal. Sparks and Bottoms write of control within prisons being manifest in, as well as the signs, symbols and rituals of the prison, its education and healthcare.[104] Foucault implicated educationalists in prison's technology of the soul.[105] Teaching within prison means teaching in space managed for security considerations, space governed by military-like rules and regulations and monitored by officials of a military-like prison service.[106] As outlined, the power structure in the women's prisons in Ireland is that of a quasi-military regime and a patriarchal order. Students within prison space must contend with all these issues, while their abilities and means to cope with the exigencies of imprisonment, as considered in the previous section, impact upon the educational experience afforded by prison.

The Dóchas Centre and Limerick Prison provide very different educational experiences[107] for their respective inmates. In the Dóchas Centre, 'school' takes place in a new, purpose-designed, two-storey building. For women in Limerick, 'school' takes place in a cell adapted, to some degree, for this purpose. In 2001, the range of educational and vocational opportunities offered to the women in the new Education Unit of the Dóchas Centre encompassed woodwork, computers, English and maths, cookery, food and nutrition, soft toys, pottery, art, photography, group skills, swimming, outdoor pursuits (a hill walking and canoeing opportunity offered two or three days in the academic year), parenting classes, music, clay modelling, drama, physical education and creative writing.[108] There is in the school a beauty/hairdressing salon, a craft room, an industrial cleaning programme, and in 2003 an industrial sewing programme was offered to the women. A project called CONNECT, introduced in 1998 by the Department of Justice, Equality and Law Reform, was designed to help women while in prison and on leaving, both socially and vocationally. It was EU funded and involved collaboration between the department and the National Training and Development Institute, part of the REHAB Group. The project faltered, however, due to budgetary constraints. One woman in the Dóchas Centre was engaged in an Open University course and two had commenced programmes with Oscail, Distance Education at Dublin City University (DCU). The annual Summer School had been established in 2000.[109] In the Dóchas Centre, teachers from the Vocational Education Committee (VEC) run the school, while prison officers run the beauty shop, the industrial cleaning, the craft workshop, and the gym. Foras Áiseanna Saothair (FÁS), the state training agency, ran the industrial sewing programme. In the school the prison's focus on surveillance, security and control is very evident, with prison officers keeping a note of who's coming and going. Students who sign up for classes and then don't attend are 'locked back', locked into their rooms. The prison only stopped this practice for those not attending Sunday mass with the move to the Dóchas Centre in 1999.

On one particular morning there were ten women in the school, seven in a crafts class and three in a photography class. The beauty shop opened at 10 a.m. Eight women could be accommodated there but the numbers depend on the officer and the mix of women. There were a couple of prisoners in the beauty shop; they were going to a function in the gym and wanted to look well and so were having their hair done. Hutter and Williams[110] found that pride in one's feminine appearance and the ability to fulfil a stereotype were deemed to be significant factors in the 'recovery' of mentally ill and psychopathic female patients in Broadmoor.

The prison gym is readily and regularly converted into a function hall. The officer in charge of the school remarked: 'The women don't care for the gym, they're not a sporty lot.' Two prisoners stalked out of a class; they'd been arguing, the officer hushed them and they made up sitting on stools outside the classroom. The officer said that the women were allowed to get away with too much, that if you let a child get away with something they keep pushing and pushing. One woman left a class; she asked the officer monitoring the school to call the Healthcare Unit to tell them she was on her way back. In Dóchas the woman needs the officer to make that call; if the officer doesn't make the call for whatever reason, the woman will have to stand outside the

Healthcare Unit until someone happens to come along with a key to open the door to admit her. Sometimes women prisoners clean the school: 'Might get a few cigarettes for cleaning it,' one remarks.

The signifying elements of identity within this experience were the provision of school supported by the physical strength and discipline of the discipline staff, the locking and unlocking of doors, the locking up and locking back of women, the promise of a gift, the infantilisation of the women, the paternalistic words of the officer, and the prison's beauty treatment provision. With these signs, the prominent discourse is one of danger. Positioned with that discourse the women are subjectified as infantile and recalcitrant. The expression of femininity facilitated is normative.

The Education Unit in Limerick Prison had, in the first years of the twenty-first century, for the entire prison population of about 230 prisoners, no more than twenty of whom were women prisoners, the equivalent of sixteen full-time teachers; there were about twenty-three teachers coming into the prison. The value placed on education in Limerick Women's Prison in 2001 might be calculated by the provision of 'a five-man cell' adopted, if not adapted, for the purpose of a schoolroom. This prison cell was too small and airless to use as a classroom. The widows were too small and there was no air circulation. It was a schoolroom in which, according to the head of education there, teachers were physically exhausted after two-hours' work – a schoolroom that was equally if not more exhausting, debilitating and discouraging for imprisoned women. In interview the head of education described the programme of training and education available. It ran over five days a week and ranged from stress management, aromatherapy, reflexology and yoga to arts and crafts, home economics, health education, music, and computers; in addition there would, from time to time, be invited speakers.

The main school in Limerick Prison[111] was a two-storey building with five rooms used only by male prisoners. In addition, there were two classrooms on the top of D Class, a male wing of the prison, used only by male prisoners; there were two teachers in the gym (the male prisoners' gym) and a teacher in the craft workshops (again in the male prison). The school timetable in the women's Education Unit at the time of interview was as follows: on Monday morning, English literacy, arts or crafts; in the afternoon, and on Monday night, PE; on Tuesday, Computers and Art in the morning and Music and Art in the afternoon; on Tuesday and Wednesday night, Home Economics; Wednesday morning was at that time a free slot; Wednesday afternoon, Music; Thursday all day, Arts and Crafts; Friday morning, Health Education and Awareness and Friday afternoon, PE. PE in the women's wing took place in a low-ceilinged cell adopted for this purpose.

The head teacher said that, on average, two thirds of the women would attend class, and that the response to classes would generally depend on what was happening that day. She added that the women complained about the poor part of the gender bargain they had secured in terms of educational provision in the prison, and that they constantly complained that the men got more and better educational and training opportunities than them. She pointed out, however, that the women in the prison, in terms of educational provision, had as much as the men. This was to some degree disingenuous, given the structure of the schools in Limerick Prison and the uneven and gendered distribution of educational resources. The head teacher did concede that the men had workshops that the women didn't have, woodwork and tailoring; and that the men, at that time, were engaged in a stained-glass workshop. This workshop was, she said, open to the women if they wanted to join but none had opted to do so.

The women, in this interview, were represented as dissatisfied and complaining. It is possible that such complaining could be tiresome for prison staff. In time, it could lead to the women being described as troublesome, more troublesome perhaps than the men. As highlighted, Pollack found informal agreement among prison staff that imprisoned women are more difficult to deal with than men.[112] In this case, it is evident that the education, work and training provision in the male prison is superior to that in the female prison. This was denied in the interview, and when the women prisoners complained about it, it was denied to them. Despite the reasonableness of the women's complaints, those complaints led to them being negatively represented in the discourses of the educational system within the prison.

In terms of work opportunities within prison, in both the Dóchas Centre and Limerick Women's Prison, the women replicated familial and household labour. They generally worked at cleaning, whether the landing, the house or the visiting area, the school, the stores or the corridors. In the Dóchas Centre, two women were employed in a Training For Work programme, contract cleaning. Three worked in the kitchen. Some did piece-work for companies outside the prison, packing greeting cards and sewing shoes. The women worked at these occupations for lengths of time ranging from seven or eight hours a day every day for those who worked in the kitchen, to a few minutes every day for some of the cleaning tasks. In Limerick Prison, there are no work opportunities for women; instead they do chores. The women were remunerated for their work with money, €13 a week for the kitchen jobs, €50 for sewing a hundred pairs of shoes, 15 cents for packing a small box of greeting cards. For some of the work/chores, women were remunerated with cigarettes, sweets, crisps and chocolate every now and then. A woman in Limerick Prison said: 'If you do jobs [chores] you get the extra phone call or some tobacco.' Work for Ireland's imprisoned women is a pastime; it is designed, as is much of the educational endeavour within the prisons, to occupy them. The rewards the women receive for the work they do are for the most part treats rather than recompense. The work signifies to the women the trivial nature of women's work generally, while the rewards given to the women powerfully signify the slight value of their work.

ACCOMMODATION

In the Dóchas Centre women are provided with ostensibly private personal facilities, in single ensuite rooms to which they have keys. The wooden doors are solid, while the keys to which the women have access can be overridden by the regime. One day I met one of the women who had been accommodated in the Healthcare Unit, the woman who had been sniffing paint. She had been moved out of the unit into a house. I went with her at her invitation to see her new room in Laurel House, but we couldn't get access despite having a key. I thought that perhaps she was confused about her room number but this wasn't the case. The officer in the house had locked all the rooms, overriding the keys to which the women had access. The officer suggested that if my (really very frail) friend didn't want to spend time in the gym, we could go out into the yard. It was made perfectly clear that because it was the middle of the day, when all prisoners were supposed to be engaged in some organised activity, we were not allowed to stay in the house, not even the kitchen or living area. It was the coldest day, snow had been forecast, and we went, like two orphans, out into the elements.

In the women's rooms, each door is equipped with a peephole, a small rectangular clear space at eye level in the door covered on the outside by a hinged wooden flap. There are light switches both inside and outside. The rooms are carpeted in a uniform light brown colour and painted in uniform pastel shades. Each room is uniform in terms of size and fittings. Each has a window which cannot be opened and an air vent which can; there is a single bed, a half-sized wardrobe (to prevent suicide attempts), a bedside locker and a table and chair. The door separating the bedroom from the shower room is semi-opaque and three-quarter length, the length again designed specifically to prevent suicide attempts. Similarly, the fittings in the shower room are low down on the wall. The focus is on security and on a presumed propensity to suicide among imprisoned women. The technology is that of a Foucauldian panopticism rather than a Benthamite panopticism, a subtle power designed to produce, by acting on individual subjectivities, docile bodies.

3.4: The women's exercise yard in Limerick Prison (current accommodation)

The focus on security and control is even more evident in Limerick Prison. The women there are accommodated on two floors, on one corridor on each floor, in cells designed for double occupancy. Each of the cells has bunk beds, a counter top, two lockers and a chair. There are no locks inside the doors; they can only be locked and unlocked from the outside. There are no light switches inside the cells so the women have no control over lighting. There are no clocks or watches allowed, as the Prison Service is afraid that the women will makes bombs with them, so the inmates depend on the TV or radio for time checks. The officers on the wing control the electric power and so they decide whether or not a woman has access to light or television. A woman might have batteries for a radio and so be independent of the officers in this regard, but otherwise is dependent on the goodwill of the officers for access to the radio. Each of the cells is equipped with a stainless steel flush toilet bowl. In the lock-up regime of Limerick Prison the women spend most of every day locked in their cells.

In both prisons the main engagement of imprisoned women with management happens during the daily 'governor's parade'. The governor on parade in the Dóchas Centre visits each of the houses in turn and the women may meet her/him if they wish and make requests or have a dispute resolved. In Limerick Prison the governor visits the wing and each woman may ask for a meeting. The following paragraph documents a visit to Rowan House in the Dóchas Centre. The assistant governor, in this case, with the officer in charge of the house met the women individually in the small staff office on the second floor off the recreation area of that house. At that meeting one of the women complained that she was still waiting for her clothes, which were at reception; the governor said she would take care of this. Another said that she would like her (financial) account to be sorted out; the governor said she would take care of this. Another who had been unlawfully at large for twenty-nine days, said that her father had died; the governor said that the time spent 'at large' would be added on to the end of her sentence. One woman had no cigarettes, so the governor arranged for her to get some. Another had no television in her room and she said she would crack up without it, to which the assistant governor responded: 'You can't crack up here; if you do you'll be sent to the pad.'

The absolute power and control of prison staff over imprisoned women and the authoritarian militaristic nature of that
power and control, implicit and explicit in every aspect of the
women's existence, establishes and constantly reinforces the
penal nature of the institutions and the deviant, stigmatised identities of the women imprisoned within them. These identities are
further ascribed, and inscribed, through the constant reiteration
of the prisons' rituals of control and punishment, through the
symbolism, and frequently through the experience of the prison's
most powerful recalcitrance technologies. In healthcare, the penal
culture of punishment becomes part of the medical culture. Within
the healthcare experience the women are psychiatrised and pathologised. The educational experience is provided within the security
and control structures of the prisons. The gendered provision of
education in Irish prisons is very evident. Within the prisons' structures and routines the women live every moment of every day
of their lives in prison. The capacity of the prisons' structures and
routines for discursive reiterative practice is immense and it is
through the prisons' ceaseless reiterative and citational practices
that the female prisoner is discursively produced.

NOTES

1. See Appendix for an outline of the methodology used in this research.
2. M. Foucault, *The Order of Things: Archaeology of the Human Sciences* (London: Routledge, 1974).
3. N. Elias, *The Civilising Process* (Oxford: Blackwell, 2000).
4. J. Horgan, *Mary Robinson: An Independent Voice* (Dublin: O'Brien Press 1987), p.146.
5. P. Scraton (ed.), *Law, Order and the Authoritarian State* (Milton Keynes: Open University Press, 1987), p.21.
6. I. O'Donnell and E. O'Sullivan, *Crime Control in Ireland: The Politics of Intolerance* (Cork: Cork University Press, 2001), pp.2–3.
7. E. Goffman, *Stigma* (London: Penguin, 1990).
8. E. Goffman, *The Presentation of Self in Everyday Life* (London: Penguin, 1990).
9. J. Butler, *Gender Trouble: Feminism and the Subversion of Identity* (New York: Routledge, 1990).
10. J. Butler, *Bodies that Matter: On the Discursive Limits of Sex* (New York: Routledge, 1993).
11. C. McCullagh, 'Getting the Criminals We Want: The Social Production of the Criminal Population', in P. Clancy, S. Drudy, K. Lynch and L. O'Dowd (ed.), *Irish Society: Sociological Perspectives* (Dublin: Institute of Public Administration, 1995), pp.410–31.
12. M. O'Connell, 'Is Irish Public Opinion Towards Crime Distorted by Media Bias?', *European Journal of Communication*, 14, 2 (1999), pp.191–212.

13. I. O'Donnell, 'Imprisonment and Penal Policy in Ireland', *The Howard Journal*, 43, 3 (2004), pp.253–66.
14. B. Morrissey, *When Women Kill: Questions of Agency and Subjectivity* (London: Routledge, 2003), pp.14–20.
15. U. Beck, *Risk Society* (London: Sage, 1992).
16. M. Lianos and M. Douglas, 'Dangerisation and the End of Deviance: The Institutional Environment', in D. Garland and R. Sparks (eds), *Criminology and Social Theory* (Oxford: Oxford University Press, 2000), pp.103–27.
17. M. Foucault, 'Foucault on Attica: An Interview', interview by J.K. Simon, April, 1972, *Telos*, no.19 (1974), pp.154–61.
18. S. Cohen and J. Young (eds), *The Manufacture of News: Social Problems, Deviance and the Mass Media* (London: Constable, 1973).
19. See Morrissey, *When Women Kill*.
20. See Cohen and Young (eds), *The Manufacture of News*.
21. P. Williams, *Gangland* (Dublin: O'Brien Press, 1998).
22. P. Williams, *The General* (Dublin: O'Brien Press, 2004).
23. P. Reynolds, *King Scum: Life and Crimes of Tony Felloni* (Dublin: O'Brien Press, 1998).
24. P. Williams, *Evil Empire: The Irish Mob and the Assassination of Journalist Veronica Guerin* (New York: Forge, 2001).
25. L. Madden and J. Levine, *Lyn: A Story of Prostitution* (Cork: Attic Press, 1987).
26. D. Mullins, *Ladies of the Kasbah: The Story of Ireland's Most Infamous Brothel and the Women who Worked There* (London: Little, Brown & Co., 1995).
27. P. Reynolds, *Sex in the City: The Prostitution Racket in Ireland* (Basingstoke: Pan Books, 2003)
28. N. O'Connor, *The Black Widow: The Catherine Nevin Story* (Dublin: O'Brien Press, 2000).
29. M. McCaffrey, *The Irish Scissor Sisters: The Inside Story of the Torso in the Canal Investigation and the Gruesome Homicide of Farah Noor* (self-published, 2007).
30. E. Connolly, *Lying Eyes and the Hitman for Hire* (Dublin: Gill & Macmillan, 2008).
31. O'Connell, 'Is Irish Public Opinion Towards Crime Distorted by Media Bias?', pp.191–212.
32. Reynolds, *King Scum*.
33. *Sunday World*, 18 February 2001.
34. *Ireland on Sunday*, 2 September 2001.
35. On 11 September 2003, *The Irish Times* carried a short article detailing the dismissal of a member of staff in the CMH following an investigation into an allegation of sexual abuse of a female patient there.
36. *Sunday World*, 1 April 2001.
37. *Evening Herald*, 13 June 2001.
38. *Evening Herald*, 31 May 2001.
39. *Evening Herald*, 14 June 2001.
40. *Evening Herald*, 21 July 2001.
41. *Sunday Tribune*, 19 August 2001.
42. Cohen and Young (eds), *The Manufacture of News*.
43. Morrissey, *When Women Kill*, pp.14–20.
44. J. Smith, *Different for Girls: How Culture Creates Women* (London: Chatto & Windus, 1997).
45. Morrissey, *When Women Kill*.
46. K. Silverman, *The Subject of Semiotics* (Oxford: Oxford University Press, 1983).
47. Morrissey, *When Women Kill*, p.54.
48. J. Sim, *Medical Power in Prisons: The Prison Medical Service in England, 1774–1989* (Milton Keynes: Open University Press, 1990).
49. M. Foucault, *Discipline and Punish: The Birth of the Prison* (London: Penguin, 1977).
50. D. Garland and P. Young, *The Power to Punish: Contemporary Penalty and Social Analysis* (London: Heinemann, 1983).
51. L. Irigaray, *An Ethics of Sexual Difference* (New York: Cornell University Press, 1993), p.7.

52. Goffman, *Stigma*.
53. M. de Certeau, L. Girard and P. Mayol, *The Practice of Everyday Life. Vol. II: Living and Cooking* (Minneapolis, MN: University of Minnesota Press, 1998), p.12.
54. Lianos and Douglas, 'Dangerisation and the End of Deviance', pp.103–27.
55. Ibid., p.119.
56. C. Jose-Kampfner, 'Coming to Terms with Existential Death: An Analysis of Women's Adaptation to Life in Prison', *Social Justice*, 17, 2 (1990), pp.110–25.
57. R. Sparks and A.E. Bottoms, 'Legitimacy and Order in Prisons', *British Journal of Sociology*, 46, 1 (1996), pp.45–62.
58. R. Morris, *Crumbling Walls: Why Prisons Fail* (Oakville, ON: Mosaic Press, 1989), p.105.
59. M. Eaton, *Women After Prison* (Milton Keynes: Open University Press, 1993), p.35.
60. F. Heidensohn, 'The Deviance of Women: A Critique and an Enquiry', *British Journal of Sociology*, 19, 2 (1968), pp.120–75.
61. Foucault, *Discipline and Punish*.
62. M. Foucault, *Fearless Speech*, edited by J. Pearson (Boston: Semiotexte, 2001), p 32.
63. M. Mauss, *The Gift* (London: Routledge Classics, 2002).
64. M. Douglas, *Risk and Blame: Essays in Cultural Theory* (London: Routledge, 1992).
65. Mauss, *The Gift*, p.37.
66. Douglas, *Risk and Blame*, p.157.
67. J. Pollack, 'Women Will be Women: Correctional Officers' Perceptions of the Emotionality of Women Inmates', *The Prison Journal*, 64, 1 (1984), pp.84–91.
68. C. Fennel, *Crime and Crisis in Ireland: Justice by Illusion?* (Cork: Cork University Press, 1993), p.182.
69. A. Worrall, 'Out of Place: Female Offenders in Court', *Probation Journal*, 28, 3 (1981), pp.90–3.
70. P. Carlen, *Women, Crime and Poverty* (Milton Keynes: Open University Press, 1988), p.10.
71. Foucault, *Discipline and Punish*, p.84.
72. Sim, *Medical Power in Prisons*, p.129.
73. The team considered the work of the Prison Service, the Department of Justice and Dublin Corporation with regard to accommodating women from the prison. They discussed the efforts of the NOW (New Opportunities for Women) project in terms of Everton House, a hostel for women released from prison which was blocked by the local community, the efforts of the St Vincent de Paul in the development of their hostel and the efforts of the Mercy Sisters, also blocked by the local community, in terms of the provision of accommodation for women leaving prison.
74. The activities discussed or available to the women, in addition to the formal education and training programme of the prison, included horticultural projects, gardening, the Christmas entertainment programme (including Christmas lunch, Christmas party, Kris Kindles), competitions for the best decorated house, St Patrick's Day celebrations, a céilí, some set dancing, some children in Irish dancing costumes invited in, Easter celebrations, a summer programme (including the Summer School), games rooms, pool tables, organised games, visits from football players, drama, card making, a choir, newsletters, quizzes, bingo, barbecues, health and fitness programmes, step aerobics, outdoor pursuits weeks, VEC debating competition, creative writing competition, creative writing workshops with writers like Julie Parsons, Marian Keyes, Maeve Binchy, a visit by the musicians the Furey Brothers, guest lectures, visits from poets, workshops such as industrial cleaning and industrial sewing, the beauty shop, the CONNECT project. Days were planned, such as Homelessness Day, International Women's Day, National AIDS Day, Bloomsday. Visits were arranged to services such as the Rape Crisis Centre, and there were visits from the Northside Partnership, the Alternatives to Violence Programme (AVP), the Samaritans, and the European Languages Bus. Workshops were planned around HIV, contraception, STDs, women in prostitution, and cleaning needles. A visit by the relics of St Therese of Lisieux was also organised. The group developed a yearly planner on which the activities could be plotted and an Activities Committee

was set up, comprised of officers and imprisoned women, to plan and organise the events and activities proposed for the year.

75. S. Walby, *Theorising Patriarchy* (Oxford: Blackwell, 1990).
76. S.L. Bartky, *Femininity and Domination: Studies in the Phenomenology of Oppression* (New York: Routledge, 1990).
77. H.L. Radke and H.J. Stam (eds), *Power/Gender: Social Relations in Theory and Practice* (London: Sage, 1994).
78. P. Bourdieu, *Masculine Domination* (Cambridge: Polity, 2001).
79. Walby, *Theorising Patriarchy*, p.64.
80. The vision statement of the Dóchas Centre is as follows: 'We are a community which embraces people with respect and dignity. We encourage personal growth in a caring, safe environment. We are committed to addressing the needs of each person in a healing and holistic way. We actively promote close interaction with the wider community.'
81. The mission statement of Limerick Prison is as follows: 'Our mission is to hold in humane, safe and secure custody the people committed to our care in an environment in which individuals can develop, reducing the risk of reoffending by encouraging participation in rehabilitative programmes and to promote interaction with other caring agencies.'
82. Eaton, *Women After Prison*.
83. J. O'Dwyer and P. Carlen, 'Women in Prison: Surviving Holloway', in *The Polity Reader in Gender Studies* (Cambridge: Polity, 1994), pp.305–10.
84. F. Lundström-Roche, 'The Affective Responses of Women Prisoners to Two Discrepant Penal Systems', *Criminal Justice and Behaviour*, 15, 4 (1989), pp.411–32.
85. H. Garfinkel, 'Conditions for Successful Status Degradation Ceremonies', *American Journal of Sociology*, vol. 61 (1956), pp.420–4.
86. Ibid., p.421.
87. See photograph on book cover.
88. Butler, *Bodies that Matter*.
89. F. Heidensohn, *The Imprisonment of Females* (London: Routledge & Kegan Paul, 1975).
90. L.H. Bowker, *Women, Crime and the Criminal Justice System* (Toronto: D.C. Heath and Co., 1978).
91. M. Chesney-Lind, 'Patriarchy, Prisons, and Jails: A Critical Look at Trends in Women's Incarceration', *The Prison Journal*, 71, 1 (1991), pp.51–67.
92. European Committee for the Prevention of Torture and Inhuman or Degrading Treatment or Punishment (CPT), *Report to the Government of Ireland on the visit to Ireland*, 36 (2003).
93. The small number of women (no more than three at a time from the prison system) in the Central Mental Hospital were described by one of the psychiatrists there as a biased group, very vulnerable, often with dual diagnoses of mental illness and drug abuse, some had mental handicaps, some had low IQs, some had attention deficit disorder, they had mood problems and significant social problems. This psychiatrist said that the experience of the locked ward in St Brendan's Psychiatric Hospital (in Dublin) would not be very different from the experience of the CMH. This interviewee spoke of the forensic experience in dealing with challenging behaviour, the particular expertise of the staff of the CMH in what was called the three-pronged approach: talk down patient; behaviour out of control, might require 'control and restraint', hand locks etc; finally they might require medication. The women's unit in the CMH had a padded cell that had been there since the hospital was built (1850) and nearly all the rooms could be turned into strip rooms: the women could be secluded in their own rooms on rugs and gowns (recalcitrant rugs and gowns) which would have to be prescribed by a doctor and reviewed every three hours. There were no televisions in the rooms, no budget for them, the women are locked up from 9 p.m. to 9 a.m., some of the women had their own stereos and CD players. They were allowed sheets of paper to write on in their rooms but a lot of the women would have literacy problems. This interviewee said: 'The forensic service would like to see people whose offences do not warrant incarceration diverted back into the community; people who are mentally unwell should not be remanded in custody but diverted into the appropriate service.'

94. D. Garland, 'The Limits of the Sovereign State: Strategies of Crime Control in Contemporary Society', *British Journal of Criminology*, 36, 4 (1995), pp.445–71.

95. P. Carlen, *Sledgehammer: Women's Imprisonment at the Millennium* (London: Palgrave Macmillan, 1998), p.141.

96. P. Carlen, *Women's Imprisonment: A Study in Social Control* (London: Routledge & Kegan Paul, 1983), p.210.

97. A. Liebling, 'Suicide Amongst Women Prisoners', *The Howard Journal*, 33, 1 (1994).

98. In general when a prisoner is placed under special observation, she stays within her regular routine within the prison and is closely observed in that routine by all staff who have contact with her. Some women on special observation are taken to the strip or padded cells and held there for observation.

99. P. Carlen, 'Psychiatry in Prisons: Promises, Premises, Practices and Politics', in P. Millar and N. Rose (eds), *The Power of Psychiatry* (Cambridge: Polity 1986), pp.265–6.

100. J. Sim, '"We Are Not Animals, We Are Human Beings": Prisons, Protests and Politics in England and Wales, 1969–1990', *Social Justice*, 18, 3 (1991), pp.107–29.

101. Ibid., p.121.

102. Lianos and Douglas, 'Dangerisation and the End of Deviance', pp.103–27.

103. Limerick Prison at that time could accommodate twelve women, it can now accommodate twenty.

104. R. Sparks and A.E. Bottoms, 'Legitimacy and Order in Prisons', *British Journal of Sociology*, 46, 1 (1995), pp.45–62.

105. Foucault, *Discipline and Punish*.

106. F. Corcoran, 'Pedagogy in Prison: Teaching in Maximum Security Institutions', *Communication Education*, 34, 1 (1985), pp.49–58.

107. One person working in the Department of Justice co-ordinates the programme of education in Ireland's prisons. The director of education in Mountjoy Prison, in interview, detailed the development of education in Irish prisons as follows: 'In 1972, the Department of Justice approached the VEC [Vocational Education Committee] with regard to putting some education in St Patrick's Institution [the young (male) offenders facility within the Mountjoy Prison complex]. In those days some teachers were sent down for some part of their timetable from Cabra Vocational School [a local school]. From 1976 to 1977 teachers started to come in full time; [there was] a Sister [a Catholic nun] teaching literacy to the Travellers in the prisons.' Further detail on the educational provision was taken from various reports. The Department of Education provided just over 178 teachers from nine VECs, or whole-time equivalents, in 1999/2000. Given a prison population of 3,000 at that time, the figure represents a teacher–pupil ratio of seventeen students per teacher if all prisoners in Irish prisons attended and participated in the prisons' schools, but of course they do not. So the actual ratio is considerably lower. The co-ordinator of education in the Prison Service, in interview, did comment on the high rates of voluntary participation in education in Irish prisons. He quoted the Council of Europe report, *Education in Prison*, which he said states that achieving the potential that educational activities offer to prison regimes is contingent upon the adoption of 'a wide concept of education', offering a wide variety of learning opportunities to prisoners. He pointed to *The Management of Offenders* report, the Department of Justice's 1994 policy document, in which the aims of prison education were outlined in terms of helping prisoners cope with sentences, develop personally, prepare for life after release and establish an appetite and a capacity for further education.

108. An analysis of school attendance records for the months of January and February 2001 conducted for this study established the broad range of classes offered within the prison and the low average attendance. In all, 350 classes were delivered, attended by 1,089 students. This averages out at three students per class. It should be noted that averaging the attendance in this manner masks the fact that some classes were very well attended and some very poorly attended; in fact attendance at the classes was very erratic rather than consistently poor. In all, over the two-month period

analysed, forty-five classes were timetabled and subsequently cancelled by staff. In addition to this, many of the students who signed up for classes did not attend. The reasons given for non-attendance were very varied. The following is a list of the reasons given: the woman concerned was cleaning; involved in drama; involved in voluntary work; at a meeting with Probation and Welfare; she was sick; taking a phone call; attending an interview; in a meeting with the governor; taking a visit or a spiritual visit; she had gone to the Central Mental Hospital; she had gone to Limerick Prison; she was in bed; she was too late for class and so was not allowed attend; she was at the hairdresser's; she was studying; she was with an holistic healer; she was working, painting, cleaning or working in the kitchen; the woman forgot she had a class, the woman declined to attend for no specific reason, she took the class off or was attending another class; she was with the psychiatrist, the doctor or the dentist; she was in court; she was too upset to attend class; she was out of the prison on bail or temporary release; she had no babysitter or had a sick baby and so could not attend; she was sick or in hospital; she was with the CONNECT project or she was 'locked back', i.e. being punished for something by being locked in her room.

109. C. Quinlan, 'A Journey into the Women's Prison', *Women's Studies Review*, vol. 9: 'Women's Activism and Voluntary Activity' (2004), pp.59–79.

110. B. Hutter and G. Williams, *Controlling Women: The Normal and the Deviant* (London: Croom Helm, 1981).

111. Statistics from the Irish Penal Reform Trust state that Limerick Prison currently has a capacity for 290 males and twenty females, 310 prisoners in total, www.iprt.ie/prison-facilities-in-ireland (accessed 20 June 2010).

112. Pollack, 'Women will be Women'.

Chapter Four

The Women's Perspectives

This chapter examines how women in prison in Ireland in the first decade of the twenty-first century experienced imprisonment. It draws on testimony of the women themselves in order to explore how they construct and represent their own identities, and the degree to which they resist the identities ascribed to them. To begin with, the women are profiled, the numbers of women in prison, their backgrounds, the crimes for which they were committed, and the prison sentences imposed upon them. Following this analysis, their prison experiences are examined. Finally, there is a consideration of the women's personal identities, their senses of self, as represented by themselves.

In this first section, three different profiles of the women are presented: (a) a socio-demographic profile of the women imprisoned over one year; (b) the women in prison in the Dóchas Centre on one day; (c) the women interviewed for the research. With each profile, a clearer, more comprehensive description of the population of the women's prisons emerges.[1]

THE WOMEN IMPRISONED IN THE DÓCHAS CENTRE
OVER ONE YEAR

In 2001, about 1,000 women were committed annually to prison, to both the Dóchas Centre and Limerick Prison. The vast majority served extremely short sentences. Over half were committed to prison on remand, one quarter were sentenced to days in prison, with or without fines, and 14 per cent were sentenced to periods up to twelve months. Only 3 per cent were sentenced for periods of one year or over. About half were from Dublin, nearly a quarter from outside Dublin, one fifth were foreign nationals, and there were some Traveller women and some homeless. Most of the women were imprisoned for nuisance-type offences, public order offences such as breach of the peace or public drunkenness. A substantial proportion were imprisoned for larceny and stealing, offences generally related to the women's addictions. Some were there for trafficking drugs, as were most of the foreign nationals serving long sentences. Until the first decade of the twenty-first century, there had not been, since the foundation of the state, more than three or four women in prison at any time serving life sentences for murder. In June 2005, five women were on life sentences, one who had been imprisoned since she was 16 years old; she was due to be released that year. Another was Catherine Nevin who, as explained in Chapter 3, was serving a life sentence for her part in the murder of her husband Tom Nevin. Among the other three were two Irish nationals, a woman who had killed her abusive partner, and a woman who had killed her 8-year-old son. The third woman was from the UK; she had killed a man there, her partner, and had chosen to serve her sentence in Ireland. There were also three women in prison serving sentences of eight to ten years for manslaughter.

In 2001 over 750 women were imprisoned in the Dóchas Centre. Of this group, 446 (59 per cent) were Irish nationals and 305 (41 per cent) were foreign nationals from thirty-one different countries. Details of the place of origin of the women prisoners are summarised in Table 4.1.

Most of the women were young, poor and uneducated. Few had established significant relationships beyond their immediate families. Generally unemployed, most were sentenced to short stays in prison for petty or nuisance-type offences. Their ages ranged from 16 (there were four committals of women aged 16)

Table 4.1
Geographic Area of Origin, 2001

Europe (other than Ireland)	121	Dublin	135
South Africa	17	Wicklow	75
Africa	37	Waterford	58
Asia	43	Other Leinster	82
Russia/Scandinavia	2	Ulster	40
Eastern Europe	62	Connaught	39
South America	23	Munster	17
Total	305		446

(n=751)

to 70; one woman of 70 was committed to the prison during the period examined. Almost 50 per cent were aged 25 or younger; 75 per cent were aged 32 or younger. The remaining 25 per cent were aged 33 to 70; less than 5 per cent were 50 or older. Almost 90 per cent were unmarried. The foreign nationals represented 41 per cent of the prison population. Many were 'aliens' held in the prison awaiting deportation. The largest national group of foreign women was Ukrainian; they were imprisoned for a range of offences, the most significant of which were stealing and the possession of drugs. There were twenty-one Spanish women, charged with a range of offences from money laundering to begging and vagrancy. There were sixteen South Africans, most of them in breach of immigration regulations and awaiting deportation, with three of them on charges of possessing drugs; and there were sixteen Nigerians, most of them awaiting deportation. One of these women was being held on a charge of possessing drugs.

Many had been convicted of a range of offences and each of these offences were listed on the prisoner's record. The lists were individual and almost unique to each woman. Many of the lists were lengthy and complex. This is because a person before the courts will be charged with all outstanding warrants. For homeless people or those suffering from mental illnesses or addictions there are often several outstanding charges; for the most part these would be relatively petty, for example shoplifting, being in breach of a warrant, being drunk in a public place. In the analysis carried out, the length and complexity of some of the lists of charges forced an aggregation of the data. With this aggregation, the data fell into thirty-three categories of offences or types of offence; these are detailed in Table 4.2.

Table 4.2
List of Categorised Offences Committed, 2001

Fail to appear	Forgery	Money Laundering
Assault	Importation of Drugs	Drunk and Disorderly
Breach of the peace	Possession of Drugs	Casual/Illegal Trading
Murder	Assault on Garda	Larceny/Stealing/Robbery
Fraud	Soliciting/Prostitution	Possession of a weapon
Malicious Damage	Handle Stolen Property	Breach Bail
Damage to property	Loitering	Danger to self
Fail to produce ID	Alien	Road Traffic Act
No bus ticket	Contempt of Court	Domestic Violence
Debt	Vagrancy/Begging	No TV licence

Over that year, three women were imprisoned for murder, forty for assault and eighteen for assault on a Garda; sixty-eight were imprisoned on charges of possession, importing or supplying drugs; fifty-eight for offences against the Road Traffic Act; sixteen for casual or illegal trading; six for vagrancy; eleven for begging; four on domestic violence charges and four on charges of soliciting and prostitution; two were imprisoned for not having a bus ticket while travelling on a bus, one for not wearing a seat belt, one for not having a TV licence, and one for failing to send a child to school. Figure 4.1 illustrates proportionately the crimes committed.

Figure 4.1
Crimes with which the Women were Charged, 2001

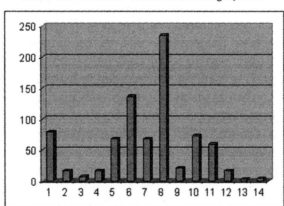

[NB this figure includes those women being held on remand, i.e. not yet convicted]
(1=Fail to Appear/Breach Bail; 2=Forgery/Fraud; 3=Money Laundering; 4=Casual Trade; 5=Assault, Assault Garda, Possession of Weapon; 6=Drunk and Disorderly, Breach of Peace, Danger to Self, Soliciting/Prostitution, Failure to Produce ID, Vagrancy, Begging; 7=Possession, Importation, Supply of Drugs; 8=Larceny, Stealing, Robbery; 9=Loitering, Damage Property, Malicious Damage; 10=Alien; 11=Road Traffic Act; 12=No Bus Ticket, No TV Licence, Contempt of Court, Debt; 13=Murder; 14=Domestic Violence)

As can be seen, more women were imprisoned for larceny, robbery and stealing than for any other offence. The next most frequently occurring offences were drunk and disorderly or breach of the peace. A large number of women who had entered the country illegally were committed to the prison that year. It is worth noting the number of women imprisoned on assault charges, in particular the fact that one third were imprisoned for assaulting a Garda. Also noteworthy is the very small number imprisoned for murder or domestic violence charges. Perhaps the most striking feature overall is the relatively trivial nature of the offences for which many of the women were imprisoned, either awaiting trial or having been sentenced. Table 4.3 provides a synopsis in percentages of women being held on remand or waiting deportation and the sentences of those women who were convicted.

Table 4.3
Remand/Deportation/Sentences, 2001

Remand	51%
Deportation	9%
Days plus fine	23%
One to twelve months	14%
One year to life	3%

(n=751)

As can be seen, over half was held on remand, almost one quarter sentenced to days in prison with or without fines, while 14 per cent were sentenced for periods of one to twelve months. Only 3 per cent of the committals to the prison represented women sentenced for periods of one year or over. While the lengthy and complex lists of offences for which the women were committed to prison indicated substantial expressions of and engagements with criminality, further inspection of the lists and the nature of the sentences imposed on the women evidenced the opposite, the generally trivial nature of female criminality in Ireland.

In terms of serious crimes, among the 3 per cent of women who receive sentences of one year and over are the foreign national women imprisoned for drug trafficking, a practice that, for these women, is neither very lucrative nor very profitable. Among drug traffickers, it is the couriers who are the most visible. Perhaps because of this visibility, their criminal activities are easily prosecuted.[2] Their crimes are constructed as serious, their trials are public and visible, and their prison sentences, when they are sentenced, are long.[3] These women helped transform the profile of the population of the Irish female prison, through the perceived seriousness of their crimes and the significant sentences they were given. Where most of the women tried for criminal offences in Ireland receive extremely short custodial sentences, these international women are generally given four to six years.

Relatively significant numbers receiving relatively long custodial sentences impact on the female prison in Ireland, on its structures and management and on the prison experiences provided.

One of the effects of significant numbers of women receiving substantial sentences for crimes constructed as serious is an exaggerated public perception of the nature of female criminality. The discourses of the criminal justice system, in criminalising the drug courier activities of the women in the manner that they do and to the extent that they do, feed the discourses of risk and danger associated with women prisoners in the press, and those of the architectural and organisational dimensions of the women's prisons. The discourses of danger fuel, and are in turn fuelled by, public perceptions of such crimes, of such criminality, and of such criminals. In reality, the women are couriers rather than traffickers. They work for the traffickers, transporting drugs for them. Disadvantaged women all of them, in the world of the international trade in illegal drugs they are insignificant. They are generally gullible women, desperate women, and/or very young women. While they present statistically as the most criminal of the women in Irish prisons, in reality they are always among the prisons' most docile characters.

A PROFILE OF THE WOMEN IN THE DÓCHAS CENTRE OVER ONE DAY

The records of the women imprisoned in the Dóchas Centre on one day in March 2001 were examined. This analysis yielded a representation of the day-to-day population of the prison. On that day there were eighty-two women inmates. They were aged between 18 and 54, with almost 50 per cent aged 26 or younger; more than 75 per cent were aged 31 or younger. Almost 50 per cent were from Dublin; five were of no fixed address. There were fifteen non-nationals, representing 18 per cent; seven were from South Africa, two from each of Jamaica, Brazil and the UK, and one each from Switzerland and Romania. The rest of the women, nineteen in total, were from the following Irish cities/towns or counties: one from each of Dundalk, Westmeath, Navan, Carlow, Laois, Fermanagh, Kildare, Kilkenny, Longford, Wicklow and Waterford; two each from Donegal and Limerick, and four from Meath (excluding Navan). These nineteen women accounted for

23 per cent of the population. In addition, there were two Traveller women, and two homeless women who before being imprisoned had been staying in hostels for the homeless in Dublin.

The women had been imprisoned for a wide range of offences, fifty in total. Larceny, robbery and stealing were prominent, as were drug-related offences; the most commonly occurring offence was possession of drugs with intent to supply. Fifteen were imprisoned for that offence, among them the seven South Africans. South African drug couriers have in recent years represented up to 25 per cent of Ireland's imprisoned women. Others among the women were imprisoned for assault, breach of the peace and public drunkenness, and a small number for prostitution. There was one woman, an illegal immigrant, awaiting deportation on that day. Three were on murder charges, all serving life sentences, and one on a manslaughter charge; another was charged with arson. Over 85 per cent of the women were serving sentences in excess of one year. There were fourteen women on remand. Less than 25 per cent were married or in a significant relationship. In all, 84 per cent had been unemployed on their committal to prison. Of the 16 per cent who had been employed, one was a machine operative, one a sales assistant, one an artist, and one a secretary; there was one self-employed woman. Two said that they were homemakers. In terms of education, four had Group Certificates, the lowest level of state certification in Ireland, fifteen had Junior Certificates, one had Leaving Certificate, and one had participated in third-level education. Most, on admission, had claimed to be literate, three said they were illiterate, one said she couldn't read but could write a little, and one claimed that she was semi-literate.

This analysis highlighted two main subdivisions in the female prison population, the division by prison management of women into two groups of those designated trustees and those not. The process of designating some women prisoners trustees, as explained in Chapter 3, resulted in the 'othering' of the rest of the population. Through the othering process, the othered women were seen to be further dangerised. In fact, this division of the women into two groups was a division between addicted and non-addicted women. Among the prisoners, addicted women came generally from Dublin's inner city. They tended to be chronically addicted, young and unemployed. The non-addicted women, either Irish or non-national, tended to be mature, reasonably healthy, reasonably well educated, and relatively well resourced.

In 2006, 960 women were committed to prison, of whom 409 were committed under sentence.[4] A profile compiled of the eighty-two women in prison on 6 December 2006 showed that twenty-two (27 per cent) were serving sentences of twelve months or less while nineteen (23 per cent) were serving more than twelve months but less than two years. The latest figures available, for 2008,[5] detail that a total of 1,484 women were committed to prison that year: 676 were imprisoned under sentence, 552 were on remand and 256 were in violation of immigration regulations and were in prison awaiting deportation. The number of women committed to prison have risen over the first decade of the twenty-first century, from a daily average of 100 at the start of the century to 104 by 2008.[6] On her resignation in protest over the deterioration in conditions in the Dóchas Centre, governor Kathleen McMahon said that the prison had become chronically overcrowded, with up to 137 women being held in that facility which had been designed to accommodate just eighty-three (eighty-five if the two padded cells were included), and which currently, according to the Irish Prison Service, has an official capacity for 105 women. The 2009 Report of the Irish Prison Service shows that 1,456 women were sent to prison in Ireland that year.

THE WOMEN INTERVIEWED FOR THE RESEARCH

The women interviewed were Irish and non-nationals. The youngest was 17, the oldest 53. The women fell, broadly speaking, into two subgroups: non-addicted women and addicted women – trustees and others. In general, trustees are non-addicted women and in this way the appellation serves to delineate and formalise the main cultural division in the female prison population. The divide between trustees and others is, in effect, the divide between trustees and addicted women. The divide is a useful construct within which to explore the impact of the discourses of the prison on the women's senses of self.

Within the Dóchas Centre, it is through a presentation of self that a woman becomes and remains a trustee. The designation 'trustee' is another gift within the remit of prison management. This gift is, within Douglas's concept of the gift,[7] not a free gift, but one that engages the women in permanent commitments articulating the ideologies of the dominant institutions. Trustees enjoy more freedom in the prison; they are less subject to surveillance and less liable to punishment. The capacity to produce a performance capable of securing the designation of trustee is substantial. Such a performance is related to prison management notions of civility and incivility.

Bourdieu[8] wrote of cultural capital as the ability to engage in valued forms of cultural activity upon which the power of the bourgeoisie is in part based; he detailed[9] as outward signs expressing social position, clothes, bodily as well as linguistic language, manners, ways of speaking, accents, postures, ways of walking and standing, table manners and taste. Elias's analysis of notions of civility and incivility, the civilised and the uncivilised, provides insight too into the manner in which a class-based criminal justice system can facilitate the further punishment and exclusion of particular groups and individuals.[10] Carlen described the more extreme experiences of imprisonment of poorer offenders, suggesting that in prison such individuals are likely to be labelled difficult and so subjected to more intense surveillance and correction than offenders from other classes.[11]

There were twenty-one trustees among the women interviewed in the Dóchas Centre, accounting for 30 per cent of the interviewees. There were also three women from Limerick Prison of the eleven interviewed there who could also, if the term had been used in that prison, have been described as trustees. Of this population of twenty-four trustees, eight were Irish and sixteen were non-nationals. They ranged in age from 23 to 53. As explained, in general it is the non-addicted women who serve the longest sentences; the longest among these women was life, the shortest was eighteen months. The three women serving life sentences for murder were Irish, and they were all trustees. Another of the trustees was serving a seven-year sentence for fraud, one a three-year sentence for dangerous driving causing death, another a two-year sentence for fraud and dangerous driving. One was serving eighteen months for possession of cannabis with intent to supply, and another, a Traveller woman, was effectively serving life through instalments. As detailed in Chapter 2, Carey wrote of what penal historian Sean McConville described as 'life by instalments', by highlighting the 'little and often' syndrome of female imprisonment in Ireland.[12] This woman had seventy or eighty convictions for larceny, mostly hotel and post office robberies. She served many years in prison, in both Limerick and the Dóchas Centre. She was in fact in the first decade of the twenty-first century the only really serious and substantial career criminal among the women in the Irish prison system.

There were sixteen non-nationals among the trustees. Ten were from South Africa, six black women among them. There were two Brazilians, two Britons, one German and one Jamaican. All but two were serving sentences for drug trafficking. One was serving five years for money laundering, and one was on remand facing charges of credit card fraud. The fourteen drug traffickers were serving substantial sentences of three to seven years. The South African women were from the cities of Pretoria, Durban, Cape Town and Johannesburg; they were convicted of bringing cannabis into Ireland. One woman was from Swaziland, and she, the two Brazilians and the Jamaican were all convicted of trafficking cocaine into Ireland. The Briton was convicted of bringing in ecstasy.

All but four of the trustees were serving their first prison sentences. The four trustees who acknowledged previous prison sentences were as follows. The woman on remand for credit card fraud had previously served thirty-three sentences in the UK, 'all for the same thing, credit card fraud'. The Briton charged with trafficking ecstasy had served, she said, 'about thirty previous prison sentences, mostly for petty things, some for prostitution, one six-year sentence in Holland for importing cocaine from South America'. The Traveller woman had had, as stated earlier, many previous convictions, while the woman serving a two-year sentence for fraud and drunken driving had twenty-six previous convictions, 'all for the same thing'.

These women were aged between 23 and 53, the average age being 34. They were predominantly single, either widowed, separated, unmarried or unpartnered, with one to four young children to support. Three were childless. One of the South Africans was pregnant during her stay in the prison; she was deported before the birth of her baby. In terms of education, seventeen of the trustees had school certificates, two had additional management training, two had some training as hairdressers, and the Traveller had been on a Traveller training programme. Seventeen had had jobs, in shops, as hairdressers, and as child minders. One had been a fitness instructor. Three had been business people: one had owned her own business, one had been a director of a business, and one a business manager. The others had worked in shops, in factories, as street vendors, selling vegetables from home, and in the sex trade. One of the women was an artist, and was so described in the media in Ireland, but she had never painted for a living. She featured several times in the press while serving her sentence. She was more usually represented there as a drug mule, and, as detailed in Chapter 3, as one of Catherine Nevin's 'prison pals'.

Although non-addicted, the Briton on the fraud charge was a drug user, as was one of the white South Africans. One of the Irish women serving a life sentence had only ever used drugs, cannabis and cocaine, in prison. Her life sentence had been imposed on her at 16 years of age; she was 25 at the time of interview. The Traveller woman, who didn't drink alcohol, had started using drugs in prison – cannabis, ecstasy, crack, speed and cocaine. 'I started in the old prison, I got off it as soon as I came down here [the Dóchas Centre].' The woman serving the two-year sentence for fraud and drunken driving was a binge drinker: 'not at home or during the day, I'd go out with someone and go on somewhere else on my own, twice a week, serious drinking.' The woman serving eighteen months for the cannabis charge used drugs recreationally – ecstasy, coke, speed, acid, magic mushrooms – 'just the odd weekend ... never a case of needing to have it'. Apart from these women, none of the trustees used drugs or alcohol to any significant extent.

There were five young non-addicted Irish women, aged 18 to 33, who were not addicts and were not designated trustees. Their status as other than trustees would have related, in the case of two 18-year-olds in Limerick Prison serving sentences of twenty months and four years respectively, to their youth and assertiveness. In the case of the other three women, a 20-year-old, a 22-year old and the 33-year old, they were not designated trustees because they had just recently been committed to prison and were being held there on remand.

The eight Irish women among the trustees had stable homes and family backgrounds. All but one had established their own homes separate from their family homes; the one exception was the 25-year-old who had been in Mountjoy Prison on a life sentence since she was 16. They were all embedded in their families. There were four mothers among the women, two of whom were mothers of adopted children. All received regular visits from family members and spent a great deal of their time in prison planning and preparing for these visits. The South African women were all struggling to hold on to their homes. They were trying to pay South African bills from an Irish prison, rent and utilities and school fees. They got some help with this from the Sisters of Mercy.

The rest of the women, 51 in total (64 per cent of the interviewees), were young Irish women, except for one Briton. They were all either serious drinkers or alcoholics and/or drug addicts. They ranged in age from 17 to 42; eight were teenagers, thirty-five were in their twenties, nine were in their thirties, and one was 42. They had erratic, short or no work histories. Those who had worked were employed in shops, bars and factories, as cleaners, waitresses and hairdressers. Twenty-two (43 per cent) had school certificates and one had spent a year in college. About 25 per cent did not construct their activities as criminal. In interview they said that they were sick, or that they did stupid things, but they were not criminals.

The women who did construct their activities as criminal were mostly shoplifters. They were immersed in a culture of shoplifting, many of them doing so to feed chronic drug habits. One woman, Rose,[13] described this culture as follows: 'The girls are kind of in a gang, for shoplifting, and I'm classed as being in the gang with them. There's no leader and it's up to yourself whether you want to go or not. There are no fellas, just the girls. They hang out together and that's what they do, shoplift, they make big money.' Another woman, Jackie, said:

> I'd shoplift for my regular customers. They'd buy made-to-order from me. They'd tell me what they want and I get it for them. I'd get one-third of the shop price. One of my regular customers was going to the Galway races and she asked me to get her the oddest looking hat I could find. I got a hundred and fifty quid for that. I was very professional, a real junkie, jeans and runners, I'd organise transport and fleece one town after another. Your face gets known and you have to move on. I'd wear different wigs and disguise myself. I was making

ridiculous money. I spent it all on heroin. It would have killed me to spend it on anything else.

The addicted women were generally serving relatively short sentences. Among the teenagers, the longest sentence was seven months for assault on a Garda; this girl had four previous convictions for shoplifting, for being drunk and disorderly and for assault. The longest sentence among the women in their twenties was four years for assault. Two of the women in their twenties were serving three years, one for mugging and shoplifting, and one for a syringe robbery. One was serving two and a half years for drug trafficking, four were serving two years for pick-pocketing and shoplifting, thirteen were serving three to eighteen months for shoplifting, fraud, robbery, burglary and larceny. Fourteen were on remand facing charges of assault, fraud, possession of heroin with intent to supply, shoplifting, robbery, assaulting a Garda while intoxicated, having false tax on a car, and missing a probation appointment. Of the nine women in their thirties, three were on remand, one for breaching the peace and two for shoplifting. One had 'stolen forty fags from a shop in Ennis ... I had a few drinks taken'. Of the sentenced women, one was on a thirty-month sentence for shoplifting, and one a ten-month sentence for assault and for being drunk and disorderly. Two were on two-month and three-month sentences respectively for assaulting members of the Garda, and one was on a one-week sentence for abusive behaviour and for being drunk and disorderly. The 42-year-old was on remand charged with being intoxicated and a danger to self. Homeless, she lived on the streets in Dublin and begged for her money, 'tapping' she called it. She said it was an honest living, and that she had been 'in and out over the years, for drink, and once for shoplifting ... a couple of dopey teddy bears'.

Of the teenagers, one 19-year-old said that she used every drug – sleepers, hash, ecstasy, magic mushrooms, gear, coke, speed, acid. She said that she would also drink seven or eight pints of Budweiser once a week. One 17-year-old said she had started drinking the 'odd one' at 11 years of age and was 'drinking properly' by the time she was 15. Of the thirty-four women in their twenties, thirty-two were drug addicts and two were alcoholics. One was the Briton, charged with intoxication and assaulting a Garda; she had a serious alcohol addiction and was living on the streets in Dublin. One of the alcoholics said that she would drink 'twelve bottles of beer every night', another would drink 'three bottles of cherry wine and twelve cans of beer every night and every morning'.

The drug-addicted women used every kind of drug. They described how they swallowed, smoked, snorted and injected drugs of every description. They sniffed aerosols, glue and paint. They drank bottles of Benylin. They took Valium, cannabis, magic mushrooms, acid, speed, cocaine and methadone. They took ecstasy to get high, and heroin to come down. One woman, Linda, said that she would take 'really any sort of tablet' and would smoke heroin three or four times a day. She started taking cannabis at 13 years of age: 'There used to be an older gang sitting on the corner, drinking and occasionally they'd smoke cannabis, and sometimes I'd take a drag.' She started taking ecstasy at 14 at discos, and acid for the first time when she was 15, at her first rave. She regularly injected heroin and coke, 'to be one of the gang'. She said:

> When you're on drugs, that's your first priority, your money for drugs, style or getting your hair done wouldn't rate at all. I need drugs to feel normal. I'd feel sick if I didn't have my drugs. The buzz from heroin makes me feel confident. I can express myself more. It's relaxing as well. It's just like all your worries are lifted. It's just great like, and the E, Jesus, I love taking ecstasy. I do. I just love it. I'm confident. I love everybody. Nobody can do no wrong. I would never dance without E. I'd just sit and watch. I'd be worrying about who was watching me.

Of the nine women in their thirties, two were binge drinkers, two were alcoholics, four were chronic drug addicts, and one was chronically addicted to both drugs and alcohol. One woman drank vodka, 'three bottles a day. I'd always make sure I had it.' Another drank three bottles of wine and ten cans a day. The 42-year-old said that, with her boyfriend, she drinks 'maybe three bottles of vodka and a few cans of cider every day'.

The women said that they started using drugs for many reasons: because they were curious, because they were trying to lose weight, because their friends were using drugs, because members of their families were using drugs, because they were selling drugs, because they were with a clubbing crowd, going to parties, going to raves, because they were trying to escape something, trying to block something out. They said they continued to use drugs because they liked the buzz, because they wanted to be one of the gang, because they became really badly 'strung out' on them (addicted to them). They said that they enjoyed it, that they couldn't stop, that they were better with it. They were relaxed and could sleep, they weren't worried, they weren't, as some of them said, thinking madly. They said it made everything go away. It made them forget about things, just forget about everything. They were in a different world.

When the addicted women talked of home they generally talked of the family home, the home of their families of origin. Few had established homes of their own. Four of the five non-addicted non-trustees lived in their parents' homes; one lived alone in a flat. Five of the eight teenagers lived in the family home, two were homeless and one had lived on the streets from 14 years of age but was at the time of interview back living with her Mum. One 24-year-old, Lorraine, described how she became homeless:

> I had my own place and I was able to take care of my son. Then I got bad on the heroin. I wasn't cooking proper dinners. Then he started missing days at school and I wasn't doing his homework with him. I didn't want him to be a victim of me, so I gave him up to be fostered. It was horrible. Then I was found with drugs in my flat. It was a corporation flat and they made me give it up. Then I was homeless.

Of the thirty-two women in their twenties, eight were homeless, while twenty-four still lived in the family home. Three had established their own homes. One was married. The other two lived in bedsits, one in Galway, one in Dublin. The homes the women lived in were in many cases more traditional, two and three-generational homes. Poorer women, within such circumstances, are likely to be more subject to the patriarchy of our society, and more controlled by it. Mahon[14] acknowledged the persistence in Ireland of a class-based private patriarchy. She concluded that women in Ireland, through educational achievement and access to middle-class jobs, were making significant gains. She acknowledged that such gains had resulted in 'a certain polarisation' between women in terms of class and income.

All but one of the eight addicted women over 30 was homeless, the one being the Traveller woman, living in a trailer in Ennis. In all, eighteen women, 35 per cent of those chronically addicted, said that they were homeless. It is likely that some or many of the rest of these women were also homeless or experienced homelessness from time to time. Jacinta, a 22-year-old on remand for shoplifting, talked about her experience of homelessness:

> I grew up in a hostel. We all lived there, the whole family. We used to live in a flat in Ballymun. It was a three-bedroomed flat. We all lived there, me Ma, me three brothers, me two sisters, and me. I used to feel horrible. Me Ma used to get battered by me step-Da. One day we all left, because it was his flat, and we went to live in the hostel. I left the hostel when I was 18 years old. I went to the UK.

The three profiles presented above detail women's engagement with criminality in Ireland. The analysis establishes that that engagement is now, as it was historically, primarily related to addiction. Almost two thirds of the women interviewed were chronic addicts. Of the other one third, twenty-four women in all, fifteen were imprisoned for drug-related offences. One was an Irish woman serving eighteen months for possession of cannabis with intent to supply. The other fourteen were non-nationals serving sentences for drug trafficking. The impact of globalisation on the population of the women's prison is manifest in the international makeup of the population, a consequence of the global trade in illegal drugs. The drugs problem really developed in Dublin in the 1980s, and as it did, the female prison population began to expand. From a daily average in 1974 of twenty-four women, the population grew to a daily average of 104 in 2008.

Most of the 100 women imprisoned in the first few years of the twenty-first century were incarcerated for engaging in petty crimes to feed addictions or for being deemed public nuisances, through their addictions. The majority of the rest were imprisoned for dealing or importing drugs. The substantially petty nature of much of the offending of the chronically addicted women indicates that they use the prisons as shelters, as they did in the nineteenth century (Chapter 2). These women tend to be on the fringe of the lower class, constantly in contact with the police and law. As Carlen wrote,[15] since the nineteenth century prisons have been used to disproportionately discipline the socially disadvantaged. Many Irish theorists have found that Irish prison populations are, by and large, characterised by poverty and multiple disadvantage. Specifically in relation to women prisoners, this has been established in the studies of Carmody and McEvoy[16] and Monaghan,[17] both of which found women in prison to be overwhelmingly from lower socio-economic backgrounds with substantial healthcare and addiction problems.

Prison Experiences

The women described the manner in which the prisons' discourses hailed them. In doing so, they echoed Lefebvre.[18] They also echoed Irigaray's expression of space as a container or envelope of identity.[19] As detailed in the preceding chapter, the two prisons provide very different experiences of imprisonment for women. Yet within both, as evidenced by the women, all understood themselves to be positioned within discourses of risk and danger. The women of both prisons described similar feelings of control in terms of the regimes and their day-to-day experiences within them. The most powerful signs in both prisons are the closed, confined, locked and guarded spaces, the symbols of militaristic discipline, and the degradation rituals. The discourses of the prisons spoke to the women through the powerful signifying capacity of the physical conditions of the spaces within which the imprisoned women were confined.

While the physical conditions in the Dóchas Centre are vastly superior to those in Limerick Prison, the culture of control, the restrictions on space and on movement in space, the experiences of being managed by a quasi-militaristic regime, are similar for women in both institutions. The discourses communicated with the women through the discipline regimes of the spaces, through the constant control, the recalcitrant technologies, the infantilising punishments, through the endless waiting, and through the engagement in the organised activities into which the women were encouraged and ultimately coerced. In terms of semiology, these experiences were the women's denotative experiences of those spaces. Connotatively, these experiences signified for the women their prisoner status, their degraded stigmatised identities. At this level of signification, these experiences communicated to the women, very clearly, and in every moment of every day, their spoiled identities, their deviant subject positioning within the discourses of the prisons.

Experiences of Control

The women detailed the manner in which their every-moment-of-every-day experiences within prison were controlled. They said that they were everywhere and in every way controlled and very obviously controlled. They were in fact, they said, rendered helpless by the level of control imposed upon them, and by the subsequent degree of passivity enforced on them. Anne said: 'You are completely helpless. You lose all your power. You can do nothing. You can arrange nothing. You can't make a phone call. You can do nothing on your own.' Bernie spoke of the experience of being so controlled and of how that subjection to control manifested itself in the relationships in the prison. Through her description of that control, the power differential between the women prisoners and the staff of the prisons was illustrated; as was the disciplined ways of being of the imprisoned women. Bernie said:

> You are not in control of yourself at all. It's all yes sir, no sir, do what they tell you to do. You just have to do what they want; otherwise you're just making life hard for yourself. I get on with the officers. I keep myself to myself. I don't cause trouble. I'm not a cheeky person, I don't answer back, you know. Just tell me to do something, I do it.

The women said that they themselves had no control over anything. Not only that, they said that everything was out of their control. They experienced the controlling structure and design of the prisons, the prison regimes, and the management and staff of the prisons, as denials of their adulthood. As Carlen wrote,[20] the constitution of women within and without adulthood in Lombroso and Ferrero's theory of female penology persists among prison administrators. One of the women, Carol, said:

> I'm treated like a 2-year-old all the time. I know very well that my intelligence matches theirs. I know that I can look them in the eye and match them word for word but sometimes the words don't come, because I'm undermined somehow. So I get tongue-tied and I never know if I'm saying the right

thing or the wrong thing. If I was on the outside and I met them, it would be totally different.

For the women, the daily routine in the prisons is structured through queuing, crowding and waiting. The women spoke of the waiting, the waiting for everything, waiting to go to school, waiting to go to lunch, waiting for phone calls, waiting for lock-up, waiting for a smoke. Deirdre talked about shop orders, the mechanism through which prisoners may buy the goods on sale in the prison, cigarettes, soft drinks, sweets and so on:

> You have to wait to make a shop order, then wait for it to be delivered. Then you have to wait for the shop to open, so that you can go and pick it up. Then when you do go to pick it up, there may be too many people there, queuing for shop orders. Then the officers will chase you away, tell you to wait and come back when things are quieter. Then when you come back, the shop may be closed. Then you have to wait for it to open again. You know you will get your shop order, you just don't know when. That's what it's like in here, waiting for this, waiting for that. It's always waiting. When I'm waiting for things, I just have to pretend to myself that it doesn't matter, and just wait and wait and wait.

This experience of waiting is the women's every-moment-of-every-day experience of the prison. As is the experience of being 'chased around' or 'run around' the small enclosed guarded space that is both female prisons by uniformed officers and staff. These experiences are reiterative elements of the experiences of penal control to which the women are subjected. Another inmate, Elena, said:

> Here people sometimes can make me angry. For instance the officers, you should hear the way they talk to us. One day I heard one say, 'oh, let's give the monkeys their medication, it will keep them quiet.' Today I told the nurse that I had my period three times this month. She replied, 'oh, lucky you.' My skin was dry and I said it itched and I couldn't sleep at night. She said, 'take less showers.'

The women felt degraded and disempowered by the staff, in terms of the ways in which many members of staff engaged with them. They readily interpreted such communications from staff within which they understood their interpellation as prisoners. It is in this way that prisoner identities are ascribed and more deeply inscribed.

Prison Structures

As detailed in Chapter 3, with the progressive atmospheres of the new prison, new structures have been instigated in the Dóchas Centre: among them the civilian dress of the discipline staff; and in the 'family or home-like' structure of the prison. There are no such new structures in Limerick Prison. The women in the Dóchas Centre described better relationships with the prison officers than the women in Limerick. This is related to the relatively greater autonomy of the women in that prison. In the Dóchas Centre, the women are more independent of the officers. They have more options in terms of how they spend their time and they have more control over those options. As detailed in Chapter 3, the regime in Limerick Prison is a lock-up regime. Frances detailed that experience as follows:

> They open the door at 9 a.m. You have to be up and dressed, with your shower taken and your room cleaned and gone to the yard at 10 a.m. They lock the door to your cell behind you. If you stay in your cell, you are not let out again until dinnertime (12.30 p.m.). If you are out of your cell, you are not allowed back in until dinnertime. You eat your dinner locked in your cell. Then the same thing happens again at 2 p.m., you are unlocked and you can choose to leave the cell or stay in it. You are locked up again at 4.30 p.m., and again unlocked at 5.30. Then lock-up for the night is at 7.15 or 7.30 p.m. If we want to go to the toilet at night we have to wait for them to unlock us. When they do, they lock the door behind us. Then we have to wait on the corridor, for maybe half an hour, until they think they are ready to open our door for us to let us back into the cell. Then they lock us in again.

The women in Limerick Prison expressed their dependence on the officers, their relative powerlessness and their resulting frustration. According to Geraldine:

> The worst thing about the prison is not being able to do things for yourself. When you ask for the post they tell you it's not there. They tell you they've made a phone call when they

haven't. We don't matter to them I suppose, so it doesn't matter whether or not I've spoken to my Mam and Dad. I don't even want to think about it.

Hilary outlined her relationship with prison staff:

> I try to manage them now. I negotiate with them. When I was younger I used to think that I could take them on. I used to try and I'd get killed. Jesus, they would kill me, corner me, throw me down, strip me, and lock me in a punishment cell. They'd leave me there until the governor came to talk to me. He would ask me how I felt and decide whether or not I could be allowed out. I was held there once for four days. You feel stupid when you're in it. You feel totally in the wrong. You feel alone and upset, more ashamed than anything.

In the prison system, formal punishment involves a prisoner being put 'on report', punished formally within the penal system: almost 40 per cent of the women interviewed had been on report at some stage and some had been on report 'loads of times'. Imprisoned women are placed on report for breach of prison discipline. Generally, the women are placed on report are being punished for any show of disrespect towards an officer of the prison, towards the authority of the prison. They are reported for shouting at an officer, for being cheeky with an officer, for swearing at an officer or for fighting, with officers or with other prisoners. In keeping with the patriarchal order of the prisons, they are punished for such minor breaches of discipline as recalcitrant children might be punished. They are scolded or told off and/or sent to their rooms. In the Dóchas Centre, the women said that the prison is structured around constantly changing petty rules and regulations; one of the biggest issues, they said, was the fact that there were no written rules, no set of rules on the back of the door, no dos and don'ts.

Of the activities in that prison, Imelda said:

> You always have to be doing something. If you're not doing something they want to know why you're not doing something. The whole place reminds me of boarding school. I know that I can pick up brownie points by going to school.

They love that, when you go to school. So I go and I pick up my brownie points even though the whole school bit drives me bonkers.

Walklate commented that the concessions offered to women in prison can create an imagery of women's prisons as boarding schools; she cites evidence which establishes the reality of the brutalising nature of women's imprisonment experiences.[21]

The main issue of concern for the women imprisoned in Limerick was the space that is that prison and the condition of their accommodation there. The women felt very trapped, and very confined in that small space. The prison, they said, was too small, that there was no place to go within it and nothing to do. They said that they had 'no space at all and no air at all'. According to Janet, 'There is no chance at all for exercise, only in the gym. You can't walk, not even up and down stairs. You can ask to be allowed out into the yard when you are unlocked, but there's nothing out there, there isn't even a bench to sit on. There is nothing to do.' Another inmate, Kay, said that in the small space that is the prison there would be 'about twenty girls, always fighting'. Linda said that the 'new' women's wing in Limerick Prison was better than the old place, the old female wing where the women had been held until 2001. Linda was discussing the interim move; the women had not at this time moved into the accommodation they currently inhabit. She described conditions in the old cells:

> At least here you have glass in the windows. You didn't over there. We used toilet rolls ... full rolls ... You stick them in this way into the window, length ways. Two would fill each space where the glass should be. Two rows of ten rolls of toilet paper where the glass should be, keeping the wind out. Then take two down if you needed a little air. Take them all down in the summer time.

In the Dóchas Centre, almost 30 per cent of the inmates spoke about the isolation they felt in the new prison, living in different houses in two separate yards. They had been used to the closeness of the old women's prison at Mountjoy or the closeness of their accommodation on the outside. Many of the women came from the flats complexes of inner-city Dublin, from Traveller trailers, from homeless shelters, and from skips (sleeping rough). Marion said: 'I get lonely in here. I miss me family being around me and talking to me all the time. At home I sleep in with me sister. I think it's the same for everyone here. It is the same for everyone, we're all locked up. But I suppose for Travellers, we're usually very close physically to each other.'

Ten of the women felt that the structures of the new prison divided them, that somehow they had been more united in the old prison. They felt that the new prison was stricter, more controlled, as Nikki explained:

> It's not like old Mountjoy, it's different here [the Dóchas Centre]. The door into the prison works on electric, and the door into my room is a wooden door. But it's still the same really. I mean they're still going to close the door in on me till I'm due me time out. I mean the key [the keys the women have to their rooms] is fuck all, it doesn't mean anything.

Only fifteen of the women interviewed had ever heard of the Visiting Committee, the only structure within the prison system through which the inmates can get a hearing that is not of the control or management structure of the prison. Members of the Visiting Committee at Mountjoy Prison said, in the group interview held with them, that they believed the new female prison to

4.1: The Big Yard, Dóchas Centre

be a 'holiday camp'. They said that the two open yards in the prison, with their flowerbeds and shrubs and the few benches arranged around them, made the prison look like a holiday camp. They suggested that the holiday camp experience of the prison was also evident in the relative freedom that the imprisoned women enjoyed.

Prison Discipline

The boarding school and/or holiday camp representations of the Dóchas Centre are difficult to sustain in light of a consideration of prison discipline, which manifests itself in various signs, symbols and rituals within that prison. Among these signs, symbols and rituals are the lock-ups and the lock-backs; the obsequies; the queuing; the rigid hierarchies; the punishments, both formal and infantilising; the tellings-off; the scoldings; the degradations; the stripping; the searching; the surveillance; the random drug tests; the strip rooms and padded cells; and the prison transfers, from the Dóchas Centre to Limerick Prison and from either of these to Dundrum, the Central Mental Hospital, the state's only forensic psychiatric facility. Fifteen of the women interviewed said that they had been threatened with being sent to Limerick Prison as a punishment. All imprisoned women are subject to the discipline of the prisons. All live with the threat of being stripped, restrained, locked into a strip cell or a padded cell, transferred to Limerick Prison and/or the Central Mental Hospital.

The women described the process of becoming a prisoner as a very short, very sharp, degrading process. As detailed in Chapter 3, the process is a ritualistic degradation ceremony through which the individual becomes 'reconstituted' as a prisoner. The person's individual identity is removed, and their prisoner identity is ascribed, and in this way a female prisoner is brought into being. Phil said: 'They take everything that's yours from you and you are left in a holding cell with nothing but a concrete slab that looks like a bed. There's graffiti all over the walls and you can see pain everywhere.' Rita said: 'As soon as you come through the gate, that's when you realise ... words like prisoner, offender and incarcerated bounce off your head. Words you thought you'd never in your life hear. Those are the words the officers use.'

The women discussed the strip-searching that is always part of the process. They agreed that all the women prisoners are subject to it, all of the time, regardless of their physical or psychological state of being, their age, their culture, their status, remand or sentenced, their criminal status or their drug habits. Susan said:

> Yes, I was strip-searched coming in. Oh, I was so shocked. It was my first time to be in a position like that. I really didn't know that, that you can be naked in front of the people. I really didn't know. Every time now when I go to court, they say I must lift my bra up and you have to take down your underpants. I don't feel good every time, I don't feel good. I feel bad and disgraced, every time I go to court.

Teresa described the experience as follows. Her description, as the description above, is of an experience far removed from the professional descriptions of strip-searching detailed in Chapter 3:

> It's an awful invasion of your body. You pull your knickers down and then they tell you to jump in case you've something inside you. You shower in front of them; they check your ears, your nostrils, between your toes. It's awful. All these women around you searching you, checking your hair; it's like you don't belong to yourself anymore.

Úna said that she had psoriasis all over her body; she felt very embarrassed stripping off in front of the officers. Valerie said that when she had a period, they wanted her to show them the sanitary towel. Alice said: 'I've been strip-searched about twenty-five times. It's horrible and degrading and I do mind. I wouldn't tell anyone about it, not my family, no one. We're ashamed of it. It's degrading.' Some of the women had been strip-searched hundreds of times. Evidencing the different control, discipline and punishment experiences of the addicted women, they said that 'when a woman is into drugs they really go to town on her.' Cara's was a case in point: 'Coming into prison this time was horrible, I was dying sick. I didn't have me medication. After being in the police station all night you're dirty. They strip-searched me. This time I wouldn't strip for them, so they pinned me to the ground and took all my clothes off. They must have strip-searched me 200 times.' Although male officers were never involved in this searching, one woman said that, 'in the old place, if a riot broke out, the men might be involved,' adding, 'they'd just strip you and give you a hiding and that would be it.'

All of the women are subject to prison discipline, to surveillance, control and punishment, but the experience is more intense for some. Gina said: 'They know everything. The know when I wake up, they know when I leave my room, they know when I have a shower. Anytime the governor wants to search my room I have to allow it. Every week I have a urine test and a nurse stands in front of me and watches me pee. I have no privacy.' The black South African women were among the most docile of all the prisoners. Sara said: 'Yes I am being watched, but it doesn't bother me. And yes I am being controlled in ways, but it doesn't bother me because I know why I am here, I have committed a crime and so I have to be here, to be punished.' The photograph below, from the current accommodation in Limerick Prison, illustrates the surveillance technologies: the small shared accommodation, the blue fluorescent light, the lock on the door which only locks from the outside and the peephole on the door are clearly visible. Also evident, lower left of the photograph, is the stainless steel shield for the toilet.

The electric lights in the prison are part of the control system; the women said that the lights are always on. They discussed the

4.2: Double cell, Limerick Prison (current accommodation), 2003

fact that they can't leave the door open at night because of the lights on in the corridor, and the fact that while the women may sleep in dark rooms, officers checking the sleeping women peep in at them, turning on a blue florescent light to illuminate the room. Room searches are part of the surveillance rituals. Almost 60 per cent of those interviewed, most of them addicted women, said that they had had their rooms or cells searched. According to Diane, they were 'routine spins [searches] for drugs or workses [needles]'.

The padded cells were central to the disciplinary controls of the Dóchas Centre, as were the strip cells of Limerick Women's Prison. Over 40 per cent of the women interviewed had been at some time accommodated in the padded cells, many sent there for accommodation when the prison was overcrowded. Elaine, who had been under observation in a padded cell, said that she had spent nearly all her time inside asleep in a padded cell: 'In a gown, no knickers, no bra, hair all over the place and you can do nothing. It feels fucking cold; there's no heat at all in there, a mattress on the floor and padded walls. It's horrible, cold and dreary looking.'

The women who were sent to the pads for punishment tended to be addicts. Jackie said:

> They treat you like a piece of dirt, food is thrown in at you, milk is put on the floor and when you're punished, the way they drag you to it. They treat you like a rag doll and start striping you off down to your jewellery. They drag you all around and put the gown on you and then they put their arms over their faces and heads and run out.

Karen said that a nurse would often suggest to a woman that she might like to go to the pads if she needed time alone or needed to hit something, saying that she could scream and go crazy in the pad if she wanted. Lucy said that sometimes women were tricked into going to it: 'It's horrible; when you're there; you think you're mad.' Many women, including Mary, echoed this:

> I think they put me in the pad because they were afraid I might take my own life. The cameras were the scariest thing about it. I thought that they were probably watching me all the time. I wanted to bang on the walls and go mad, but I was afraid to, because maybe they were watching me, and

they might think that I was mad and then they might want to strap me down.

Some of the women, evidencing Carlen's contention that the women are 'horribly at home within psychiatry',[22] said that they would ask to go there. Three of the women spoke of using the facility of the padded cell in lieu of company, in lieu of confidantes, in lieu of support; they talked of desperately needing someone to talk to and not having anyone, and of asking to go to the pads so that they wouldn't harm themselves. Nuala said:

It's horrible, feels real claustrophobic. Nothing in it, it's boring, you don't even know what time of day it is or anything. The gown is degrading cos you're not allowed wear any underwear, but it's a good idea. It keeps you safe and that's important, especially for me and for people like me. I'm suicidal from time to time and they often take me to the pad to keep me safe.

Kate said:

I would ask to go to the pad. I was often depressed. The pad

4.3: Padded cell: Dóchas Centre

would depress you more, but sometimes you need someone to talk to and there's nobody to talk to and so you go to the pad so you don't harm yourself. Sometimes I cut my arms. I think I'm just trying to get the anger out of me. I was raped by my brother-in-law when I was 14 years old. I think I'm still trying to get that anger out.

All of the women accepted the padded cells with its referents of madness as part of their lives. They accepted the padded cells and the role they played in the controlling structures of the prison. They accepted the control, the degradation and the signs of insanity implicit in the padded cells as part of their world, their lives and their identities. These were women who could, if they did not behave, be dragged to padded cells, stripped and locked in those cells until they behaved. All the women were subject to these punishments and all learned to live with the threat and reality of such punishments. All also learned to adjust their behaviour, their senses of self, and their personal identities accordingly.

There was very little evidence of resistance among the women. This relates to Sue Richardson's comment on her experience of imprisonment (Chapter 2), that resistance was always individual and likely to manifest in the form of verbal protest or self-injury. One of the main sites of resistance in both of the women's prisons were the peepholes on the door of the rooms or cells. Laura said:

I don't like when people look into holes, it bothers me. I get actually annoyed about it because I think if you want to see someone or talk to them, you open the door, look them in the eyes, and talk to them like that. I just don't like it. It's not right to look through holes at people, why not open the door and speak to them?

Pamela had similar issues with the peephole:

When I want some privacy I cover the peephole with some paper. You are not allowed to do that and you would get told off for doing it. I covered the peephole one time when I was having a shower and I forgot to take the paper down when I was finished. I was told off big time for that. So now I leave the door open all the time, even when I'm in the shower. With the door closed I never know when I'm being watched and I just couldn't have that, and so I leave the door open.

In Limerick Prison the peephole was a big deal. Where in the Dóchas Centre the women would be 'told off' for covering a peephole, in Limerick the women would lose their privileges for a week or two, no shop orders, no phone calls, no visits or screened visits, and locked up for the night every day at 4.30 p.m.

Personal Identities

As will be seen, the women's identities emerge in part from the women's engagement with the powerful penal discourses of the media, the criminal justice system, the Irish Prison Service and the structures of the women's prisons, as detailed in the previous chapter. In his investigation of power, Foucault wrote of the constitution of subjectivity through power relations.[23] Garland spoke of individual subjectivity as being socially and culturally constructed.[24] Bosworth's focus was on how women, as agents, negotiate power within prison. She focused on how imprisoned women negotiate the various discourses of prison and, through these negotiations, construct their own identities.[25] Carlen and Worrall questioned the extent to which an individual is free to shape her own actions and identity independently of the circumstances in which she finds herself.[26] It seems, from the analysis presented in this book, that identities are progressively and dynamically achieved through discursive practices. It is through the reiterative use of signs, words and phrases, symbols, rituals and behaviours that social reality is constructed, that roles and identities are ascribed. The prison's signifying capacity does most emphatically ascribe the identity of prisoner to all the women, and all of the women who engaged with this study very readily identified themselves as prisoners.

The Sub-Cultures

There were many different groups of women among the interviewees. As well as the 'trustees' and others, there were Irish women and non-Irish women, older women and younger women, black women and white women, addicted women and non-addicted women. There were women serving long sentences and women serving short sentences. There were Traveller women and homeless women, city women and women from provincial and rural

Ireland. In prison women tend to become close to, and to stay close to, women who were similar to them, women with similar life experiences.

Susan said: 'There are very many different groups in the prisons; the different floors in Cedar House in the Dóchas Centre tend to stay together, the Traveller women stay together. For me it's difficult to have friends. Well, you can be close with one or two, but not in general; because they know each other from outside and they stay with their friends.' The women serving long sentences, the better-educated women, the women with the more stable lifestyles, generally the 'trustees', tend to bond with each other. It is clear that the women tend to bond with women they identify with, and so their friendships can be seen, as suggested by O'Connor, as serving to elaborate and perpetuate the structures of their society.[27] One woman in the Dóchas Centre, Terri, talked of the young addicted women who come and go from the prison:

> The women here never got a chance. They don't know right from wrong. They don't even behave in Church. They've never been taught anything. They all have sad stories. Every one of them has had a very bad experience at home, with their families. Those women are in the houses where at night they are locked in their rooms. When everything is locked up you hear them shouting to each other, screaming. If they hear bad news and they are locked up, they can set fire to their rooms or cut themselves. It happens at night.

There is evidence in this testimony of the differential experiences of imprisonment in the Dóchas Centre, where although all women are locked into the house within which they are accommodated, only some are also locked into their rooms at night. In relation to this differential treatment, Vicky said:

> We get searched all the time. Even after a visit we get searched. A black person wouldn't get searched. Someone doing life wouldn't get searched. They get to spend a longer time on their visits. They're all in for big stuff, murder or for drug smuggling, and they walk straight into a 24-hour house [a house with no lock-up at night] and they get all the privileges. We're all in for petty crimes, and we're stuck in the small yard.[28]

Vicky's testimony evidences in part the role of the prison's design and regime in shaping prisoner culture. She identifies very strongly with her group or sub-culture, the other Irish addicted women, the 'we' of her discourse. She differentiates herself and her group from the others, the 'they'. These elements of the prison experience play a part in the subject positioning of the women. It is through such experiences and the reiterative nature of the experiences that the women come to know the identities ascribed to them.

In prison some of the women develop very close bonds of friendship with other women. Paula, one of the 'trustees', remarked:

> Women get closer together than men. Women can become deeply intimate with each other, without that intimacy being sexual. When the door to the house is locked at night we spend hours together, talking, drinking tea, in each other's rooms. We are all sad in here. We spend half our time counselling each other. The love we have for each other and the intimacy we share really helps in here.

These close friendships sustain the women in their prison experiences and through their prison sentences. Within prison the friendships between the women are encouraged and supported. This is particularly the case of the friendships among the 'trustees'. O'Connor suggests that friendships 'are attractive because they offer a definition of self which is under the control of the individual'.[29] The friendships among the addicted women are more controlled. One of the women, Stacy, discussed the manner in which she managed her relationship with the other women:

> I try to keep to meself a good bit, cos they're always gossiping and fighting. See, a lot of bitchiness goes on, jealousy; always have to have something to say about you. What you've got and what you haven't got. You have to be careful. You can get roped into the conversation, and before you realise it, you've said something you shouldn't have, and then they say it back and then you're in trouble before you know it.

The women related the manner in which power is wielded among the inmates. Amy discussed the way in which she engaged with prison staff and management:

You have to be strong, that's all. You have to learn in prison to be strong. Prison can make or break you. You have to let a lot of things pass. In your mind just pretend its not happening. Just walk away. If I wanted something, I'd fight for it. Maybe I'll get it, maybe I won't. It's just up front and ask. There's a chance you might get it, but you can't work it, that's all.

Brenda said: 'The officers can bully you and threaten you. Half of them would put you going, wind you up like, like they're the boss. I tell them they're not the boss; the governor's the boss. And they say the governor's not the boss, that they're the boss.' Delia highlighted the level of surveillance in Limerick Prison:

> The women watch as the officers watch, everyone watches: the girls watch for a chance to go into your cell and rob it and the officers are watching you to see if you are trying to rob the other girls' cells. I trust them both the same, the girls and the officers. I don't trust either of them. Sometimes you have to watch the girls alright. In case they robbed something out of your cell. They wouldn't rob my cell now cos they know I wouldn't leave them rob it. They know that if something went missing I'd search their cells until I found it.

The power the women discussed was the power to intimidate, the power the officers had and used to intimidate the women, and the power some of the women had and used to intimidate other women. In Limerick Prison in particular, the women also discussed the threat of physical violence. Catriona spoke of the old female prison at Mountjoy, when inmates were accommodated on a wing of St Patrick's Institution, before the Dóchas Centre was built: 'During meal times the doors to the cells would be open and girls were going in and taking stuff from your room, you know robbin' stuff, cigarettes and stuff, and now [in the Dóchas Centre] you can lock your room and you know that nobody is in it.'

Most of the young women in Limerick, because of the lock-up regime there, preferred sharing their cells, although the older women felt that they would not survive their prison sentences if they had to share a cell. Since 2003, all of the cells in Limerick have been equipped for double occupancy and the prison is almost always at full occupancy. One of the women there, AnneMarie, was almost 50 years of age. She said that the other women were all young, 19, 20 or 21, and she explained her isolation:

> Most of the women are from inner city Dublin. Most of them are drug addicts. Some are from Cork city. There's fighting all the time between the two gangs, Cork and Dublin. Sometimes we have women here from Athlone town as well. Then we have faction fights. The Athlone crowd back the Cork crowd against the Dublin crowd. There's tension all the time and fist fights and head butting. I saw one girl putting her fingers up another girl's nose and she was pumping blood. She thinks she has a broken nose but I don't think it is broken. She got a kick in the head yesterday. She has a mark there and a mark on her eye. I think she got five beatings in a week and a half. She doesn't cause any hassle really but she gets on their nerves.

The aggression and violence manifest in Limerick Women's Prison is absent from the Dóchas Centre. The bleaker accommodation at Limerick provides the setting for, and probably the incentive for, physical aggression among the women imprisoned there; this aggression is absent in the Dóchas Centre with its contemporary, novel and personal design, and it's relatively relaxed management.

The Addicted Women

As addiction is the critical issue in experiences of criminality and imprisonment for many, if not most of the women, this section considers the women's experiences of addiction in more detail. In terms of addiction, about 85 per cent of all those interviewed smoked cigarettes, 75 per cent drank alcohol. Over two thirds, 64 per cent, acknowledged that they were drug addicts. Over 60 per cent used cannabis while 45 per cent used other illegal drugs. The women used prescription drugs, among them methadone, sleeping tablets, Valium, Prozac and anti-depressants. Over 49 per cent of the addicted women had overdosed at some stage in their lives. Only 16 per cent of all of the interviewees had ever received counselling or therapy. Donna told her story:

I was 12 years old when I started using cannabis. Then I tried all the others, speed, acid, Es. I only tried coke once or twice. I was tricked into taking heroin. It's five years since I stopped all that. I just use hash now. I started using it because my brother used it. I liked it. It made me feel good, it still does. It doesn't bother me, I can go without it, but nobody would stop me from using it.

Most of the women engaged very seriously with their addictions. Elizabeth said: 'I tried it to see what it was like. Then I just got addicted to it. It was a weekend thing, then every day, then taking acid, heroin, ecstasy and cocaine. I'm much more confident when I'm taking drugs.' For these women their identities were completely immersed in their addictions. Sabrina said:

I'm a smoker and a drinker, big time; two bottles of vodka a day every day. I use prescription drugs, sleeping tablets, phy' [physeptone] and Valium. I use cannabis regularly and I use cannabis in prison, just a little, a drag off the girls. I used heroin in the old prison, smoked it. I started using drugs nine years ago when I was 22 years old. I had been drinking since I was 14. The last time I snorted a bit was in the courts the day before I was brought in. I took it just to take away the pains of withdrawal. But it didn't even help that. Both alcohol and drugs ruined my life. Cocaine really fucked me up, the heroin too. I started because everyone else was, the drugs were there in front of me face all the time, the guys I was with. Then I got addicted to them. You get to like the buzz. Then you get to the stage when you're just normal on them.

Marie outlined her addiction: 'I'm a smoker and a drinker. I drink shorts, Pernod and black. I use prescription drugs, Valium, methadone, a couple of others. I use cannabis regularly. I started using drugs when I was 15. I use everything. I started for the novelty, not through peer pressure. Then I liked it too much to stop.' These women were alcoholics and drug addicts, their lives were the lives of alcoholics and drug addicts, their associates were alcoholics or drug addicts or drug dealers, their routines were those of alcoholics or drug addicts, their habits were those of alcoholics and drug addicts and their concerns were those of alcoholics and drug addicts. Mandy said:

> I'm here for a week. I got nicked on Wednesday and I was
> brought in on Thursday, drunk and disorderly and abusive
> behaviour, outstanding warrants for the same thing and for
> not turning up. I don't shoplift or anything like that. I tap
> for my money. I have six or seven previous convictions for
> drunk and disorderly mostly, once for damage to a car. I'm
> homeless. I drink vodka, Cork Cream wine, and bottles or
> cans of cider. I drink every day. It depends on the money. I use
> prescription drugs. I use hash now and then. I use heroin, I
> inject it.

Alana also told her story:

> I came in on Thursday and I'm on remand, for failing to
> appear. I was shoplifting and they found an old warrant. I
> had two bottles of Smirnoff and I went into a shop for three
> cans of Fosters. The security guard said I hadn't paid for the
> vodka. I have about ten previous convictions, for larceny,
> house breaking, driving offences and soliciting. As a drug
> addict the prison is great for a week. When you go out you
> get a great hit from the heroin.

As did Katherine:

> I drink cider, ten cans and wine as well. My boyfriend and I
> would share about three bottles between us everyday. I take
> Valium and I use cannabis every day. I was 14 when I started
> using cannabis, I started using solvents when I was younger,
> magic mushrooms when I was 15, LSD at 17, speed at 18,
> rocks, cocaine in rock form, at 21 and heroin at 23. I suppose
> I'm trying to escape, trying to obliterate.

And Louise:

> I started drinking when I was 14 or 15. I first used cannabis
> when I was 17, then ecstasy, cocaine and speed at 17 or 18.
> I started using heroin when I was 21. A lot of the people I
> did drugs with over the years are dead now, dead from
> drugs. I didn't know when I started that it would destroy
> me, all the robbin' I did, all me friends dying.

The women used drugs in prison. They get them from people visiting them, from people coming in on a sentence or returning to

prison from temporary release. Some women are bullied into bringing drugs into the prison, while some want the notoriety of bringing them in. The dealers among the imprisoned women and among the women's associates on the outside want the profits and the dependency to be had from getting drugs in. Drugs are 'kissed over' into the prison on visits. They come in sewn into the lining of clothes; people outside send drugs in with gifts. Women bring drugs into the prison in plastic bags pushed into containers of hair gel or body lotion. Most popularly, they bring them in internally, in the women's vaginas, 'bottled', in prison vernacular. There are no internal searches in prisons in Ireland. There are random strip-searches, random room searches, and random drug tests.

Sexuality

The women discussed their experiences of sex and sexuality. All but three of the eighty interviewees said that they were heterosexual. The interviews highlighted the absence of sex in the lives of the women. Alex said: 'I never think about it. It's not a problem for me. To my knowledge there really isn't any sex in the prison. I'm sure nothing like that goes on here. I don't know how other people feel about it, it's not discussed.' Maria added: 'There's no sex in here. I never actually seen gay people in the prison. Nobody ever came on to me.' Olivia said: 'There was this girl yesterday; she came on to me in the yard. I thought she was buzzed [stoned]. She wasn't. So I went to swing out of her. The officers stopped me. I would genuinely have punched lumps out of her.' Nina said: 'There's no sex, but I do sometimes do a bit of kiss-chasing in the yard.' Other women said things like 'sex is not really a problem' or 'no, I never think about it.' Ellie declared that she was 'anti-sex really', while Rachel said: 'As far as I know there's no sex in here. My own sexuality doesn't bother me. I'm straight, but I never really had much sex. The first time I did, I got pregnant, so now I'm terrified. I've had sex maybe ten times, that's all.' Sally, who was in a long-term heterosexual relationship, said: 'There's no sex in the prison. I don't miss sex as much as I miss just cuddling up. I miss him when I go to bed. He always cuddles up to me. I miss being near him, sitting on his knee watching TV. I don't miss sex. I miss the closeness. I miss holding him.'

Only eight of those interviewed expressed interest in sex.

Three were 'trustees', and all eight were mature white women, two of them grandmothers. The oldest of the interviewees said:

> I miss sex. I miss men. We've got the male officers and I want to talk to them all the time, because I miss the attention of men. I think it's dreadful the way the male prison is separate from the female prison. It's so unnatural. It's terrible if you're a woman who likes to be with a man. It's terrible, so lonely.

The black South African women who were in a relationship were deeply committed to that relationship, while those not in a relationship were deeply committed to the thought or the ideal of a relationship. Joy said:

> I am married and I have one little girl and I am pregnant. When I go home my husband will be there with my little girl. He tried to stop me from coming here. He works part-time at a bank. We argued one time and I stopped telephoning him. Then he started to telephone me. Since then things have been better between us.

Ruth said:

> I am closest to my boyfriend, he is from Nigeria. He helps me a lot while I am here. He helps my baby and he helps my Mum. She is not OK. She has AIDS. People are just dying of AIDS and there is no treatment at all if you have no money. She is in and out of hospital. He sends her money.

Two women spoke of women prisoners having relationships with male prison officers. One said: 'There is sex, between an officer and one of the women. One of the officers is having sex with one of the women, and everyone knows it. He is in her room with her every night. They are sleeping together. Of course he is going to protect that person more.' As part of 'normalising' the prison environment (see Chapter 3), there are a lot of men, prison officers and prisoners, working in the women's prison every day and there are many close friendships between these men and women. This has several implications. There is the advantageous change that male company represents, the naturalness in having both sexes represented among the staff. But there is also the power differential between staff and prisoners, which may sometimes be even more pronounced between male staff members and female prisoners. This power differential can render the women vulnerable to sexual abuse, even if the encounter or relationship appears consensual. One of the women, Trish, spoke of the sexual abuse she suffered at the hands of a male employee while being held in the Central Mental Hospital (see Chapter 3): 'I was sent to Dundrum for a week, they kept me there for five weeks and I was abused, sexually. It's not the only incidence of abuse in my life. I just don't want to talk about it.'

Nearly half of all the women interviewed, 44 per cent, said that they had been abused at some time in their lives, abused by men – men in their families, men who were friends of their families and men who were strangers to them. The abuses the women had endured included sexual abuse, molestations and rape, verbal abuse and threats, beatings and other physical, emotional and psychological abuses. Seven of the 'trustees', 29 per cent of them, had been abused. Caroline said: 'I was sexually abused by my brother at home from when I was 10 until I was 13. In the end I got him charged. He was 19 and 20 years old at the time. He's at home now. I don't speak to him or associate with him. I don't have a brother any more.'

Abuse of every description featured in the lives of the addicted women. They dealt with it regularly. It was a part of their life experience, a feature in the world of drugs of their female roles. Of the fifty-one chronically addicted women, four of the eight teenagers had experienced all kinds of abuse; 61 per cent of those in their twenties had suffered sexual and other abuse, all but two of the women over thirty had been raped and beaten. Dee said: 'My father would beat me with bars and belts; he hit me with shovels, hatchets, knives and forks. He smacked me one day with a shovel across the back of the head. He smashed a mirror over my head another day and then tried to choke me.' Helena said:

My father used to give me alcohol and then he'd abuse me. He did it to all of us. My Ma wouldn't believe me until a babysitter made an accusation against my Da. Then my brother remembered being raped by my Da. But how could me Ma not have known? Even now I can feel the anger coming up in me.

Rose had been 'raped by a fellow in a park in Ballinasloe': 'I don't know who he was. I'd taken sleeping pills and drink an' all and my friends woke me up and asked me what had happened. I was covered with blood. Some fella had raped me.' One of the women, a 19-year-old, at the end of the interview showed her back which was covered from her shoulders all the way down to the top of her jeans with scars from whippings she had received from her father:

> I never really had a childhood. It was a nightmare, full of crazy violence and abuse. I left home when I was 11 years old and went on the streets. At home my Dad watches TV alone in the dark in the living room; my Mum, with all my brother and sisters, watches TV in the kitchen. My Dad is fierce and physically very strong and everyone at home is terrified of him.

In general, very few of the women were imprisoned for prostitution. Among the interviewees, three of the trustees had had long careers in prostitution – two Britons and one white South African. The Briton on the trafficking charge said: 'I worked on the streets for thirty years and I'm a dealer as well, although that's only a recent thing.' The Briton on the credit card fraud charge said: 'It's eighteen years since I had a job and then I had a few. I worked in an old people's home. I worked in bars and in shops. For the past eighteen years I've been working as a prostitute. I work in a massage parlour and from my own flat.' The white South African said: 'I've worked as an escort for ten years, sexual encounters and conversing with people. It's mostly business people. I have a wardrobe in work and I can dress up any way, I do whatever they want.'

While very few of the women were imprisoned for prostitution, very many, particularly those with chronic drug addictions, engage in prostitution. Carrie said:

> I love scoring good stuff. It's terrible when you do everything you can to get the few bob [the money] and then you get gear [heroin] or coke, cos I'm into both, and it's really crappy stuff. You could get gear and it wouldn't be real strong. You might be on the street for ten hours and maybe only get fifty quid.

Within prostitution, the women are fiercely disciplined to a utilitarian sexual functionality. This brutal disciplining, within and to prostitution, is a most extreme manifestation of the patriarchal social order. This brutality was evidenced in the documentary series *The Underworld*,[30] where women's experiences of prostitution in Ireland and women's experiences of trafficking and of being trafficked for the sex industry into Ireland were documented.[31] These uses of the women's bodies evidence many women's experiences of the patriarchal social order, and they evidence an understanding that many of the women had in relation to women's roles and place in society. They also evidence many of the women's internalised sense of self; their learned sense of the physical utility of female sexuality. This learning adds another dimension to the women's vulnerabilities. One of the women, Jennifer, described for me an incident that occurred in the prison when one of the women prisoners searched her, and other women, internally. She said: 'Gold chains went missing and a young one put her hand up inside me to see if I had them. One was doing it in one of the rooms and another was keeping a lookout. I had to submit to it or I would have had me head bashed in.' The experience of prison was an ordeal for all of the women. The poorer women experienced more violence and degradation in their lives, and they experienced more violence and degradation within prison. They did not have the cultural capital necessary to manage that environment, to perform presentations of self to prison management that would have earned them the designation 'trustee'.

The Media

Within their controlled, controlling and defining prison experiences, many of the women felt further controlled by the media. One quarter of those interviewed had featured at some point in the media, in the press, and on television and radio. They felt prey to the press. Many said that the new prison was also prey to the press, as a result of the changes and developments introduced in the new prison. The women believed that they were treated differently in prison depending on what was in the press. As detailed in Chapter 3, the media has a major role in the development of penal policy through its influence on public opinion and on ministerial and government departmental opinion. These opinions, influenced as they are by the press, shape in turn the penal policy which controls and orders the prison experiences of these women. The women believed that 90 per cent of what was published in the media about them and about the prisons to be untrue.

They experienced the press coverage as upsetting, humiliating, degrading and embarrassing, and believed themselves to be subject to hostile media discourses. Carol said:

> The media can do with you what they want. They don't check their facts. They write what they want to write. It doesn't matter whether what they are writing is true or not. I was in the media even before I was in court. I never had a chance. I couldn't answer back. I couldn't defend myself. First they make up stories, and then the way they present them ...

Jean agreed:

> I was in the newspapers when I was first in court for the robberies. It was degrading, and very embarrassing for my family. The newspapers mostly tell lies. They were adding stuff onto the story about me, saying a girl got stabbed an' all. That wasn't true, nobody got hurt. It's mostly all lies, for five lines of fact you can have two pages of made-up stuff. After you come into prison they can literally say what they like about you.

Debbie said: 'I think sometimes they go on too much about the women, making them out to be real down-and-out junkies and bad people. They're not. Some of them are real good people.' The women said that the invasions of privacy they experienced in the prison were mirrored in their exposure in the media. Even within their seclusion in prison the women felt and were exposed to the press. The newspapers could say apparently anything they wanted about the women and they could say it apparently with impunity. The women felt powerless and exposed in the face of press scrutiny, as Yvonne outlined:

> I know about two articles that have been published about me. One was in a local newspaper for being drunk, and the other was in a woman's magazine for being homeless and begging. I was shocked more than anything else. They brought up my illness, that I was HIV positive and everything. I thought that that was private. Both of the articles made me feel terribly ashamed.

The 'trustees' were generally more concerned with the press coverage than the other women, although some of the addicts were also concerned. Martine suggested that there was no need for the addicted women to be concerned because the media was only interested in big crimes, while the addicts generally commit only minor crimes or public order offences. The women believed that the public had a poor view generally of women in prison and many felt that that view was shaped in part by the press. As Niamh said: 'Everyone in here is always on show; a topic for people to talk about. You can't be left alone to do your sentence and it's all lies as well. I think that the people out there believe a lot of the crap they read in the paper.'

In terms of public discourses, the women said that the general public were likely to think that imprisoned women were 'down-and-outs and low-lifes', 'scumbags and junkies', 'animals', 'criminals and jailbirds', 'all rowdies'. Maeve said: 'I think they despise people who are in prison', while Celine added:

> I think they believe all that stuff they read in the papers. I don't think that they see us as human beings. I think that they see us as outcasts who should be treated without mercy. This is totally wrong. We are human beings who made mistakes and are paying for them. We shouldn't be treated as anything less, or stigmatised for it.

The degradation implicit in the status of prisoner within the structures of the prison served to render the women visible and vulnerable to the press. Women prisoners have no defence against the scrutiny of the press. In addition, women prisoners have no other public representation. The women themselves believed that the identities ascribed to them in the press are the identities ascribed to them by the public.

Prisoner Identities

The women discussed their own sense of themselves as women and as imprisoned women. They constructed their identities around phenomena external to themselves. Their identities were grounded in notions of themselves in relation to others, grounded in relationships, in their families and in their children; 75 per cent of those interviewed were mothers. The women identified themselves as mothers, daughters, sisters, wives and girlfriends.

They generally did not feel in control of their lives; only 12 per cent felt that they were. Those women who believed that they had roles in society believed that those roles were the roles they had in their families.

Some, like Pauline, talked of the problems of being a woman: 'You can get bullied, by fellas and bigger women than you', while Aileen said: 'It's very hard being a woman. It's so demanding. I mean I think it's hard being a woman, the rules of society, what a woman should and shouldn't do. A lot of things men get away with; if you as a woman do it you're shunned or seen as a bad or immoral person.' The women generally felt that an experience of imprisonment was worse for women than for men, that the entire experience of imprisonment was more degrading for women. Gail said: 'Women don't belong in prison. Prisons are not designed for women. Prisons do not cater for women, they cater for men. Whoever thought that women should be in prison? Females feel lost in prison, they are not equipped for it.' Gillian said: 'It's terrible, it's very bad for a woman to be here, to experience jail, to be arrested, to be searched, everything. It's shameful. I feel it's worse for a woman, a lot worse.' Bartky writes of women's profoundly disempowering shame, which she says manifests in a pervasive sense of personal inadequacy.[32] It was apparent that most of the women, over two thirds, internalised their prison experiences in a manner that shaped both their senses of self and their personal identities. For some, particularly the chronically addicted homeless women who experience pain and degradation throughout their lives, the prison's shaming capacity was simply another painful, degrading episode in their troubled lives. When asked how many prisons they had been in, one third of the women said they had been in one prison, one third in two, 11 per cent in three and 5 per cent in four prisons; one woman had been in five prisons and one in twelve. Some had slept in many prison cells, two said they had slept in hundreds.

The women felt that the prisons undermined their personal identities, their senses of self, that their identities as women were degraded by their prisoner identities. Eithne said: 'In the prison you're just a number. You're stripped of your identity, your integrity and your honour. Your womanhood is taken away from you, and all you are left with is trying to keep your head up and yourself focused.' Some, like Veronica, talked of the infantilising experience of prison:

> In the prison the women are like dolls in a doll's house. The worst thing is that you are not in command of yourself. In here I feel like a child, but I am 34 years old and I have children. Some of the women here are in their thirties, their forties and fifties. Many of them have children and grandchildren. They are all, in here, treated like children.

On leaving prison the women believed that they were taking with them the prisoner identities so carefully crafted for them by the prisons and the penal discourses. With these carefully constructed identities, they had many concerns about leaving prison. One of the concerns was not to come back. Another was the worry of getting their lives together again, of getting a place to live, of keeping away from drugs and/or alcohol. About 60 per cent felt they had improved in prison, 21 per cent had used the prison to detox. They had put on a bit of weight, calmed down, come off drugs. About 22 per cent said they had used the prison as a shelter or refuge. Others were grateful for the educational opportunities they had while inside. One or two said they could see things clearly now, they believed that they had 'copped on'. One or two said they had learned their lesson.

About 20 per cent believed their time in prison had done nothing for them. About 36 per cent were acutely conscious of the damage they had sustained through their prison sentences and through the loss of the time they had spent away from their families and their lives. They were acutely aware of the damage they had sustained through their experience of imprisonment. About half of those leaving prison worried about being 'normal', about being 'like a mother and doing what normal mothers do'. Their main concerns related to their children, their families and friends, and to how these people would react to them. One quarter did not believe that those outside would expect to be reunited with them. They were fearful of the manner in which, and the degree to which, the prisoner identities ascribed to them would influence their relationships with their families, friends and relatives. They worried about being given a chance by society, about having a stigma attached to them. Emma said: 'The prison experience was like a tattoo, a tattoo of shame and pain; I don't know how long it will remain with me, perhaps it will remain forever. I think that we have been punished enough. I don't know how I will think back on this place.' This tattoo, she felt, she would have forever. The women's experiences of their representations in the various discourses could be likened to Kafka's 'apparatus' the harrow, from his short story *In the Penal Colony*,[33] where the condemned is strapped to the harrow, which deeply inscribes, deadly and decoratively, on the body of the condemned, the crime for which they have been condemned. Goffman discussed stigma symbols, visible signs of stigma as signs carrying social information.[34] Such signs, Goffman wrote, can become a permanent part of the person. Clearly, the power of the discourses of the identities of ascription, discourses which ascribed to the women infantilised, powerless, shameful, deviant identities, profoundly affected the women and their personal identities and senses of self. The women could not, as agents, 'subjects capable of designating self in a signifying world', privilege their own senses of self over the discourses ascribing identity to them.[35]

NOTES

1. C. Geertz, *The Interpretation of Cultures* (London: Fontana, 1993).
2. International drug couriers in Ireland are currently dealt with in the courts under the Criminal Justice Act 1999, which amended the Misuse of Drugs Act 1977, legislating for a mandatory minimum prison sentence of ten years for anyone caught in possession of more than £10,000 (€12,700) worth of drugs for sale or supply. When this legislation was introduced, there was a degree of disquiet over the issue of mandatory sentences interfering with judicial independence. However, the judiciary has exercised independence and this independence is manifest particularly in the disparate sentences imposed. Since mandatory sentencing was introduced, some women have been sentenced to ten years, some to seven years and some to four years; some were released on review and some on appeal and some are serving or have served their entire sentences.
3. *The Economist* presented the case for legalising drugs in an article in 2001. The case for a liberal approach rests, it suggests, on the fact that the 'harms' from the ban on drugs fall disproportionately on poor countries and on poor people in rich countries; according to the article, among those involved in the trade in illegal drugs, it is poor people who end up in prison: 'The Case for Legalisation', *The Economist*, 28 July 2001, pp.11–12; see also 'A Survey of Illegal Drugs', unpaginated, in the centre of the magazine.
4. C. Quinlan, 'Ireland's Women's Prisons', Jesuit Centre for Justice and Faith (2008), available at www.cfj.ie/content/view/243/3/ (accessed 20 June 2010).
5. *Annual Report of the Irish Prison Service, 2008*, available at http://www. irishprisons.ie/documents/IPSannualreport2008e.pdf (accessed 20 June 2010).
6. 'Prison Facilities in Ireland: The Dóchas Centre', Irish Penal Reform Trust website, www.iprt.ie/prison-facilities-in-ireland (accessed 20 June 2010).
7. M. Douglas, *Risk and Blame: Essays in Cultural Theory* (London: Routledge, 1992), pp.155–66.

8. P. Bourdieu, 'Cultural Production and Social Reproduction', in R. Brown (ed.), *Knowledge, Education and Cultural Change* (London: Tavistock, 1973), pp.487–511.
9. P. Bourdieu, *Language and Symbolic Power* (Cambridge: Polity, 1991).
10. N. Elias, *The Civilising Process* (Cambridge: Blackwell Publishing, 2000).
11. P. Carlen, *Women, Crime and Poverty* (Milton Keynes: Open University Press, 1988), p.6.
12. T. Carey, *Mountjoy: The Story of a Prison* (Cork: The Collins Press, 2000), p.138.
13. To preserve the women's anonymity, pseudonyms are used throughout.
14. E. Mahon, 'Ireland: A Private Patriarchy', *Environment and Planning*, 26, 8 (1994), pp.1277–1296.
15. Carlen, *Women, Crime and Poverty*, p.19.
16. P. Carmody and M. McEvoy, *A Study of Irish Female Prisoners* (Dublin: Stationery Office, 1996).
17. M. Monaghan, *A Survey of Women in an Irish Prison*, unpublished MPsychSc dissertation, University College Dublin, 1989.
18. H. Lefebvre, *The Production of Space* (Oxford: Blackwell, 1991), pp.141–2.
19. L. Irigaray, *An Ethics of Sexual Difference* (New York: Cornell University Press, 1993), p.7.
20. P. Carlen, *Criminal Women* (Cambridge: Polity, 1985), p.3.
21. S. Walklate, *Gender, Crime and Criminal Justice* (Abingdon: Willan Publishing, 2000), p.190.
22. P. Carlen, *Women's Imprisonment: A Study in Social Control* (London: Routledge & Kegan Paul, 1983), p.210.
23. M. Foucault, *Discipline and Punish: The Birth of the Prison* (London: Penguin, 1977).
24. D. Garland, *Punishment and Modern Society: A Study in Social Theory* (Chicago: University of Chicago Press, 1990).
25. M. Bosworth, *Engendering Resistance: Agency and Power in the Women's Prisons* (Aldershot: Ashgate, 1999).
26. P. Carlen, and A. Worrall, *Analysing Women's Imprisonment* (Abingdon: Willan Publishing, 2004).
27. P. O'Connor, 'Women's Friendships in a Post-Modern World', in R. Adams and G. Allan (eds), *Placing Friendship in Context* (Cambridge: Cambridge University Press, 1998).
28. The most secure, more controlled, of the two yards in the prison.
29. O'Connor, 'Women's Friendships in a Post-Modern World', pp.117–36.
30. 'The Underworld', a documentary film, Parallel Films for RTÉ, Dublin, 2003.
31. Ibid. According to the documentary, the 1993 Criminal Law (Sexual Offences) Act moved women off the streets and into brothels, and so organised prostitution began. In 1999 *In Dublin* magazine was making up to £20,000 fortnightly from advertising massage parlours and escort agencies. The magazine was censored, its editor Mike Hogan investigated, and the magazine eventually folded. The pimps identified in the documentary were 54-year-old Marie Bridgeman, who was beaten to death shortly after her conviction for running a brothel; Tom McDonald, who was described as a millionaire; Brian Byrne, who was said to have brothels in north central Dublin; Samantha Blanford Hutton, who made an estimated half a million pounds annually from her brothel 'Penthouse Pets' on Pearse Street in Dublin; and Peter McCormack, an ex-RUC reservist who moved to Dublin in 1995 and had, within one year, six brothels operating across the city. McCormack, identified as the biggest pimp operating in Ireland, was said to have a nationwide prostitution business. The documentary detailed the development in Ireland from the late 1990s of lap-dancing clubs, of which there was initially a benign view. There were a number of clubs in Dublin and around the country operating publicly, among them 'The Barclay Club', 'Strings', 'La Petite' and 'Angels'. When the Gardaí launched their 'Operation Quest' investigation, ten clubs around the country were raided and seventy-one women from eastern Europe, Russia, Africa and Mongolia were found to be working illegally. The clubs were considered fronts for prostitution and many of the women working in them were believed to have been trafficked into Ireland for the purposes of prostitution.

The women, victims of traffickers, were treated as criminals by the Irish criminal justice system. They were prosecuted and imprisoned.

32. S.L. Bartky, *Femininity and Domination: Studies in the Phenomenology of Oppression* (London: Routledge, 1990), p.85.
33. F. Kafka, 'In the Penal Colony', in N. Glatzer (ed.), *The Complete Stories* (New York: Schocken, 1995), pp.140–67.
34. E. Goffman, *Stigma* (London: Penguin, 1990).
35. P. Ricoeur, *Oneself as Another* (Chicago: Chicago University Press, 1994), p.113.

Chapter Five

The Scholars' Perspective

In the literature on women prisoners and women's imprisonment, there are two strands of analysis, one of which tends to represent women in prison as victims, and one which represents them as resisters. The debate is about, on one side, the degree to which women are victims of penal regimes, these accounts detailing generally the appalling experiences of women in prison, and, on the other side, the degree to which women can resist those regimes, studies which tend to represent imprisoned women as powerful agents, agents capable of overcoming the exigencies of the penal regimes within which they are imprisoned. In a relatively recent contribution to this debate, Carlen and Worrall pointed out that while some researchers have established that particular female prisoners may in some instances be capable of resistance, in prison it is in fact the phenomenon of prisoner resistance which actually activates the prison's disciplinary and security mechanisms. [1]

We live in a social world; that world is historical, it has an ever-accumulating past which shapes it and shapes our experiences of it; and that world is fundamentally and ontologically spatial. The concern in this chapter is with exploring in the literature the manner in which space, and in particular female prison space, engenders and shapes identities. One of the key debates in sociology is the extent to which individuals actively participate in shaping their own identities. The debate is about the extent to which human beings, as agents, are able to shape their own identities, make choices, and take responsibility, and the extent to which their identities are influenced, even determined, by factors outside their control. Woodward highlights the overlap in the literature between the terms self, subject and identity. [2] She suggests that preference is often given to the term identity, because the term accommodates the interrelationship between the personal and the social, and the complex possibilities of an interplay between agency, personal choice, personal power and personal responsibility, and social construction or constraint.[3] A key concern in this book is with the manner in which the individual's sense of self, the individual's subjectivity, is constructed. Subjectivities are not constructed in isolation but in relation to the historical experience, and in relation to the social and spatial milieu which individuals inhabit. Identities are constructed by means of a conjoining of the personal with the historical, the social and the spatial. The individual within this triple dialectic constructs her subjectivity.

IDENTITY, CRIMINALITY AND PENALITY

Criminal identity is a very powerful identity. The individual who has been identified by the criminal justice system as criminal may be punished by the state with a prison sentence. The model of crime and punishment that embraces imprisonment as its ultimate sanction consistently and insistently reduces deviance to the level of the individual where the individual, generally a member of the 'fringe of the lower class which is constantly in contact with the police and law', is deviant, and responsible for that deviance.[4] Within the construct that is prison, despite its abiding centrality in our model of social control, structural causes of deviance are not recognised, acknowledged, challenged or corrected. In the utilitarian (actions and consequences) vision of justice[5] and in Bentham's quantification of morality by reference to utilitarian outcomes (extrapolated from Hume's work), the notion of sacrifice becomes formidable, where justice is defined at the expense of the individual in terms of maximising good for the majority.[6] The Rawlsian theory of justice equates justice with fairness and equality, where inequalities may affect initial chances at the start of life, the situation into which one is born, inequalities in terms of contributions to society, inequalities in terms of competencies.[7] The anti-sacrificial element of Rawlsian justice holds that potential victims must not be sacrificed even to the common good. As Ricoeur wrote, 'The social contract appears to be capable only of drawing its legitimacy from a fiction … because peoples … do not know they are sovereign, not by reason of an imaginary contract, but by virtue of the will to live together that they have forgotten … [and] the desire to live well with and for others in just institutions.'[8]

The construct that is prison emerged from an imperative of social control. Internationally, many writers have considered the subject of social control and the state, and many have considered the subject of social control, prisons and imprisonment. From restorative justice to bureaucratic justice from feudalism to capitalism, from the development of total institutions dedicated to the reformation of deviant individuals, to the state's strategies of control of late modernity, the state has unflaggingly supported the institution of the prison. It has given imprisonment a role as the strategy of ultimate sanction, centralising imprisonment and, in terms of identity, prisonerising[9] and dangerising prisoners.[10] The idea of dangerousness meant that the individual must be considered by society at the level of his potentialities, and not at the level of his actions. Penality has the function of correcting individuals at the level of their behaviour, their attitudes, their dispositions, the danger they represent – at the level of their supposed potentialities.[11] 'You [society] signalled to us [prison guards] that they [prisoners] are wild beasts; we signal in turn to them. And when they have learned it well behind their bars, we will send them back to you.'[12]

In Ireland, the discourses of criminal deviance are in part constructed by the Irish state and the deviances it chooses to identify and then punish. McCullagh[13] details the Bantry Bay oil disaster (1979) in which fifty people died, after which there were no criminal convictions; the Goodman investigation, a corporate fraud case, again no criminal convictions; tax evasion, criminal convictions very rare; insider dealing, an offence only since 1990; the Stardust night club disaster (1981), in which forty-eight people died, no criminal charges. He juxtaposes these events with statistics on larceny where in 1993 just over 47,000 larcenies were recorded, 44 per cent involved amounts less than £100, 63 per cent amounts of £200 or less, with only 8 per cent involving amounts of £1,000 and over. Fennel demonstrated in her analysis how in Ireland crimes are mainly committed by men, poorer men, who represent the types of dishonesty engaged in by working-class people and the criminalisation of that type of deviance.[14] Fennel found that women in prison in Ireland represent a tiny minority of prisoners, that they are mainly poor and are also representative of the type of deviance that is criminalised in Ireland. Since Fennel wrote this there has been in Ireland a decade of court cases about child sex abuse. Many, if not most, of those prosecuted for the offences have been middle-class men. Women have not featured as defendants in these cases although female religious orders have formally apologised and made reparations to individuals who suffered child abuse in their institutions. The Irish state's strategy of signalling effective criminal justice through its construction of criminality was demonstrated by McCullagh,[15] who outlined how violent crimes and property crimes, many of them drug related, are allied in Ireland to the public image of the typical criminal.

Many other Irish writers have demonstrated the use of criminality and the prison by the state in signalling an effective criminal justice system. Kirby et al highlighted how the Irish state is currently imprisoning more people than ever before.[16] They found that between 1997 and 2000, some 2,000 new prison places were created; that there were three successive tax amnesties, 1988, 1993 and 2001; that in 1999–2000 there were twenty times more checks on social welfare claims than on tax returns; and that as the economic life of the country is becoming more deregulated, the social life is becoming more regulated through the expansion of CCTV and information surveillance technology.

The reactive nature of the Irish state's strategy for constructing criminality was demonstrated in a recent analysis of social control and the state, O'Donnell's and O'Sullivan's study.[17] This study traces the development by the Irish state of a 'triple lock' of criminal justice policies, in part to the 1996 murders in Ireland of Detective Garda Jerry McCabe and two weeks later journalist Veronica Guerin.[18] These murders resulted in, according to O'Donnell and O'Sullivan, a textbook case of moral panic.[19] The state's response to that panic was the institution of triple lock criminal justice policies. The force of the panic generated an equally forceful criminal justice response.

The individual within this system, when established in court as having offended, is vociferously identified and represented as criminal. When criminalised, the individual is imprisoned, stigmatised and dangerised. Lianos and Douglas discuss the concept of dangerisation in relation to high levels of risk awareness, to public perceptions of danger, to the primitive fear of otherness, and to the institutional environment.[20] Beck writes of 'risk society', of contemporary societies being increasingly characterised by struggles to escape 'bad' things rather than struggles to attain 'good' things. In this risk society, the effect of incarceration, imprisonment or confinement in an asylum or prison appears to be a perceptual exaggeration of the pathology of the incarcerated, an emphasis of the separateness of the individual, mad and/or bad, from the community.[21] According to O'Mahony, 'for most prisoners the message of their prison experience, the physical, psychological and social conditions in which they are forced to live, is obvious and stark. They know themselves to be neglected, rejected and, in some minds, totally demonised.'[22] He writes that the Irish criminal justice and penal systems blame people for what they are, and attribute the things that people do to what they are, while scrupulously refusing to consider what it is that makes people what they are.

Women who have been criminalised and imprisoned have new spoiled identities or they have old spoiled identities reinforced. Goffman wrote that the spoiled identity or stigmatised self has to be managed, as any identity has to be managed.[23] He wrote that we think of individuals with stigmas as not quite human, further that we see any defensive response on their behalf to their stigma as a reflection of the condition, 'a direct expression of defect'. He concluded that, for society, both the stigma and the defensiveness occasioned in the stigmatised by the stigma are expressions of 'just retribution'. Goffman drew on George Herbert Mead's work in presenting the individual as having many roles and multiple identities, who in the course of a lifetime is required to present different selves.[24] Goffman developed Mead's understanding of roles, in his analysis of the performative in human interactions. He divided identity into social and virtual, into the public and private self, into front-stage and back-stage performances. He noted the obligation on all of us in society to be who we are expected to be, that the cripple must be crippled, just as many women must be what men expect them to be.

This book considers the manner in which, and the means by which, imprisoned women play the part of imprisoned women, how they adopt the role, persona and identities of imprisoned women. According to Ricoeur,[25] it is the self, as agent, the subject capable of designating self that negotiates identity within power relations. This negotiation is always between more and less powerful agents. This power balance, or imbalance, that is most pronounced within prison. The spoiled identity of the imprisoned woman is an ascribed identity, fundamentally an identity of the gazes. For imprisoned women the discourses of the gazes of the prison and the criminal justice system transdiscursively, or intertextually, ascribe to them their spoiled identities. For each woman then, the transdiscursively ascribed identity, like a badge, a label, an emblem or emblems of identity, is attached to the self. It is something worn by the self, a phenomenon separate and apart from the self. The individual woman responds to this process. The response on the part of the individual is performative. Bell writes of how identities are produced, embodied and performed.[26] The individual copes with and responds to this transdiscursively ascribed identity through performativity. The individual internalises the ascribed identity. Then, having absorbed the ascribed identity and incorporated it into their personal identity, the individual performs an identity for the gazes.

Judith Butler, drawing on the work of Erving Goffman, developed the notion of performativity in post-structuralist and psychoanalytic critiques.[27] Butler posited identity not as some authentic core self but rather as the dramatic effect of performances developed through imitation, fabrication and manipulation.[28] Butler holds that identity is performatively constituted. She writes of acting as power, suggesting that it is through acting, the power to act, that will is produced; but that it is through the invocation of convention that acting derives its power. Further, she wrote that performativity must not be understood as a single or deliberate act but rather as the reiterative and citational practice through which discourse produces the effect that it names. Although Giddens[29] suggests that a person's identity is not found in their behaviour or in the judgement of others but in their capacity to 'keep a particular narrative going', it seems likely that the capacity to keep a narrative going rests fundamentally with the judgement of others. For Ireland's imprisoned women it is more, as Ricoeur suggests, the identity of the story which makes the identity of the character.[30] One idea fundamental to Foucault's investigation of power is that of the constitution of subjectivity through power relations, the intention of power to teach, to mould conduct, to instil forms of self-awareness and identities. Garland[31] argues that penal institutions positively construct and extend cultural meanings as well as repeating or reaffirming them. Punishment like any major social institution generates its own local meanings which contribute to the bricolage of the dominant culture. Subjectivity, personhood and personal identity are all socially and culturally constructed, and penality, according to Garland, plays a part in this 'making up people', helping to form subjectivities, selves and identities.

Discourse is constitutive. Discourse, according to Sunderland, means a broad constitutive system of meaning or, she suggests, different ways of structuring areas of knowledge and social practice.[32] Discourses in this sense, she says, are indistinguishable from ideology. For Foucault, discourses are intrinsically ideological flows of information.[33] Within discourse, identities are constructed. Discourses are 'ways of seeing' the world.[34] They are ideological flows of information through which the social is constructed and communicated. Discourses are constituted through power; the power that constitutes them also transmits them, or communicates them. This is Foucault's order of things, his knowledge/power nexus. For Foucault, social reality is always discursively produced. Highlighting the strength of the constitutive potential of discourses, Butler said that discourse has the capacity to produce that which it names.[35] Thus, discourse is more than just perspective, discourses call into being particular realities. The powerful, through discourse, create knowledge and circulate it, and in this way produce that which is known, that which is real.

GENDER AND CLASS: THE CRITICAL DIMENSIONS

Gender has been and is a defining feature shaping women's experiences of imprisonment. Women's criminality has long been established as being different from men's criminality. Women's experiences of social control and the state are and have been different from men's experiences of social control and the state. Carlen wrote of women as being by and large a law-abiding lot, and she suggested that the different modes of social regulation for women have resulted in particularly female patterns of law-breaking, of criminalisation and of penal regulation.[36] Ideological constructions of appropriate femininity are frequently, if not generally, patriarchal.

Scraton outlines the socio-legal-political potency of patriarchy: 'It combines the use of force and violence against women with the language, ritual, convention and legal discourses of subordination.'[37] Scraton points to McKinnion's statement that the state is male in a feminist sense and that power is institutionalised in a masculine and indeed masculinist form. Morris recounts the thoughts of an imprisoned woman: 'A woman in the system is ten times, 100 times more devastated, because it's a man's world in and out of the system ...'[38] Eaton details the rigorous control exercised over women in prison, where from their appearance at the prisons' reception areas, every woman's sense of self is 'subsumed into the identity "prisoner"'.[39]

The control that is imprisonment, 'existential death' according to Jose-Kampner,[40] is manifest in the architecture, in the regime, in the rules and regulations, in the discipline, in the linguistics of the prison.[41] It is manifest in the signs and symbols of the prison, in its rituals, its education and healthcare, its organised physical coercion.[42] And as Eaton points out, it is manifest in the presence of men who 'reiterate a model of coercive control' with which female inmates are already familiar.[43] Chesney-Lind[44] urges a feminist analysis of the state's increasing willingness to imprison women, which she attributes in part to judicial policies such as the 'war on drugs', in order to develop our understanding of the role of imprisonment in the maintenance of patriarchy. Chesney-Lind calls for a rebuilding of the literature on women's prisons, particularly that relating the incarceration of women to patriarchy. Walby, in her consideration of patriarchy, explores women's subordination in contemporary society, 'the depth, pervasiveness and interconnectedness of different aspects of women's subordination'.[45] She points to women's everyday experiences for the causes of women's subordination, the family as the site of women's oppression, the confinement of women to the private sphere. She points to housework and wage labour as sites of women's exploitation by men, and writes of the threat and fear of male violence. She speaks about men's flight from responsibilities, the flight from fatherhood, of patriarchal sexual relations, of sexual violence, of compulsory heterosexuality and of the sexual double standard. Walby contends that gender differentiated forms of subjectivities are generated everywhere within patriarchal cultures, within institutions which create, within a patriarchal gaze, representations of women. Mahon explored Ireland's public and private patriarchy.[46] She highlighted the significance of Catholicism in the maintenance of patriarchy, and argued that, in Ireland, the Catholic Church formed part of the cultural superstructure. O'Connor in her work considered the discourses of Irish society and their role in the partisan treatment of women.[47] She suggested that while patriarchy is recognised as a key element in understanding the experiences of women in Irish society, there is a need for discussion in Ireland on the extent and nature of male control. She said that it is necessary to go beyond identifying this, to explore the practices and processes through which it becomes a reality; the discourses and processes which legitimate and/or obscure these practices.

In relation to male control of Irish society, Galligan details that, with the exception of the appointment of Countess Markievicz as minister for labour in the government elected by the first Dáil in 1919, no woman held a cabinet post in Ireland until 1979;[48] in 1979 Marie Geoghegan-Quinn was appointed minister for the Gaeltacht. Galligan found that of the 136 people who held full ministerial positions from independence to 1993, only five (4 per cent) had been women; before 1993 there was never more than one woman in the cabinet at any time; in 1993 there were sixteen parliamentary committees with a total of 285 members, forty of whom (14 per cent) were women. Galligan found a similar pattern in women's representation in local government. In 1967, 3 per cent of seats at local government level were held by women; in 1974, 5 per cent; in 1979, 6.8 per cent; in 1985, 8 per cent; and in 1991, 11 per cent. In 1970, the report of the *Commission on the Status of Women* further detailed Ireland's patriarchal culture, noting that there was only one woman among the board members of the ten leading state-sponsored bodies. Galligan found that, in 1992, women represented 15 per cent of the total of 2,073 members of state boards.

The number of women in influential positions in the organisations of the 'social partners', trade union, employer and agricultural interests, were low; none of the senior official positions in the Confederation of Irish Industry, the Federation of Irish Employers, or the Irish Farmers' Association in the decade preceding 1993 had been held by a woman. There was a similarly poor record of women's representation in the senior levels of the civil service. Research published in 1991 established that there were no women among the senior positions of secretary and deputy secretary, the majority of women filled lower-level clerical and typing grades.[49] The same pattern was found in the judiciary where, in 1993, there were six women justices (14 per cent) out of a total of eighty-four. There were five justices in total in the Supreme Court, one of whom was a woman. Ms Justice Denham was the first woman appointed to the Supreme Court; she was appointed in 1992. There were sixteen justices in the High Court, one of whom was a woman; seventeen in the Circuit Court, with no women among them; and forty-six in the District Courts, among them four women. At this time, about half of all solicitors and one quarter of barristers were women.[50] Research conducted by Bacik et al found that, at the start of this century, women constituted 21 per cent of judges in Ireland, 34 per cent of barristers and 41 per cent of solicitors; only 9 per cent of senior barristers were women and only one managing partner from thirteen larger solicitors firms in Dublin was a woman.[51]

In addition to gender, class was and still is a defining element of women's experiences of imprisonment. Carlen says that, since the 1800s, prisons have been used to discipline disproportionate numbers of the poor, the socially inept, the socially disadvantaged.[52] She adds that, still today, lower-class offenders, disadvantaged by powerlessness and poverty, are more likely to be over-criminalised than offenders from other classes. She describes the more extreme experiences of imprisonment of poorer offenders, suggesting that, in prison, such individuals are likely to be labelled 'difficult' and so subjected to more intense surveillance and correction than offenders from other classes. Elias in his analysis of civility and incivility, the civilised and the uncivilised, gives insight into the manner in which a class-based criminal justice system can facilitate the vilification, punishment and degradation of particular groups and individuals in society.[53] He writes that, in some cultures, the value which a person has by mere existence, without any accomplishments, is very minor. He discusses Western concepts of behaviour typical of 'civilised' people, and states that there is almost nothing which cannot be done in a 'civilised' or 'uncivilised' way. Bourdieu explored the relationship between cultural reproduction and social reproduction, and the role of cultural capital in the reproduction of the structure of relations between classes, in the perpetuation of class distinction, and through it, class inequality;[54] Bourdieu detailed the manner in which social classes, through language and action, are discursively produced.[55]

O'Mahony, in his work on Irish prisons, states categorically that in Ireland the issue is class; that the Irish prison population appears to be drawn in a much more concentrated way than in England and Wales, from poor, socially and economically disadvantaged sectors of society.[56] Bacik and O'Connell[57] in their research found residing in an economically deprived area of Dublin to be a strong risk factor for District Court appearance; they suggested that their data in fact indicated that the institution that is the Dublin District Court system is there *for* people from deprived areas. O'Mahony held that the Irish prison population is highly homogenous and Irish prison populations are by and large characterised by poverty and multiple disadvantage.[58] The impact of the class system on the female prison population has been considered by Monaghan,[59] by Carmody and McEvoy[60] and by the General Health Care Study of the Irish Prison Population.[61] All three highlighted the impoverishment and marginality of Ireland's imprisoned women. All found that many of the women imprisoned in Ireland are so poor, powerless and disadvantaged they might be described as being of an 'underclass'. The underclass is the undeserving poor, the lumpenproletariat, as opposed to the deserving poor. Functioning as an agent of control, this class serves to warn of the perils of not participating in society.

The nature of Irish female criminality in the 1970s was illustrated by McCafferty where she detailed some of the cases of women appearing in Dublin courts: among them the grandmother who stole a babysuit and sweater and went to prison for three months; the story of Rosie who wanted to go to Mountjoy Prison 'for a rest'; and the case of the street traders, 'four barrels of Guinness standing on the street with baskets or boxes of flowers laid out on top', obstructing traffic and discommoding the flower shops in the area.[62] In the 1980s, Rottman in a study of the socio-economic characteristics of those arrested for an indictable offence in Dublin, found the female offenders (16 per cent of his population) to be young, unemployed or in marginal employment, and from the inner city.[63] In recent years, there have been some changes in the structure of Irish criminality and of Irish prison populations. These changes relate particularly to the imprisonment of large numbers of middle-class men for child sex offences, detailed already, and the imprisonment of large numbers of male and relatively large numbers of female international drug couriers, manifestations of globalisation within the Irish prison population. The globalisation of the Irish female prison population has had, as has been demonstrated, a profound effect on the Irish female prison and perceptions of female criminality in Ireland.

HISTORICAL REPRESENTATIONS OF CRIMINAL WOMEN

Foucault's phrase, a saturnalia of punishment,[64] is useful in attempting to develop a synopsis of the history of punishments inflicted upon women and the performatory, dramatic and entertaining elements of these punishments. Dobash et al[65] detail that 80–90 per cent of the thousands of people executed as witches between the fourteenth and seventeenth centuries were women.[66] Famous burnings of Irish women for witchcraft include the condemnation for witchcraft and heresy of Dame Alice Kytler by Bishop Richard Ledrede and the burning of her maid Petronella in Kilkenny in the 1320s;[67] the burning to death in 1895 by her husband, family and neighbours of 26-year-old Bridget Cleary, believed to be a changeling left by fairies who had taken the real Bridget away.[68] Bourke details many nineteenth-century newspaper accounts in Ireland of similar incidents, most of them involving elderly women or severely disabled small children, burned, beaten, drowned or otherwise tortured and/or killed in order 'to put the fairy out'. Dobash et al suggest that witch-hunts were a tool in the arsenal of the powerful in controlling the superstitious populations.[69] 'Women's bodies were the instruments for exorcising political and social evils, establishing the power of institutions, and for the symbolic marking of boundaries of appropriate female behaviour.'[70] Dobash et al discuss the physical punishments, pillory and stocks, and the symbolic punishments, misrules and charivaris, of the eighteenth century, and they conclude that these punishments were often directed at women and men who offended the patriarchal order of society. Where male dominance was considered the natural order, female leaders risked being labelled public nuisances, shrews, nags, viragos; cucking and ducking were devices used to control such women, as was the scold's or gossip's bridle.[71] The power to punish was patriarchal.

Confinement has long been used to control and punish women. Dobash et al discuss the confinement of women in nunneries, monasteries, castles and watchtowers from the Middle Ages.[72] According to them, voluntary entrants were usually aristocratic and upper-class women.[73] Women forced into convents were usually 'political prisoners, illegitimate, disinherited, physically deformed or mentally defective'. Unwanted women or 'nuisance' women could be deposited in convents by fathers or husbands; imprisoned within the rules and confinements of convent life. In the 1500s the first houses of correction opened.[74] By the seventeenth century prisoners in penal institutions were being categorised and segregated and trained to labour within the institution's economic production system. Women confined in prisons were put to labouring to maintain the institution within which they were incarcerated; they were taught a trade, through whatever commodity production the institution engaged in, or were leased out to merchants and manufacturers. Dobash et al detail how modern penal institutions dealing with the crimes and deviances of women are responses shaped by gender and class assumptions through institutional and ideological patterns associated with patriarchy and early capitalism.

Through history, within the more hierarchical model of crime and punishment the ruling classes, or the person or body with whom or with which power rested, defined crime and devised punishment as was deemed appropriate within the power investiture. This model of crime and punishment was supported in the early and mid-centuries of the last millennium by the 'Theatre of Terror', the *amende honorable* and the 'Bloody Code' (capital punishment), instruments of the ruling classes, or elites, employed by them to secure their positions and their assets. Ignatieff[75] details some of the offences deemed capital offences by the elites of the 1600 and 1700s as highway robbery, housebreaking, beast stealing, grand larceny, murder and arson. He explains how new statutes of this era, for example the Riot Act, made offences capital that had long been subject to lesser penalties. Stealing hedges, underwood, fruit from trees and timber, damaging orchards, or woodland, taking fish from ponds became, according to Ignatieff, criminal acts, criminalised through the Black Act. 'The Black Act was enacted to make possible the conviction of the small farmers and tenants who were waging a guerrilla-style resistance to the encroachment upon their customary forest rights by nouveaux riches estate holders and royal foresters in the woodlands of Hampshire and Berkshire.' Ignatieff outlines how the first forty years of the eighteenth century witnessed a proliferation of new forgery and counterfeiting statutes. These statutes, he says, may be explained as 'an attempt by banking and commercial interests to secure protection for the new systems of paper credit and exchange created in response to the rise of a national market'. According to Ignatieff, two-thirds of those convicted of forgery throughout the nineteenth century were executed. He explains how in one case, after taking the unusual decision to hang a man in chains, 'the justices admitted that they had been urged to do so by "very many respectable Gentlemen and Merchants in and about Halifax and Rochdale, who felt that such a notorious and public example" would deter others from making counterfeit coin.' Dobash et al state that by the end of the eighteenth century over 200 offences were capital offences in Britain.[76] According to Philips, most of these were property offences but the enforcement of these laws was arbitrary and erratic and prosecution was 'haphazard'.[77] However haphazard, the spectacle and terror of the *amende honorable* and the *Bloody Code* were employed by the powerful to impress their power upon those subject to it. In a similar fashion, the prosecutions during these years of social theorists and pamphleteers such as the Jacobins, the Chartists, and religious such as the Quakers, and later the Fabians and the suffragettes, the suspension from time to time of civil rights and habeas corpus, document a justice system defined by the powerful to protect their power base.

The analyses of earlier theoretical representations of female criminality, among them Lombroso and Ferrero,[78] Pollak[79] and Thomas,[80] established a gendered concept of female criminality. Female criminality was analysed and represented as deviant femininity; the discourse generally was one of biologism. Women who engaged in crime and criminal activity were unnatural, lacking in female or maternal instincts and characteristics. Women were generally represented as being psychologically unbalanced; they were socially, psychologically and economically dependent; they were innocent and defenceless in the world as children are innocent and defenceless in the world. The criminal woman was deemed to possess all the criminal characteristics of the criminal male and the worst characteristics of women – cunning, spite and deceitfulness; they were deemed to be more male than female. While for men, criminality was deemed in earlier studies to be part of their natural characteristics and in later studies a product of their socialisation, criminality in females was deemed unnatural and was evidenced in maleness and masculinity. In the earliest work, a nineteenth-century classic of criminal biology, Lombroso and Ferrero studied the skull, brains and facial and bodily 'anomalies', including tattooing, of female criminals in an attempt to establish criminal types, categories of deviants. Their lengthy examination of the crimes of women consistently highlighted the gendered nature of female criminality. The crimes that women engaged in were prompted by their female role. Women committed infanticide, aborting or killing their babies, or they committed crimes against property, stealing or begging for sustenance or adornment.

In their consideration of the under-representation of women in crime statistics, Lombroso and Ferrero[81] noted the conservative tendency of women, the cause of which they located in the immobility of the ovule compared with the activity of the sperm, a theory in common with Freud and his grounding of women in biologism and sexual passivity,[82] and synonymous with Thomas's catabolic male's outward flowing creative energy and anabolic female's storing energy, motionless and conservative.[83] Thomas discussed the widely acknowledged and widely accepted concept of woman's superior cunning, which he contrasted with the openness and directness of males; he drew an analogy between cunning and constructive thought, positing that due to the limited and personal nature of female activities this 'trait has expressed itself historically in womankind as intrigue rather than invention'. Thomas responds to charges that women have no characters at all by stating that women's life experiences have equipped them rather to accommodating the personalities of men than to dealing with the solid realities of the world. Thomas finds that modesty imprisons women as the patriarchal system imprisons women, through exclusion and marginalisation; he outlines how woman lives in the white man's world of practical and scientific activity but is excluded through biology, through history and patriarchy; although this is not the word he uses it is the sentiment he expresses, and he discusses man's contempt for woman's degradation in her exclusion from owning or developing property and her objectification in her treatment as property, and man's superstition of women, the fear of contamination by woman's weakness. He outlines how 'chivalry, chaperonage and modern convention are the persistence of the old race habit of contempt for women and their intellectual sequestration', and writes of modesty restraining her, guarding her from freedom in her 'unfreedom'.

Pollak highlighted the checking of natural aggression in girls, the passive role of women in establishing relationships, the fact that a woman's economic and social future was dependent upon securing a male she could not be seen to be pursuing, one she could not freely pursue, as social mores engendering deceit in females.[84] Kingsley Davis,[85] in his analysis of prostitution, stated that the social behaviour of women in general, including women's behaviour in terms of marriage, may be defined 'simply as the use of sexual responses for ulterior motives'. Within marriage women, according to Davis, trade sexual favours for an economic and social status supplied by men. Pollak's Freudian loyalties are evident in his description of young women's experiences of menstruation as 'a narcissistic wound to their self-esteem. Setting the seal so to speak upon their womanhood, it destroys their hope ever to become a man, which until then they may have preserved, and intensifies any feeling of inferiority which they may have had about their sex.'[86]

Pollak discussed the psychological imbalance wrought in women by menstruation and women's claim to special consideration because of it.[87] He hypothesised that female crime was under-reported and under-detected and when detected and reported treated more leniently, that culturally men are protective of women and this cultural norm impacts on the treatment of female criminality and thus on female crime statistics. Cowie et al found the position Pollak assumed in relation to female offenders to be uniquely his own.[88] They outlined the universal agreement among criminologists that women commit far less crime than men and that they are under-represented in official crime statistics which reflect the extent to which crime presents as a serious problem for society because they 'cause much less wilful damage to society than men do'. Bishop's[89] work on women and crime is notably on two counts – his denouncement of feminism and his conviction of the accountability of the female sex for the increase in crime in the 1920s. The latter he explains in terms of the former, outlining his belief that the feminist 'is engaged in unsettling the women of the nation with disastrous results'. Crites tested three propositions: that the women's movement contributes to increased female criminality; that female criminality is increasingly violent and aggressive; and that female offenders continue to benefit from the paternalism of the judiciary; and she found none of them to be substantiated.[90]

The common denominator in the earlier works on female criminality was their propensity to look to the individual characteristics of offenders, characteristics believed to be inherently female – dishonesty, promiscuity and insanity – for the aetiology of female crime. The feminist critique of such representations of female criminals and female criminality emerged in the 1970s. These works challenged the moralistic underpinnings of the representations of the deviancies and delinquencies of criminal women of earlier works.

Smart[91] and Carlen,[92] in their respective critiques of the work of Lombroso and Ferrero, Pollak and Thomas, find misogynous themes throughout. Klein, in her aetiology of female crime, concluded that gender and sexuality are fundamental to the definition and categorisation of female crime.[93] Heidensohn wrote of folk myths about the inherent nature of women, and Carlen[94] of the 'misogynous mythology' that permeated through the ages women's experiences of social control.[95] Smart attacked criminology's lack of interest in female criminality; the widespread acceptance of sexual stereotyping in female criminality; the cultural stereotypes and the ideologically informed explanations of female deviance; and indeed the anti-feminist ideology which she found in the work on female criminality.[96] Carlen in her critique finds women who commit crimes depicted as cunning and evil, not only offending against society but against their true nature.[97] Smart's critique of the solutions proposed to the problems of deviance was that they were centred on the modification of individual perceptions of their situations, rather than 'making structural changes to the social order'. Carlen highlighted the fact that these theories ignored the economic and cultural factors and the class system which forced many women into deviant sexual behaviour and criminality. Carlen stated that Lombroso and Ferrero's nineteenth-century theory of female penology persists, constituting women criminals as being both within and without femininity, criminality, adulthood and sanity, and manifesting itself in the misogyny of judges and prison administrators.

CONTEMPORARY REPRESENTATIONS OF CRIMINAL WOMEN

Fennel outlined how the Irish legal system, partisan in nature, is informed by stereotypical assumptions and myths with regard to male and female roles which, she says, operate to disproportionately disadvantage women: 'Currently woman's treatment by the criminal justice system is dependent upon the extent to which she conforms or fails to conform to her perceived appropriate role.'[98] Fennel's assertion supports research conducted by Lyons and Hunt into the effects of gender on sentencing in Dublin. Lyons and Hunt describe how most research points to the concepts of chivalry and male paternalism to explain the more lenient treatment of women by the criminal justice system.[99]

Worrall[100] describes how the majority of female offenders are not seen as real criminals and are therefore treated more leniently than men before the courts. Women are more likely to be sentenced with a view to their personal circumstances than simply in terms of the offence they have committed. Provided a woman is prepared to play the part, the stereotypical female role, she will convince the court that she is out of place there. If this strategy cannot be adopted, one of psychiatric disturbance is utilised; see Luckhaus for a study of pre-menstrual tension as a successful plea against incarceration.[101] In the interests of 'taking female crime seriously', Worrall,[102] while acknowledging the possible drawbacks for individual women, calls for these myths to be challenged, and so too does Morrissey.[103] Worrall states that such stratagems serve to render female offenders invisible, that the gender contract permits the female offender's life to be presented or represented in terms of its domestic, sexual and pathological dimensions.[104]

In opposition to this representation of criminal women is the concept of the 'evil woman'. This representation results in harsher treatment of women before the courts, not only for the crime committed, but for exceeding the bounds of gender-appropriate behaviour. Lyons and Hunt concluded that women before the courts receive lenient sentences for traditional female-type offences such as petty theft, and they receive harsh sentences for non-traditional-type offences such as assault.[105] This argument was supported by Bacik, who wrote that Irish District Court judges were found to place more weight on factors such as marital status, family background and parenthood in sentencing women.[106]

In 1996 a total of 5,202 persons were convicted of indictable offences in Ireland; of these, only 476, or less than 10 per cent, were women. In 1998, 4,281 indictable convictions were recorded, and women accounted for 553 (12.9 per cent). From an overall total of 2,341 convictions for indictable offences in 1999, women offenders accounted for 309 (13 per cent), and their convictions were overwhelmingly for crimes against property, some 9 per cent of those convicted were convicted of drugs offences. However, women in the early years of this century made up only 3 per cent of the Irish prison population, indicating that even when convicted, women are less likely to go to prison than men.[107] In a study of Dublin District Court sentencing practice, Bacik et al found that a 'significantly higher proportion of women received no conviction' (62.8 per cent of women as against only 42.8 per cent of men), while only 14.6 per cent of women defendants were sentenced to prison as against 29 per cent of male offenders.[108] The comparison is made between sentencing practices, not between recorded offences.

Chesney-Lind explored judicial enforcement of the female sex role and challenged the chivalrous view of the judiciary's treatment of female offenders with the contention that the judiciary in fact sanctioned more severely female adolescents than their male counterparts.[109] To support this contention Chesney-Lind pointed to gynaecological exams to which adolescent women were subjected, even when charged with non-sexual offences. In addition to this, she pointed to the increased likelihood of female offenders being sent to pre-trail detention.[110/111] Lengthy detentions were used to thoroughly examine the women and their delinquent propensities, the greatest approbation being reserved for girls deemed immoral or incorrigible; she writes of young women violating their sex role rather than the law. Carlen described the 'status' offences of girls in residential care in the UK in the early 1980s, among them running away from home, and staying out late at night.[112] Chesney-Lind supported the chivalry hypothesis in that she found that the police were less likely to arrest a young woman than a young man as long as she behaved in stereotypical ways and the offence was not a sexual offence. She found that judicial paternalism resulted in custodial sentences for young women deemed sexually delinquent. She concluded, however, that the chivalry hypothesis was in fact 'the product of the fact that women have less serious offences'.

Heidensohn explained the small numbers of women in prison using two phenomena: the trivial size and personal nature of the thefts carried out by women and the informal controls exerted upon them.[113] She pointed to early socialisation and its rewards for conformity, communities and their agents of control, and lengthy remands imposed upon women in order to give the judiciary time to amass reports on the female offenders and who then frequently 'punished' women more. Carlen[114] highlighted Seear's and Player's[115] analysis of official statistics which indicated that there was considerable evidence to support the thesis that at least some women are treated more leniently by the criminal justice system.[116] According to Carlen,[117] these women are living more conventional lives. Unregulated women, single women, de-gender controlled women, unemployed women, homeless women are, she holds, more likely to be sentenced to imprisonment.

PRISON SPACE

Use of imprisonment has been traced back to Roman times, to the Mamertine Prison begun in 640BC by Ancus Martius and to the acoustics of the dungeon at Syracuse where Dionysius I amused himself listening to the conversations of his prisoners.[118] Many writers have detailed medieval places of detention, fortresses, castles, watchtowers, the abutments of bridges, town gates, cellars of municipal buildings and private dwellings. Prisons were used to coerce payment of debts; they were used as chambers of torture, as a prelude to execution, for banishment or transportation, or used in lieu of these penalties for privileged individuals. There are a myriad of prison designs, possible prisons and possibilities for imprisonment: ecclesiastical prisons, civil prisons and military prisons; island prisons, such as Robben Island, where Nelson Mandela was incarcerated, Sakhalin in Russia where Anton Chekov conducted his prison research,[119] and Ireland's prison island, Spike Island in Cork; citadel prisons such as Mont St Michel in France; plantation prisons like Angola and Cummins Farm, prisons of the cotton plantations of the southern American states;[120] colonial prisons, the plantations of Maryland and Virginia, the West Indies, Australia and Van Diemen's Land; floating prisons such as the 'hulks', the superannuated warships used in the UK;[121] and even conjugal prisons, as described by Maria Edgeworth in her novel *Castle Rackrent*.

Panopticon, as explained earlier, is the title given by Jeremy Bentham to a sketch he made in 1791 of a penitentiary. Panopticon, as designed by Bentham, is the radial-style prison designed for maximum observation, an instrument of total control through surveillance. In Bentham's vision of the penitentiary, control was wrought through rendering space visible, the experience of prison space was the essence of the experience of imprisonment. Punishment was present within the very architecture of the prison. 'Bentham placed both prisoner and guard alike under the constant surveillance of an inspector.'[122] Where the prisoner was in a space not visible s/he was 'to be buried in a solitude where s/he had no companion but reflection, no counsellor but thought ...' Thus the space the prisoner occupied in Panopticon was a space of solitude and of torment, through simultaneously intensely personal yet mechanistic and relentless control.

Prisons, whether systems-based or treatment-based, attempt the construction of separate worlds; prison is in effect 'the creation and manipulation of a total universe'.[123] The individual is incarcerated in this total universe, this separate world with its separate space and its separate use of space. Sim emphasises the control within prison that manifests itself around cellular spaces and routines and timetables.[124] Within prison, space takes the place of matter; where there were obligations, commitments, employments and relationships, now there is time and space. Giddens, according to Lash and Urry, placed the analysis of time and space at the heart of contemporary social theory.[125] 'Humans live in time and with the knowledge of passing time, humans grasp their time-experience sub-consciously as well as consciously and the movement of individuals through time and space is grasped through the interpenetration of presence and absence.'[126]

Both time and space are the apparent fundamental elements of the experience of imprisonment. The punishment that is imprisonment is the confinement of the individual within a small specified controlled space for a prescribed period of time. The state defines time for the imprisoned individual: time beyond its judicial carcereal signification ceases to exist for the individual incarcerated in prison space, beyond the prisoner's abstract sense of real time/prison time, and it is prison space that becomes the critical dimension of the prison experience. Within prison, when time has been judicially defined, 'being' happens entirely within prison space.

Bachelard's essence of being is expressed in terms of space.[127] Massey observed that, in its broadest formulation, society is constructed spatially.[128] Ardener[129] suggests that women and men experience the world differently, that they individually and collectively live in different worlds. Men and women occupy space differently. Grosz posits that men occupy space as territory to map and explore while women occupy space as place, as occupation, as living, women and dwelling, chora, the space in which place is made possible … the space that engenders without possessing, that nurtures without requirements of its own, that receives without giving and that gives without receiving.[130] Bartky discusses women's experiences of enclosure and confinement within space.[131] Rose considers women and space and the confinement of women within space, the space available to women as constricted.[132] It is suggested in the literature that women are conditioned, by our culture, our society, by our relationships and by our own self-policing, our relentless self-surveillance, to take up as little space as possible. Rose contends that spatial location for women is about vulnerability.[133] She says that women sense space to be a hazardous arena, something tricky, something to be negotiated. Irigaray wrote of space as containers, envelopes of identity.[134]

Goffman held a person's world to be divided up spatially by their identities.[135] Our identities dictate where we may go, where we will be permitted or accepted and where we are threatened by our identities. De Certeau et al hold that cultural practices are the elements of everyday life, decisive for the identity of an individual within a group because they allow the individual to 'take up his or her social position' within the group.[136] According to Giddens, 'Positioning ... is to be understood in relation to the seriality of encounters across time-space. Every individual is at once positioned in the flow of day-to-day life ... in her/his life span ... in institutional time ... and in multiple ways within social relations.'[137] Individuals have degrees of freedom and make decisions within the scope of that freedom and within the confines of habit. Bourdieu defined his concept of habitus as patterns of perception, thought and action.[138] The routines of routinised everyday lives are vital components of ontological security.

Adopting de Certeau et al, in the construction of the separate world of the prison, for prisoners the neighbourhood of the prison is an outgrowth of the prisoner's room/cell. For the imprisoned individual the neighbourhood of the prison amounts to the sum of all trajectories initiated from the prisoner's room. De Certeau et al write of the inscription of the neighbourhood in the history of the subject as a mark of indelible belonging. Lash and Urry quote Irigaray, who said that there is no need for us to remember, our bodies remember for us.[139] Bachelard writes of the spaces of our past moments of solitude remaining indelibly within us.[140] Both Bachelard and de Certeau discuss the journeying with us of our successive living spaces: 'we bring our lares with us'[141] and 'we leave them without leaving them.'[142] Bachelard writes of the liaison our bodies make with unforgettable houses and of how our houses live on in us.[143]

There is within space the capacity to shelter, and Bachelard describes the feeling of shelter, the feeling of well-being generated by retreat: the sense of refuge, the covering, the huddling, the hiding, the snug concealing, the primitiveness of refuge, its animality. Baudrillard writes of the houses of our childhood and their depth and resonance in memory.[144] He relates this to the complex structure of interiority, to notions of inside and outside. He writes of objects within space as symbolisations. He writes of the emotional value of objects, of their 'presence', of objects becoming spatial incarnations of emotional bonds. Social space, according to Lefebvre, is related to three general concepts: form, structure and function.[145] He writes that space is marked by signs, either abstractly or by means of discourse, through which it acquires its symbolic value. Space, he says, does indeed speak.

Discourses and representations of women in prison are structured in large part through or by the space the women as prisoners occupy, the *architecture parlante*, of the penal institutions, the signs, symbols and rituals, the narratives and discourses, the gazes of the female prison. Heidensohn considered the 'special' approach to women's imprisonment which emerged from the work of Elizabeth Fry in the 1800s. Heidensohn suggests that Fry's sexually segregated system and female regime differed from male prisons only in detail. As highlighted in chapter 3, she said that 'despite gallons of pastel paint and ... flowery curtains over windows the effects of the old institutions remain.'[146] Both Bowker[147] and Chesney-Lind remarked that women were an afterthought in the construction of a jail that was built primarily to hold men.[148] Carlen has written extensively on the dreadfully deleterious effects of prison experiences on women. With Worrall, she wrote of young women absconding from care in order to escape the 'muzzle', the effect of incarceration and isolation, a word evocative of the concept and experience of the medieval scold's bridle.[149] She considers, among other issues, the developing punitive rhetoric of the UK, and the effect of prison sentences on poor women, on isolated women, on depressed women, prison sentences with their implicit downward spirals of poverty, isolation and depression, 'the snowballing effects of imprisonment ... felt long after release'.[150] The biographical and autobiographical works, such as those of Peckham,[151] Evans,[152] Gregory[153] and Wyner,[154] give insight into individual experiences of various female prisons and evidence the inability of the female prison to accomplish much that might be considered positive in the lives of those women.

PENAL GAZES

Within the space of the traditional Panopticon prison the individual was caught in the gaze of the institution. Within the modern prison the individual is subject to various gazes. The technology of the modern prison produces a Foucauldian panopticism rather than a Benthamite panopticism. Within Foucauldian panopticism there is a subtle power in all disciplining institutions and it is designed to produce, by acting on individual subjectivities, docile bodies. Bourdieu writes that the gaze is more than a simple universal and abstract power to objectify; rather he says it is a symbolic power dependent upon relative positions and evaluative schemes understood by the person to whom they are applied.[155] Berger states that 'the way we see things is affected by what we know and what we believe.'[156] He says that we never look at things in isolation but always in light of the way the object of our gaze relates to us. The 'gaze' serves in modern society as a weapon for effective control through surveillance.

For Foucault,[157] power is based on detailed knowledge, we are controlled by discourses used to observe and define us. He refers to the threefold aspects of surveillant panopticism as supervision, control and correction.[158] Bartky agrees that panopticism is a form of surveillance, a discipline which 'encourages us to watch ourselves because we imagine ourselves observed by others'.[159] Bartky believes that modern women have become like the inmates of Panopticon, policed subjects subjected to relentless surveillance. However, the modern woman is unlike the inmates of Panopticon, again according to Bartky, in that she is self-policing and 'self committed to a relentless self-surveillance'. Rose considers women's self-consciousness, women watching themselves being watched and judged, women's experiences of surveillance.[160] Within a feminist theory of imprisonment, panopticism, relentless self-surveillance, and the ubiquitous 'male gaze' with its evaluative function, may be combined with a female surveillant and evaluative gaze and the judicial, structural and electronic surveillance endured by imprisoned women. Notwithstanding the political and structural surveillance all imprisoned women suffer, some must also endure pervasive media surveillance. Women in prison space exist under a networked regime of constant surveillance, perpetual surveillance, the superpanopticon of the surveillant assemblage, the great pyramid of gazes.

MEDIA GAZE

The issue in terms of media gaze is how, in the media, deviant feminine subjectivities are constructed and represented, and to what effect. The media is a major instrument of social control, and is in the business of manufacturing and reproducing images of the social world for commercial ends.[161] Media representations of imprisoned women impact on our understanding of what it is to be a woman, of what is the feminine, and of what it means to be a woman prisoner, a woman in prison. As Fiske said, 'when signs make myths and values public, they enable them to perform their function of cultural identification.'[162] It is for this reason that such representations should be examined. In the literature many authors have taken exception to the manner in which the modern media constructs and represents the feminine. The issue is the problematic representations of the feminine presented. Particularly problematic is the discursive subject positioning of the female criminal and/or female prisoner, the manner and means of the construction and presentation of media images of these women, the subsequent mass public consumption of those images, and the ultimate passing of the images into public consciousness.

There are, broadly speaking, three socially constructed discourses of crime: official, media and public discourses.[163]Public discourses of crime, are, according to Cohen and Young, constructed by a lay public with little 'expert' knowledge of crime.[164] The public is, they suggest, 'massively dependent' for their conceptions and perceptions of crime and criminality on media and official discourses. The media has the means and the mandate to mediate the social to the public. They work in partnership with the public. They cannot exist without a public willing to purchase and consume their product. The media serve their markets and must, to survive, provide their markets with consonant images of society. It is in this way that the media 'constructs' reality.

This media-constructed reality, according to Cohen and Young, is not a new reality but a reflection of reality as it has already been 'pre-constituted by the powerful'.[165] It is in this way that the media serves as an institution of major ideological significance for the maintenance of the status quo in society. As Hall explained, there are two aspects to the signification of news: the first is news value, the second is ideological significance.[166] Hall et al argue that the media's basic model of contemporary western society is one of a democratic consensus.[167] This democratic consensus legitimises particular social, economic, political and moral perspectives on society. The model precludes the media from selecting stories for publication opposing or contradicting the consensus. In fact, in order to maintain consensus the media defuse challenges to it. They do this by representing such challenges as meaningless or senseless, as misunderstandings of society rather than alternative interpretations of society. Media discourse necessarily incorporates official and public discourses. There is, as Morrissey details, a symbiotic relationship between the media and mainstream legal institutions.[168] This is evident in, she suggests, the manner in which the media generally faithfully report the criminal narratives of criminalised individuals of the criminal courts.

The media select, from the vast array of information available, the information they present. We considered the effect of this on Ireland's imprisoned women in Chapter 3. Through this presentation of selected information the media provide us with guiding myths which shape our sense of our world. In terms of accuracy in reportage, as discussed in Chapter 3, there is much evidence that the media 'consistently get things wrong' and report less than factual accounts of issues or events. Indeed their accounts can be fictional, often even mythical.[169] Van Zoonen considers the content of myth in the familiar formulaic narratives of the media, which, she says, resemble mythic story telling.[170] She considers the ritual view of communication which focuses on the construction of community through rituals, shared histories, beliefs and values. Fiske and Hartley referred to this as the bardic tradition in communication.[171]

Morrissey outlines the media's process of constructing narratives.[172] Narrative, she writes, is the staple of the news media. Every item in the news is termed a story. Journalists, she tells us, construct or reconstruct events using narrational techniques such as dramatisation and personalisation; characters in the narratives are subjectified through the principles of storytelling. The storytelling the media engages in is limited to a number of stock tales or narratives arising from popular stories or myths, as detailed in

Chapter 3. One of the most common of these stock narratives is that of the morality play. This play places the forces of good, generally the state, its institutions and 'good' people on one side, and the forces of evil, the character(s) of the narrative, in the case of crime reporting generally individual criminals, 'bad' people, on the other. The media, in mediating the event, within the imperatives of limited time and space, reduces and simplifies often complex stories to easily understood, easily judged tales. Within this process individual subjectivities can become stereotyped, victimised, even mythified. Through the process, the media provides images and narratives which construct, shape and record the order of things, the order of culture.

The media reflect society's dominant social values. In western societies generally, there has been a tendency to dichotomise women into good girl and bad girl categories. Morrissey details that while male behaviour is seen to exist on a continuum, good to bad, female behaviour is polarised, either good or bad.[173] Women are saints or sinners. This dichotomisation of female behaviour lends itself readily to the simplicity of media narrational techniques and their stock narratives. Heidensohn, in her work, considered media stereotypes of female criminals, among them the witch, the whore and the bewildered mother.[174] Cohen's media amplification spiral is a process by which issues and events are vested in an escalating manner with public significance.[175] It is useful in describing the manner in which media images of deviant women are juxtaposed with images of 'shocked middle-aged women' and 'sincere housewives' and the general moral panic concerning female criminality and the assertive, aggressive nature of liberated women. Smith considered the 'unnatural' representation in the media of women killers Myra Hindley and Rose West.[176] As explained in Chapter 3, in the media, Rose West was represented as the Black Widow drawn into a pact of friendship with fellow serial killer Myra Hindley, the White Devil. Morrissey studied, among others, the case of Aileen Wuornos, represented in the media as 'the world's first female serial killer', and the case of Tracey Wiggington, represented as 'the notorious lesbian vampire killer'.[177]

We can only make sense of ourselves and our experiences within the limits of the meaning systems available to us. An Althusserian perspective would interpret this as the construction of individual subjectivities through interpellation by ideology. The Althusser term interpellation was defined by Morrissey (see Chapter 3) as the process through which individuals are compelled to identify with the representations which their culture supplies.[178] Van Zoonen outlines the view that the interpellation of women in pornography, for example, fixes women within patriarchal ideology as objects of the male gaze, and perpetuates both the objectification of women and perspectives of women as available objects for men's domination.[179] McRobbie in her study of gendered resistances to dominant cultures, the gendered subversion of hegemony, found that such opposition was more difficult for the feminine than the masculine, primarily because of the limited sphere of the feminine, the fact that the feminine is primarily confined to the private sphere.[180] McRobbie in her analysis of *Jackie* magazine found an articulation of capitalist and patriarchal ideologies. She found four codes of connotation: the codes of romance, of personal/domestic life, of fashion and beauty, and of pop music. She found that, through these codes, readers were encouraged to engage in the personal. Throughout the magazine the emphasis was on the personal life. The readers' interests were emphatically in the private sphere. They were hailed as heterosexual. Above all, they were to get and keep a man. To this end, they were constantly and consistently engaged in programmes of self-improvement, programmes focused on fashion, cosmetics, diet and beauty. In even the fourth code, that of pop music, McRobbie found that, instead of being encouraged to engage with or create music, readers were encouraged, through picture-poster presentations of male musicians, to fantasise about heterosexual romance. The medium, *Jackie* magazine, was found to be a mechanism of social control, steeped as it was in the communication of stereotypical, patriarchal and hegemonic values about the female and the feminine.

In Ireland, McCullagh wrote about the myth of the media, the media's self image as a window on society, providing a faithful reflection of what is going on in society.[181] He presented two Irish media myths, the so-called Bugsy Malone crime wave of 1977/8, an epidemic of juvenile crime, and the joyriding of 1985, and the ensuing moral panics. McCullagh found that sensational coverage of crime in the media generated anxiety which, at times, because of the nature of the coverage, develops into fear and hysteria.

O'Connell argued that, despite relatively low crime rates, the Irish public believed itself to be experiencing a law and order crisis.[182] This, he held, was due to the nature of media crime coverage in Ireland. He found that there were four ways in which the press skews the representation of crime: bias towards extreme and atypical offences; bias towards those extreme offences in terms of newspaper space; bias towards stories involving vulnerable victims and invulnerable offenders; and bias towards pessimistic accounts of the criminal justice system generally. Horgan highlighted a major trend in the media towards the sensationalisation of court proceedings.[183] He suggested that the coverage was legal but unfair and concluded that there is a temptation in the press in Ireland to treat the administration of justice as an extension of the entertainment industry.

McCullagh highlighted the reliance of members of the government on the media for access to the public mood, and outlined the manner in which the media impacts upon policy decisions and how media coverage can generate an atmosphere in which controversial policy decisions can become commonsensical.[184] He found no counter-images to the hegemonic images of the dominant discourses. Indeed O'Connor in her work highlighted the role of the media in Ireland in reinforcing and reproducing values rather than radically altering them.[185] The images McCullagh searched for and did not find were images of joyriders, for example, as young people bearing the brunt of a recession, or of young people reacting to increasingly heavy policing of working-class areas. He did find that where the media were prepared to interpret attacks on the Royal Ulster Constabulary (RUC), the police force of Northern Ireland at the time, politically, they would not do so in the case of attacks on the Garda (the police force in the Republic of Ireland).

The power of the media and the traditional power of the print media, the press, in particular in Ireland in shaping Ireland's culture, and Irish society signals the primary role of the press in shaping the construct that is woman in Ireland. The press has a major role in the development of penal policy through its influence on public opinion and its influence on ministerial and government departmental opinion. These opinions, influenced as they are by the press, in turn shape the penal policy which orders and controls imprisonment experiences. The press, within Hall's discursive democratic consensus, helps shape the Irish public's perception of the women's prison and the women imprisoned within it. Representations of women in prison in the press help shape women's experiences of imprisonment, which in turn shape those women's constructions of their personal identities and their senses of self. The discursive subject positioning in the press of the female criminal and the female prisoner works trans-discursively or inter-textually in media, official, public and private discourses to produce the narrated and performed subjectivities of the Irish female prisoner.

EXPERT GAZE

In prison, the expert gaze represents the state in structuring, ordering and controlling prisoners. Foucault discusses the 'micro-court, the permanent petty tribunal' of prison officers and governors, from morning to night judging and punishing prisoners.[186] He outlines how the prison's technology of the soul, the educationalists, psychologists and psychiatrists, fail to conceal the instrument and vector of power that is the prison, a whole technology of power over the body. He explores the normalising gaze where surveillance and normalisation became the great instruments of power in the 1800s and comments that 'the harshest prison says to the prisoners I shall note the slightest irregularity in your conduct.'

Pollack[187] outlines the informal agreement among prison officers that female offenders are more difficult to work with than male offenders. Women are said to be more emotional, more prone to anger outbursts, more likely to engage in verbal assaults on staff. Women 'have a shorter fuse', are more hysterical, less in control.[188] Dobash et al contended that men are deemed bad and normal, needing legal punishment, while women are deemed mad and abnormal, needing a welfare/treatment model.[189] Ussher states that 'men are positioned within criminal discourse while women are positioned within psychiatric discourse.'[190] Heidensohn states that 'women offenders were seen as sick and in need of treatment',[191] while Hutter and Williams state that women offenders are represented as 'sick rather than sinful'.[192]

Sim developed an analysis of the experiences of female prisoners in England between 1774 and 1989 of medical power in prisons, and in his work on the professional dimension of women's historic experiences of imprisonment he states that the female experience of regulation, discipline and normalisation was quite distinct from the male experience.[193] He said that returning women to their normal roles warranted a degree of intervention and surveillance which was much more intense than the experience of men.[194] According to Hahn Rafter, the founding of institutions like Albion extended the mantle of state control and made it possible to punish (or 'help' as the reformers put it) such women more extensively than men who had committed the same acts.[195] Men simply were not sentenced to state prisons for promiscuity and saloon visiting. To control women's bodies, especially those of 'promiscuous' women, the Albion reformatory used three approaches: incarcerating women, parole revocation and transfer of intractables to a custodial asylum for 'feeble-minded' women at Rome, New York, where they could be held indefinitely.[196]

Women were judged to need not only preventive but protective detention. There was a culture of domesticity within which female sexuality was pathologised and within which a concept of femininity constructed around an image of motherhood prevailed as the norm. Female sexuality was seen as being linked to female criminality and female deviance. Women who were sexual were morally defective, weak-minded or ill, they were nymphomaniacs, lesbians or prostitutes. Smart found a critical attitude in juvenile institutions, of 'feminine' emotional reactions, 'hysteria', and 'feminine' interests in hair, clothes and cosmetics.[197] Smart determined that female prisoners were expected to be feminine in terms of their domestic role but not their sexual role. Cowie et al[198] found descriptions of delinquent girls with 'psychiatric' symptoms such as tensions, anxiety, insecurity and feelings of inadequacy. Sumner[199] calls this the censure of femininity, one of the master censures of a hegemonic masculinity. In an exploration of the construct that is woman, emphasising the socio-historical construction of corporeal self rather than the biological construction, Irigaray writes of the repression of instincts in order to produce 'femininity' in the growing girl child.[200]

Carlen highlighted the propensity of prison staff to pathologise resistance to their regimes when, in fact, she suggested it was perhaps imprisonment itself that was responsible for depressed or bizarre behaviour.[201] Sim points out that the rationality of negative responses of those imprisoned to their circumstances has only emerged since the 1970s.[202] Ussher explores the role of surveillance in the reproduction of madness,[203] while Sim outlines how the internalised anger and powerlessness of imprisoned women manifests itself in self-injury, arm-slashing, head-banging against walls, attempted suicide and suicide.[204] Women's prisons are closed, frightening and damaging places; sources of violence include both physical and pharmaceutical control; imprisoned women have no effective way of countering prison controls or abuses; as explained in Chapter 3, in the absence of legitimate grievance strategies some prisoners 'can only stave off their prison-induced fears of death, madness and institutionalisation and general loss of identity by engaging in survival strategies that may seem inexplicable'.[205] Worrall, in a study of women on probation, described how the women internalised pain and self mutilated 'in an attempt to remain independent of others' inroads upon them'.[206] A number of authors have written about women and medicine within prisons and penal institutions. Many feminist writers have considered the female experience in medicine and psychiatry. Their writings on these experiences make for harrowing reading. The clear issue within penal medicine and psychiatry, as articulated by Carlen, and as detailed in Chapter 3, is the fact that within prison the state pays the medics and psychiatrists who examine imprisoned women.[207] The women don't consult the medics; the state consults the medics about the women.

As outlined in Chapter 3 Carlen discusses 'moral management' and its techniques of manipulation in engendering moral states and the more coercive elements of group therapy: the subversion of the individual, the legitimisation of unanimous decisions, and the pressure towards conformity.[208] Garland states that:

> ... in the original vision of penitentiary reformers such as Howard, prisoners were to be continually addressed by moral exhortations, lectures and sermons until they were convinced of the sinfulness of their actions and the right-eousness of their punishment. Similarly, the advocates of rehabilitation in the twentieth century urged that the offender be made a participant in a therapeutic encounter, through

which he or she would come to learn a set of norms and attitudes better adapted to normal social life.[209]

Therapy is considered by Garland to be a 'developed form of persuasion'. Daly[210] discussed the 'new theology of therapy' and 'perpetual therapy'. Sim cites the benign and benevolent developments of psychiatric care as being defined by Foucault, rather than progress, as 'strange regression'.[211] He points to its elements of control manifest in its implements: drugs, straitjackets and cellular confinement, referents for power. Heidensohn[212] said that the different and special approach to treating women in prison is 'based on the notion that those few offending seriously and frequently enough to warrant imprisonment must be physically and/or mentally in need of therapy'. So, she says, the female prison system is therapeutically oriented. She remarked on the constant stress in New Holloway for 'more and better-qualified therapy-oriented staff'.

Ussher denounces 'therapy as tyranny'.[213] She says that the medical establishment followed its colonisation of women's bodies with its colonisation of women's minds. She outlines the feminist view of therapy as based on patriarchal principles supporting a patriarchal and misogynistic culture encouraging women to conform, to submit to control. Ussher's chapter 'Routes to Madness' points to issues such as: poverty; the burden of care; the ceaseless demands on the nurturer; the never-ending work of the home maker; women's vulnerability; woman as a reflection of man's glories; women's lack of opportunity; marital status, the fact that married women are more likely to be depressed; the tyranny of marriage and family violence; the threat and act of sexual violence; the mirror; images of women; the body beautiful; advertising women 'signified by lips, legs, eyes or hair, which stand metonymically ... for the sexual woman'; and silent women; as the engenders of madness in women.

In 1967 the Home Office, without regard for the fact that it was comparing a tiny (female) population serving short sentences for petty crimes with a large (male) population serving long sentences for serious crimes, said that 'severe personality and emotional disturbances were more prevalent among women and girls than among men and boys committed to custody.'[214] Liebling, as explained in Chapter 5, in an exploration of despair and medicalisation among prisoners, found that women use the word depression and men the word bored to describe the same sensation, and where men could externalise the problem, blaming the prison, the pressures they were under, the failures of others, women internalised them.[215] Sim points to the use of psychiatric labels such as personality disorder in continuing to reinforce the subordination of the women and he quotes Carlen's contention that imprisoned women feel 'horribly at home' within psychiatry.[216] Sim concludes that British penal institutions are particularly suited to disciplining women into woman's most appropriate role, that of the child-rearing homemaker.

THE IRISH FEMALE PRISON EXPERIENCE

The degree to which the Irish penal system, with its own permanent petty tribunals, attempted or attempts to 'normalise' the behaviour of imprisoned women has not been documented as Sim has documented the English experience. However, the models have developed on similar lines, evidenced in Ireland's former colonial relationship with the UK, in the architectural and organisational dimensions of Limerick Prison and the Dóchas Centre, and in the word 'normalisation', frequently used, as will be seen, in management circles in Irish female prisons. Corcoran outlines the use of 'normalisation' in the management of, rather than the eradication of, differences between female political prisoners and the penal regime in Northern Ireland, from hunger strikes, no-wash protests and dirty protests, to a momentum towards the reduction of conflict within the prisons with more circumspect cultures of intervention being adopted by the penal regime.[217] As detailed in the first chapter, there have been few studies of women's experiences of imprisonment in Ireland. The writers who have written on the topic have focused on the nature of female criminality in Ireland and the gendered treatment of women by the law; a few have written about women's experiences of imprisonment. The studies primarily focus on the demographics of the female prison population and on the health issues among that population.

The historical studies consist primarily of the works of Ward, McCoole and Curtin, while Cullen Owens, Cooke[218] and Carey[219] also give some detail.[220] In addition there is Buckley's autobiography[221] of her experience as a revolutionary prisoner. Both Ward and McCoole focus on revolutionary women in the early decades of the twentieth century.[222] McCoole details the experiences of these women in Kilmainham Gaol and in the North Dublin Union.[223] Curtin's focus is on the women of Galway Gaol in nineteenth-century Ireland and the criminality of those women.[224] The historic female experience of incarceration is to some degree detailed in Reynolds' study of psychiatric care in Dublin since 1815, in Finnegan's[225] study of women's experiences of Magdalen asylums, and in Raftery and O'Sullivan's[226] study of industrial schools.[227] The studies of women in prison all document generally the unpleasantness of the prison environment and experience. The impact of experiences of imprisonment on women and the structures of the societies shaping women's prison experiences are given little consideration.

In recent decades, four reports were published on prisons and prisoners: the McBride Report, commissioned by the Prisoners' Rights Organisation; the 1983 report *The Prison System*, from the Council for Social Welfare: A Committee of the Catholic Bishops' Conference; the 1985 Whittaker Report (*Report of the Commission of Enquiry into the Penal System*), commissioned by the Irish government; and the Prison Service's five-year plan, *Management of Offenders*. In general, the reports focus on penality and on Ireland's prisons, their structure and effect. The Whittaker Report focused in part on the shortcomings of the facilities and services for prisoners and on the inadequacies of much of the prison accommodation. Just four full pages in that report are dedicated to women prisoners. At the time of that research (1984) there were daily averages of around forty women and 1,550 men in prison. The four pages on women prisoners detail the inadequacies of the women's prisons, while highlighting the needs of the prisons in terms of services and facilities for imprisoned women.

In 2001, *Towards a Model Penal System*, commissioned by the Irish Penal Reform Trust, evaluated the prison system, presented alternatives to prison, and discussed diversions, such as neighbourhood youth projects, from the penal system. In detailing the composition of the prison population, women prisoners were presented in the report in the section on young offenders. In fact, the report devoted a couple of pages only to women offenders. It described as 'especially incongruous' the presence of women in prison, if, as it says, 'prison should be used for those who represent a danger to the community or for those who have committed the most serious crimes.' The report recommended that the population of the women's prison be halved. In 2003, the European Committee for the Prevention of Torture and Inhuman or Degrading Treatment or Punishment published its report to the government of Ireland on its visit to Ireland's prisons.[228] The report noted that the Dóchas Centre was at the time accommodating ninety-three women, when it was designed for a maximum occupancy of seventy-nine. The Irish Prison Service now states on its website that the prison currently has an official capacity for 105 women. The CPT wanted measures taken to ensure that all the women imprisoned were provided with appropriate accommodation; it commented on inadequate healthcare provision in that prison, the inadequate complaints procedure in the prisons generally, and an inadequate mailing system for prisoner mail. Overall, however, the report deemed the regime in the Dóchas Centre adequate.

The completed PhDs give a great deal of information on women's experiences of imprisonment and the inadequacies for prisoners of the various prisons within which the PhDs were undertaken. Lundström-Roche[229] detailed the grimness of Mountjoy female prison in the early 1980s, the lack of activity, the high level of security, the closed nature of the institution. She highlighted the imprisonment of women who posed no threat to society, and the failure of the prisons in their rehabilitative and deterrent responsibilities, failures which were evident in the prisons' high recidivism rates. McCann James[230] detailed the closed nature and the grim aspect of the women's prison at Mountjoy in the late 1990s, when the women were accommodated on one wing in St Patrick's Institution, before they moved to the Dóchas Centre.

O'Mahony wrote of the Irish prison experience as 'punitive, damaging and painful in a myriad of ways beyond the mere loss of liberty', and how 'in many quarters, it is expected to be so'.[231] He also wrote of Foucault's contention that prisons are, in fact, rather than failures, well-disguised successes, more about social control than the control of individual prisoners.[232] O'Mahony suggested that this was evidenced in Ireland in the extreme relative social disadvantage of Irish prisoners generally, and the general absence among the Irish prison population of the more privileged classes of Irish society. He highlighted, as well as the obligations of denunciation and restitution, the obligation on the criminal justice system to rehabilitate offenders. Lundström-Roche in her work found the Irish penal system to be retributive rather than rehabilitative.[233] O'Mahony stressed the importance of explicitly acknowledging the necessity of a constructive penal system for the needs of prisoners who have, in fact, been shaped by society for crime.[234]

The issues highlighted again and again in the publications on women in prison in Ireland are the small numbers of women prisoners, the petty nature of the offences for which they are imprisoned, the inappropriateness of prison sentences for women, and the inadequacies of the prisons for women in terms of accommodation, environment and structure. But although these studies together present a rich perspective on women's experiences of imprisonment, the gaps in the research are quite substantial. All of the studies are relatively small scale. They are all situated in narrow historical contexts. They are focused, those few that are focused on women prisoners, on very few and very particular women prisoners. Since the 1900s in fact, the Irish female penal system has not been thoroughly examined. Women's experiences of imprisonment in Ireland have never been comprehensively studied. There is little empirical data on women's experiences of imprisonment. Irish penality, and its operation in relation to women in Irish society, has never been thoroughly explored. The social and cultural impact of the prison and experiences of imprisonment on individual women's lives have never, in an Irish context, been thoroughly examined. While the scope of this book is necessarily constrained, it does explore women's experiences of imprisonment in Ireland over the past two centuries. It considers the women imprisoned, the offences for which they were imprisoned, the penalties imposed upon them, the institutions within which they were imprisoned, and the society imprisoning them. The women's experiences are examined both historically and contemporaneously. There is a particular focus on the manner in which, within the space that is prison space, the identities of imprisoned women are constructed.

NOTES

1. P. Carlen and A. Worrall, *Analysing Women's Imprisonment* (Abingdon: Willan, 2004), p.89.
2. K. Woodward, *Understanding Identity (Understanding Media Series)* (London: Hodder Arnold, 2003).
3. Ibid., p.3.
4. M. Foucault, 'Foucault on Attica: An Interview', interview by J.K. Simon, April 1972, *Telos* (1974), 19, pp.154–61.
5. J.S. Mill, *On Liberty and Utilitarianism* (New York: Bantam, 1993).
6. J. Bentham, *On Utilitarianism and Government: Introduction to the Principles of Morals* (London: Wordsworth Editions, 2000).
7. J. Rawls, *A Theory of Justice* (Cambridge, MA: Belknap Press, 1999).
8. P. Ricoeur, *Oneself as Another* (Chicago: Chicago University Press, 1994), p.239.
9. J. Irwin and D.R. Cressey, 'Thieves, Convicts and the Inmate Culture', *Social Problems*, 10, 2 (1962), pp.142–55.
10. M. Lianos and M. Douglas, 'Dangerisation and the End of Deviance: The Institutional Environment', in D. Garland and R. Sparks (eds), *Criminology and Social Theory* (Oxford: Oxford University Press, 2000), pp.103–27.
11. M. Foucault, *Fearless Speech*, edited by J. Pearson (Boston: Semiotexte, 2001), p.67.
12. Foucault, 'Foucault on Attica: An Interview'.
13. C. McCullagh, 'Getting the Criminals We Want: The Social Production of the Criminal Population', in P. Clancy, S. Drudy, K. Lynch and L. O'Dowd (eds), *Irish Society: Sociological Perspectives* (Dublin: Institute of Public Administration, 1995), pp.410–31.
14. C. Fennel, *Crime and Crisis in Ireland: Justice by Illusion?* (Cork University Press, Cork, 1993), p.171.
15. See McCullagh, 'Getting the Criminals We Want'.
16. P. Kirby, L. Gibbons and M. Cronin (eds), *Reinventing Ireland: Culture, Society and the Global Economy* (London: Pluto, 2002), p.9.
17. I. O'Donnell and E. O'Sullivan, *Crime Control in Ireland: The Politics of Intolerance* (Cork: Cork University Press, 2001).
18. Ibid., p.43; zero-tolerance policing; new criminal justice legislation (the Criminal Justice Act 1999), including mandatory minimum drug sentences and a referendum to widen the grounds on which bail could be refused (November 1996, within months of the Guerin and McCabe murders); and massive expansion of the prison system (2,000 extra prison places).
19. O'Donnell and O'Sullivan, *Crime Control in Ireland*, p.2.
20. Lianos and Douglas, 'Dangerisation and the End of Deviance', pp.104–25.
21. U. Beck, *Risk Society: Towards a New Modernity* (London: Sage, 1992).
22. P. O'Mahony, *Prison Policy in Ireland: Criminal Justice versus Social Justice* (Cork: Cork University Press, 2000), p.44.
23. E. Goffman, *Stigma* (London: Penguin, 1990), pp.15–16.
24. G.H. Mead, *Mind, Self and Society* (Chicago: University of Chicago Press, 1934).
25. Ricoeur, *Oneself as Another*, p.113.
26. V. Bell, *Performativity and Belonging* (London: Sage, 1999).
27. J. Butler, *Gender Trouble: Feminism and the Subversion of Identity* (New York: Routledge, 1990).
28. J. Butler, *Bodies that Matter: On the Discursive Limits of Sex* (New York: Routledge, 1993).
29. A. Giddens, *Modernity and Self-Identity* (Palo Alto, CA: Stanford University Press, 1991), p.54.
30. Ricoeur, *Oneself as Another*, pp.147–8.
31. D. Garland, *Punishment and Modern Society: A Study in Social Theory* (Chicago: University of Chicago Press, 1990), pp.249–50.
32. J. Sunderland, *Gendered Discourses* (London: Palgrave Macmillan, 2004).
33. M. Foucault, 'The Order of Discourse', in M.J. Shapiro (ed.), *Language and Politics* (Oxford: Blackwell, 1984).

34. J. Berger, *Ways of Seeing* (London: Penguin, 1972).
35. Butler, *Bodies that Matter*, p.2.
36. P. Carlen, *Women, Crime and Poverty* (Milton Keynes: Open University Press, 1988). p.5.
37. P. Scraton, 'Scientific Knowledge or Masculine Discourses? Challenging Patriarchy in Criminology', in L. Gelsthorpe and A. Morris (eds), *Feminist Perspectives in Criminology* (Milton Keynes: Open University Press, 1990), p.21.
38. R. Morris, *Crumbling Walls: Why Prisons Fail* (Oakville, ON: Mosaic Press, 1989), p.105.
39. M. Eaton, *Women After Prison* (Milton Keynes: Open University Press, 1993), p.17. See also H. Garfinkel, 'Conditions for Successful Status Degradation Ceremonies', *American Journal of Sociology*, 61, 2 (1956), pp.420–4; and E. Finkelstein, 'Status Degradation and Organisational Succession in Prison', *British Journal of Sociology*, 47, 4 (1996), pp.671–83.
40. C. Jose-Kampfner, 'Coming to Terms with Existential Death: An Analysis of Women's Adaptation to Life in Prison', *Social Justice*, 17, 2 (1990), pp.110–25.
41. See also K. Watterson, *Women in Prison: Inside the Concrete Womb* (Lebanon, NH: Northeastern University Press, 1996).
42. R. Sparks and A.E. Bottoms, 'Legitimacy and Order in Prisons', *British Journal of Sociology*, 46, 1 (1995), pp.45–62.
43. Eaton, *Women After Prison*, p.35.
44. M. Chesney-Lind, 'Patriarchy, Prisons, and Jails: A Critical Look at Trends in Women's Incarceration', *The Prison Journal*, 71, 1 (1991), pp.51–67.
45. S. Walby, *Theorising Patriarchy* (Oxford: Blackwell, 1990), p.2.
46. E. Mahon, 'Ireland: A Private Patriarchy', *Environment and Planning*, 26, 8 (1994), pp.1277–96.
47. P. O'Connor, *Emerging Voices: Women in Contemporary Irish Society* (Dublin: Institute of Public Administration, 1998), p.30.
48. Y. Galligan, 'Women in Irish Politics', in J. Coakley and M. Gallagher (eds), *Politics and the Republic of Ireland* (Dublin: Folens, 1993), pp.207–26.
49. C. Eager, 'Splitting Images: Women and the Irish Civil Service', *Seirbhís Phoiblí*, 12, 1 (1991), pp.15–23, quoted in Galligan, 'Women in Irish Politics', p.213.
50. Research by Connelly and Hilliard (1993), quoted in Galligan, 'Women in Irish Politics', p.213.
51. I. Bacik, C. Costello and E. Drew, *Gender in Justice* (Dublin: Trinity College Law School, 2003).
52. Carlen, *Women, Crime and Poverty*, p.19.
53. N. Elias, *The Civilising Process* (Oxford: Blackwell, 2000).
54. P. Bourdieu, 'Cultural Production and Social Reproduction', in R. Brown (ed.), *Knowledge, Education and Cultural Change* (London: Tavistock, 1973), pp.71–112.
55. P. Bourdieu, *Language and Symbolic Power* (Cambridge: Polity, 1991).
56. P. O'Mahony, *Crime and Punishment in Ireland* (Dublin: Round Hall Press, 1993), p.61.
57. I. Bacik, A. Kelly, M. O'Connell and H. Sinclair, 'Crime and Poverty in Dublin: An Analysis of the Association between Community Deprivation, District Court Appearance and Sentence Severity', *Irish Criminal Law Journal*, vol. 7 (1997), pp.104–33.
58. O'Mahony, *Prison Policy in Ireland*, p.16.
59. M. Monaghan, 'A Survey of Women in an Irish Prison', unpublished MPsychSc dissertation, University College Dublin, 1989.
60. P. Carmody and M. McEvoy, *A Study of Irish Female Prisoners* (Dublin: Stationery Office, 1996).
61. Centre for Health Promotion Studies, NUI Galway, *Healthcare Study of the Prisoner Population* (Dublin: Stationery Office, 2000).
62. N. McCafferty, *In the Eyes of the Law* (Dublin: Ward River Press, 1981).
63. D.B. Rottman, *The Criminal Justice System: Policy and Performance*, Report no. 77 (Dublin: National Economic and Social Council, 1994).

64. M. Foucault, *Discipline and Punish: The Birth of the Prison* (London: Penguin, 1977).

65. R.P. Dobash, R.E. Dobash and S. Gutteridge, *The Imprisonment of Women* (New York: Blackwell, 1986).

66. C. Larner, 'Crimen Exceptum? The Crime of Witchcraft in Europe', in V. Gatrell, B. Lenman and G. Parker (eds), *Crime and the Law* (London: Europa, 1980), pp.49–75.

67. J. Brennan (Rev.), 'Bishop Ledrede and the Trial of Alice Kyteler: A Case Study in Witchcraft and Heresy in Medieval Kilkenny', in J. Bradley and D. Healy (eds), *Themes in Kilkenny's History* (Callan, Co. Kilkenny: Red Lion Press, 1999), p.37.

68. A. Bourke, *The Burning of Bridget Cleary* (New York: Penguin, 1999), pp.33–4.

69. Dobash et al., *The Imprisonment of Women*.

70. Ibid., p.18.

71. Ibid., pp.19–20. 'The branks of an iron cage placed over the head, and most examples incorporated a spike or pointed wheel that was inserted into the offender's mouth "in order to pin the tongue and silence the noisiest brawler"'. The common form of administering this punishment was to fasten the branks to a woman and parade her through the village, sometimes chaining her to a pillar for a period of time after the procession.' Dobash et al. state that while the scold's bridle was a public chastisement, in some towns arrangements were made for employing the branks within the home. 'In the old-fashioned, half-timbered houses in the borough (Congleton), there were generally fixed on one side of the large open fireplace a hook, so that when a man's wife indulged her scolding propensities, the husband sent for the town jailer to bring the bridle and had her bridled and chained to the hook until she promised to behave herself.'

72. Ibid.

73. M. Edgeworth, *Castle Rackrent* (Oxford: Oxford University Press, 1964), pp.30, 125. Maria Edgeworth (1767–1849), in her novel *Castle Rackrent*, set in Ireland, details the 'conjugal imprisonment' of Lady Cathcart (1692–1789). She was the widow of the eighth Baron Cathcart (d. 1740), her third husband, when she married Col. Hugh Maguire, an Irish soldier-adventurer and fortune hunter, in 1745. When she refused to give him her property and jewels he abducted her from their home in Hertfordshire to a castle in County Fermanagh, where he kept her confined until his death in 1764, when she returned to England, dying childless in 1789. On release, on her husband's death, she '… looked scared, and her understanding seemed stupefied; she said that she scarcely knew one human creature from another: her imprisonment lasted above twenty years.'

74. Dobash et al., *The Imprisonment of Women*, p.24. The old Bridewell Palace of Henry VIII was the first in London and gave its name to similar institutions in Britain. Idle, destitute or lewd women were usually whipped and carted through the streets of London to their incarceration in the Bridewell. Husbands, parents and masters as well as magistrates and members of the judiciary had the power to confine women in the Bridewell. In 1597 the first unique penal institution for women opened in St Ursule's Convent in Amsterdam. When this institution burned down, the Spinhuis, which opened in 1645, replaced it. 'In the beginning, the Spinhuis … housed mostly poor, wayward and "disrespectful" women and girls, but within ten years it began to house women committed for prostitution, theft and other forms of crime. It was intended to be a paternalistic house of correction as the motto over the door attested, "Fear not! I do exact vengeance for evil but compel you to be good. My hand is stern, but my heart is kind."'

75. M. Ignatieff, *A Just Measure of Pain* (London: Penguin Books, 1978), p.16.

76. Dobash et al., *The Imprisonment of Women*, p.29.

77. D. Phillips, 'A Just Measure of Crime', in S. Cohen and A. Scull (eds), *Social Control and the State* (Oxford: Blackwell, 1983), p.54.

78. C. Lombroso and W. Ferrero, *The Female Offender* (New York: Wisdom Library, 1958).

79. O. Pollak, *The Criminality of Women* (New York: A.S. Barnes, 1950).

80. W.I. Thomas, *The Unadjusted Girl* (New York: Harper & Row, 1967).

81. Lombroso and Ferrero, *The Female Offender*.

82. D. Klein, *The Etiology of Female Crime: The Criminology of Deviant Women* (Boston: Houghton Mifflin, 1977), p.17.
83. C. Smart, *Women, Crime and Criminology: A Feminist Critique* (London: Routledge & Kegan Paul, 1976), p.38.
84. Pollak, *The Criminality of Women*, p.11.
85. K. Davis, 'The Sociology of Prostitution', *American Sociological Review*, 2, 5 (October 1937), pp.746–55.
86. Pollak, *The Criminality of Women*, p.127.
87. Ibid., p.128.
88. J. Cowie, V. Cowie and E. Slater, *Delinquency in Girls* (London: Heinemann, 1968), p.165.
89. C. Bishop, *Women and Crime* (London: Chatto & Windus, 1931), pp.272–6.
90. L. Crites, *The Female Offender* (Lexington, MA: Lexington Books, 1877).
91. Smart, *Women, Crime and Criminology: A Feminist Critique* (1976).
92. P. Carlen, *Criminal Women* (Cambridge: Polity, 1985).
93. Klein, *The Etiology of Female Crime*.
94. Carlen, *Criminal Women*, p.1.
95. F. Heidensohn, *Women and Crime* (London: Macmillan, 1985), p.17.
96. Smart, *Women, Crime and Criminology*.
97. Carlen, *Criminal Women*, p.2.
98. Fennel, *Crime and Crisis in Ireland*, p.182.
99. A. Lyons and P. Hunt, 'The Effects of Gender on Sentencing: A Case Study of the Dublin Metropolitan Area District Court', in M. Tomlinson, T. Varley and C. McCullagh (eds), *Whose Law and Order* (Belfast: Sociological Association of Ireland, 1983), pp.129–42.
100. A. Worrall, 'Out of Place: Female Offenders in Court', *Probation Journal*, 28, 3 (1981), pp.90–3.
101. L. Luckhaus, 'A Plea for PMT in the Criminal Law', in S. Edwards (ed.), *Gender, Sex and the Law* (London: Croom Helm, 1985), pp.159–83.
102. Worrall, 'Out of Place: Female Offenders in Court', pp 90–3.
103. B. Morrissey, *When Women Kill: Questions of Agency and Subjectivity* (London: Routledge, 2003).
104. Worrall, 'Out of Place: Female Offenders in Court', p.79.
105. Lyons and Hunt, 'The Effects of Gender on Sentencing', p.138.
106. I. Bacik, 'Women and the Criminal Justice System', in P. O'Mahony (ed.), *Criminal Justice in Ireland* (Dublin: Institute of Public Administration, 2002), p.145.
107. Ibid., pp.135–6.
108. Bacik et al., 'Crime and Poverty in Dublin', pp.104–45.
109. M. Chesney-Lind, 'Judicial Enforcement of the Female Sex Role: The Family Court and the Female Delinquent', *Issues in Criminology*, 8, 2 (1973), pp.51–69.
110. Ibid., p.56.
111. M. Chesney-Lind, 'Young Women in the Arms of the Law', in L. Bowker (ed.), *Women, Crime and the Criminal Justice System* (Lexington, MA: D.C. Heath, 1978), p.210.
112. P. Carlen, *Women's Imprisonment: A Study in Social Control* (London: Routledge & Kegan Paul, 1983), p.126.
113. Heidensohn, *Women and Crime*, p.46.
114. Carlen, *Women, Crime and Poverty*, p.9.
115. Baroness Seear and E. Player, *Women in the Penal System* (a report prepared for the Howard League of Penal Reform, 1986).
116. In general, in the policy-driven studies undertaken in the UK, the issues highlighted are the low but rising numbers of women in prison; the issues of substance abuse, suicide and self-injury among women in prison; the high rates of mental disorder and personality disorder among women in prison; the effect of sentencing women on families and the wider community; the fact that gender and racial stereotypes were still influencing the decisions of magistrates; and the fact that women before the courts were more likely to be defined as troubled rather than troublesome.

117. Carlen, *Women, Crime and Poverty*, p.10.
118. N. Johnston, *The Human Cage: A Brief History of Prison Architecture* (Philadelphia: The American Foundation, Incorporated Institute of Corrections, 1973).
119. A. Chekov, *The Island: A Journey to Sakhalin* (Santa Barbara, CA: Greenwood Press, 1967).
120. C. Parenti, *Lockdown America: Police and Prisons in the Age of Crisis* (London: Verso, 2000), p.164.
121. M. Ignatieff, *A Just Measure of Pain* (London: Penguin, 1978), p.80.
122. Ibid., p.77.
123. R. Evans, 'Bentham's Panopticon: An Incident in the Social History of Architecture', *Architectural Association Quarterly* (Spring 1971), p.26.
124. J. Sim, '"We Are Not Animals, We Are Human Beings": Prisons, Protests and Politics in England and Wales, 1969–90', *Social Justice*, 18, 3 (1991), pp.107–29.
125. S. Lash and J. Urry, *Economies of Signs and Space* (London: Sage, 1994), p.230.
126. Ibid.
127. G. Bachelard, *The Poetics of Space* (Boston: Beacon Press, 1969).
128. D. Massey, *Space, Place and Gender* (Cambridge: Polity, 1994), p.154.
129. S. Ardener, *Women and Space: Ground Rules and Social Maps* (Oxford: Berg, 1993), p.19.
130. E. Grosz, *Space, Time and Perversion: Essays on the Politics of Bodies* (London: Routledge, 1995), p.123.
131. S.L. Bartky, *Femininity and Domination: Studies in the Phenomenology of Oppression* (London: Routledge, 1990), p.67.
132. G. Rose, *Feminism and Geography* (Cambridge: Polity, 1993), pp.143–6.
133. Ibid.
134. L. Irigaray, *An Ethics of Sexual Difference* (Ithaca, NY: Cornell University Press, 1993), p.7.
135. E. Goffman, *The Presentation of Self in Everyday Life* (London: Penguin, 1990), p.104.
136. M. de Certeau, L. Girard and P. Mayol, *The Practice of Everyday Life, Vol. II: Living and Cooking* (Minneapolis: University of Minnesota Press, 1998), p.9.
137. A. Giddens, *The Constitution of Society: Outline of the Theory of Structuration* (Cambridge: Polity, 1986).
138. P. Bourdieu, *In Other Words: Essays Towards a Reflexive Sociology* (Palo Alto, CA: Stanford University Press, 1990), p.123.
139. Lash and Urry, *Economies of Signs and Space*, p.239.
140. Bachelard, *The Poetics of Space*, p.10.
141. Ibid., p.5.
142. De Certeau et al., *The Practice of Everyday Life*, p.148.
143. Bachelard, *The Poetics of Space*, pp.15, 56.
144. J. Baudrillard, *The System of Objects* (London: Verso, 1996), p.16.
145. H. Lefebvre, *The Production of Space* (Oxford: Blackwell, 1991), pp.141–2.
146. Heidensohn, *Women and Crime*, pp.43–4.
147. L.H. Bowker, *Women, Crime and the Criminal Justice System* (Lexington, MA: D.C. Heath, 1978), p.208.
148. Chesney-Lind, 'Patriarchy, Prisons, and Jails', pp.51–67.
149. P. Carlen, and Worrall, A., *Gender, Crime and Justice* (1987), p.149.
150. P. Carlen, 'Women, Crime, Feminism and Reason', *Social Justice*, 17, 4, (1990), pp.107–8.
151. A. Peckham, *A Woman in Custody* (London: Fontana, 1985).
152. M. Evans, *The Woman In Question* (London: Fontana, 1986).
153. S. Gregory, *Forget You Had a Daughter: Doing Time in the Bangkok Hilton* (London: Vision Paperbacks/Satin Publications, 2003).
154. R. Wyner, *From the Inside: Dispatches from a Women's Prison* (London: Aurum, 2004).
155. P. Bourdieu, *Masculine Domination* (Cambridge: Polity, 2001), p.65.
156. Berger, *Ways of Seeing*, pp.8–9.
157. Foucault, *Discipline and Punish*.

158. Foucault, *Fearless Speech*, p.70.
159. S.L. Bartky, 'Foucault, Femininity and the Modernisation of Patriarchal Power', in S. Jackson (ed.), *Women's Studies: A Reader* (Hemel Hempstead: Harvester Wheatsheaf, 1993), p.227.
160. Rose, *Feminism and Geography*, pp.143–6.
161. S. Cohen and J. Young (eds), *The Manufacture of News: Social Problems, Deviance and the Mass Media* (London: Constable, 1973), p.12.
162. J. Fiske, *Introduction to Communication Studies* (London: Routledge, 1982), p.171.
163. Cohen and Young, *The Manufacture of News*.
164. Ibid., p.29.
165. Ibid., p.27.
166. Ibid., p.231.
167. S. Hall, C. Critcher, T. Jefferson, J. Clarke and B. Roberts, *Policing the Crisis: Mugging, the State and Law and Order* (London: Macmillan, 1978), pp.75–9.
168. Morrissey, *When Women Kill*, p.19.
169. Cohen and Young, *The Manufacture of News*, p.21.
170. L. van Zoonen, *Feminist Media Studies* (London: Sage, 1994), p.37.
171. J. Fiske and J. Hartley, *Reading Television* (London: Methuen, 1978).
172. Morrissey, *When Women Kill*, pp.14–20.
173. Ibid., p.16.
174. Heidensohn, *Women and Crime*.
175. S. Cohen, *Folk Devils and Moral Panics* (London: Granada Publishing, 1972).
176. J. Smith, *Different for Girls: How Culture Creates Women* (London: Chatto & Windus, 1997), pp.133–47.
177. Morrissey, *When Women Kill*.
178. K. Silverman, *The Subject of Semiotics* (Oxford: Oxford University Press, 1983). See also N. Fairclough, *Critical Discourse Analysis: The Critical Study of Language* (Harlow: Pearson Education, 1995).
179. Van Zoonen, *Feminist Media Studies*, p.24.
180. A. McRobbie, 'Jackie: An Ideology of Adolescent Femininity', in B. Waites, T. Bennet and G. Martin (eds), *Popular Culture: Past and Present* (London: Croom Helm, 1982), pp.263–83.
181. McCullagh, 'Getting the Criminals We Want'.
182. M. O'Connell, 'Is Irish Public Opinion Towards Crime Distorted by Media Bias?', *European Journal of Communication*, 14, 2 (1999), pp.191–212.
183. J. Horgan, 'Sensationalising Court Proceedings May be Unfair', *Irish Times*, 26 August 1999.
184. McCullagh, 'Getting the Criminals We Want'.
185. B. O'Connor, *Soap and Sensibility: Audience Response to Dallas and Glenroe* (Dublin: RTÉ, 1990).
186. Foucault, *Fearless Speech*, p.85.
187. J. Pollack, 'Women Will be Women: Correctional Officers' Perceptions of the Emotionality of Women Inmates', *The Prison Journal*, 64, 1 (1984), pp.84–91.
188. See also E. Genders and E. Player, 'Women in Prison: The Treatment, the Control and the Experience', in P. Carlen and A. Worrall (eds), *Gender, Crime and Justice* (Milton Keynes: Open University Press, 1987), pp.100–20.
189. R.E. Dobash, P. Dobash and L. Noaks, *Gender and Crime* (Cardiff: University of Wales Press, 1995), p.8.
190. J. Ussher, *Women's Madness: Misogyny or Mental Illness?* (Harlow: Prentice Hall, 1991), p.10.
191. F. Heidensohn, *The Imprisonment of Females* (London: Routledge & Kegan Paul, 1975), p.52.
192. B. Hutter and G. Williams, *Controlling Women: The Normal and the Deviant* (London: Croom Helm, 1981), p.21.
193. J. Sim, *Medical Power in Prisons: The Prison Medical Service in England, 1774–1989* (Milton Keynes: Open University Press, 1990), p.129.
194. See also G. Zwerman, 'Special Incapacitation: The Emergence of a New Correctional

Facility for Women Political Prisoners', *Social Justice*, 15, 1 (1988), pp.31–47 for an exploration of the 'special incapacitation' used with female political prisoners.

195. N. Hahn Rafter, 'Chastising the Unchaste: Social Control Functions of a Women's Reformatory, 1894–1931', in S. Cohen and A. Scull (eds), *Social Control and the State* (Oxford: Blackwell, 1983), p.291.

196. See also B. Brenzel, 'Domestication as Reform: A Study of the Socialization of Wayward Girls, 1856–1905', *Harvard Educational Review*, 50, 2 (1980), pp.196–213.

197. Smart, *Women, Crime and Criminology*, p.143.

198. Cowie et al., *Delinquency in Girls*, p.143.

199. C. Sumner (ed.), *Censure, Politics and Criminal Justice* (Milton Keynes: Open University Press, 1990), p.26.

200. L. Irigaray, *This Sex Which is Not One* (Ithaca, NY: Cornell University Press, 1985), pp.36–7.

201. P. Carlen, 'Psychiatry in Prisons: Promises, Premises, Practices and Politics', in P. Millar and N. Rose (eds), *The Power of Psychiatry* (Cambridge: Polity 1986), pp.249–51.

202. Sim, '"We Are Not Animals"', pp.107–29.

203. Ussher, *Women's Madness*.

204. Sim, '"We Are Not Animals"', pp.107–29.

205. Carlen, quoted in Sim, *Medical Power in Prisons*, p.121.

206. A. Worrall, 'Working with Female Offenders: Beyond Alternatives to Custody?', *British Journal of Social Work*, 19, 2 (1989), pp.77–93.

207. Carlen, 'Psychiatry in Prisons', p.242.

208. Ibid., p.244.

209. D. Garland, *Punishment and Modern Society: A Study in Social Theory* (Chicago: University of Chicago Press, 1990), p.261.

210. M. Daly, *Gyn/Ecology: The Metaethics of Radical Feminism* (Boston: Beacon Press, 1978), pp.230–1.

211. Sim, *Medical Power in Prisons*, p.4.

212. Heidensohn, *The Imprisonment of Females*, p.44.

213. Ussher, *Women's Madness*, p.76.

214. Sim, *Medical Power in Prisons*, p.163.

215. A. Liebling, 'Suicide Amongst Women Prisoners', *The Howard Journal*, 33, 1 (February 1994).

216. See Carlen, *Women's Imprisonment*, p.210.

217. `M. Corcoran, 'Mapping Carceral Space: Territorialisation, Resistance and Control in Northern Ireland's Women's Prisons', in D. Alderson, F. Becket, S. Brewster and V. Crossman (eds), *Ireland in Proximity: History, Gender and Space* (London: Routledge, 1999), pp.157–73.

218. R. Cullen Owens, 'Votes for Women', in A. Hayes and D. Urquhart (eds), *The Irish Women's History Reader* (London: Routledge, 2001), pp.37–42.

219. P. Cooke, *A History of Kilmainham Gaol* (Dublin: Stationery Office, 1995).

220. T. Carey, *Mountjoy: The Story of a Prison* (Cork: The Collins Press, 2000).

221. M. Buckley, *A Jangle of the Keys* (Dublin: Duffy, 1938).

222. M. Ward (ed.), *In Their Own Voice: Women and Irish Nationalism* (Cork: Attic Press, 1995).

223. S. McCoole, *No Ordinary Women* (Dublin: O'Brien Press, 2003); see also S. McCoole, *Guns and Chiffon* (Dublin: Stationery Office, 1997).

224. G. Curtin, *The Women of Galway Gaol* (Galway: Arlen House, 2001).

225. J. Reynolds, *Grangegorman: Psychiatric Care in Dublin since 1815* (Dublin: Institute of Public Administration, 1992).

226. F. Finnegan, *Do Penance or Perish: A Study of Magdalen Asylums in Ireland* (Piltown, Co. Kilkenny: Congrave Press, 2001).

227. M. Raftery and O. O'Sullivan, *Suffer the Little Children: The Inside Story of Ireland's Industrial Schools* (Dublin: New Island, 1999).

228. This visit followed a visit by the CPT to Irish prisons in 1993.

229. F. Lundström-Roche, 'Women in Prison: Ideals and Reals', unpublished doctoral dissertation, Department of Sociology, University of Stockholm, 1985.
230. C. McCann-James, 'Recycled Women: Oppression and the Social World of Women Prisoners in the Irish Republic', unpublished PhD thesis, NUI Galway, 2001.
231. O'Mahony, *Prison Policy in Ireland*, p.9.
232. Foucault, *Discipline and Punish*, p.272.
233. Lundström-Roche, 'Women in Prison: Ideals and Reals'.
234. O'Mahony, *Prison Policy in Ireland*, p.105.

Chapter Six

Space and Identity in the Women's Prisons

The focus of this chapter is on the manner in which the women experience their personal prison spaces and the ways in which they use those spaces as a means to recuperate their identities. In the chapter, Butler's theory of performativity is examined.[1] With this theory Butler posits identity not as some authentic core self, but rather as the dramatic effect of performances developed through imitation, fabrication and manipulation. The theory is explored in this chapter in relation to the manner in which women in prison in Ireland inhabit prison space and the ways in which within that space they construct and represent their own identities. The ways in which the women occupy and live prison space is another discourse in this study.

Discourses are constituted through power; the power that constitutes them also transmits them, or communicates them. Highlighting the strength of the constitutive potential of discourses, Butler said that discourse has the capacity to produce that which it names.[2] Thus, discourse is more than just perspective; discourses, as discussed in previous chapters, call into being particular realities. The powerful, through discourse, create knowledge and circulate it. These circulating discourses, as discussed in previous chapters, are the means through which that which is known is created and developed. It is through these discourses that reality is constructed. Reality is discursively produced.

PERFORMING IDENTITY

In a study of agency and power in women's prisons, Bosworth examined the effects of femininity on women in prison.[3] Her focus was on how women, as agents, negotiate power within prison. She found that imprisoned women are able to transform or challenge power relations within prison from their embodied positions. Building on Bosworth's study, this book examines how women in prison in Ireland engage with power relations within their prisons. Central to this study is the response of the imprisoned women to the identities ascribed to them and inscribed upon them by the powerful discourses already explored in this book, those of history, the media, management, and organisational and architectural discourses of the prisons.

6.1: In-cell sanitation in the women's prison in Limerick Prison (current accommodation)

In the reality of the Irish female prison, imprisoned women have few means through which to articulate a response to those discourses. As stated, the discourses are powerful, and many are distant. The women's loudest, their most prepared, most organised and most articulate responses to those discourses are in fact embedded in the manner in which each imprisoned woman occupies her own personal prison space. The most detailed, individual and personal articulation by the women of their own sense of their own identity was created by each of them, and performed by them, within their own personal prison space.

Through interviews, the women discussed those personal prison spaces and they analysed the photographs taken of their

6.2: A woman's room in the Dóchas Centre

rooms/cells (rooms in Mountjoy Prison, cells in Limerick Prison). In that analysis, the women considered and/or explained the significance for them of those spaces and the cultural artefacts they themselves displayed within those spaces. There is an expression of culture and identity, according to Collier and Collier, in the way in which people order their possessions, in the range of artefacts and in their placement in space.[4]

6.3: A woman's room in the Dóchas Centre

The women's presentations of self within those personal prison spaces are structured within power relations and they are manifest in two distinct discourses, one overt and one latent. The overt discourse is one of relational associational femininity, encompassing themes of home, family and relationships, myself in relation to others, myself in the world, and myself in relation to my world. The latent discourse is one of a power engagement; the women's experiences of power; and their use of their spaces in communicating with the different power bases of the prison. This discourse encompasses themes of power and control, themes of discipline, control, punishment and resistance. Bosworth writes that having agency and being an agent is about the ability to negotiate power.[5] However, while women in prison in Ireland are obliged to negotiate with the powerful discourses of their prisons, there is in all of these negotiations a power imbalance, one that is weighted very heavily against the women.

6.4: Window in a cell in Limerick Prison (accommodation 2002)

THE WOMEN'S PERSONAL PRISON SPACES

In the first years of the Dóchas Centre each woman imprisoned there was provided with a single private room. In 2010, due to over-crowding, bunk beds were introduced into some of the rooms. In Limerick Prison, each woman is given a place in a double occu-pancy cell; bunk beds have long been in place there. In these spaces the women serve their prison sentences. In these spaces they sleep, shower and change, dress, study, entertain their fellow prisoners and prison volunteers. The spaces when provided are furnished, the floor is covered and the room is painted. The women are permitted to use their own belongings, such as bed covers and bric-a-brac, to decorate their own personal space. Given this permission, the women cover every surface and space in their rooms and cells with expressions of themselves. They take possession of this prison space and they personalise it and feminise it. It is through this decoration of the spaces that these uniform prison spaces become individual signifying spaces, spaces filled with bricolage, rich in signifiers.

Within the women's personal prison spaces the critical signifiers in the bricolage of personal belongings were, for all of the women, emblems of family and friendship. The women's identities were grounded in notions of themselves in relation to others, grounded in relationships, relationships with their families and their friends. The artefacts the women arranged and displayed within the spaces were in fact material representations of relational, emotional ties. Baudrillard wrote of objects becoming spatial incarnations of emotional bonds.[6] In many cases the women's rooms, and especially their dressing tables, were in effect cultural shrines to home, family and friends. The artefacts that the women displayed were all association pieces; each piece was associated with a person, a place or an event; each piece was given to the woman by family members or friends. The sentiments aired by the women in relation to the artefacts were sentiments of association; association with people, family, friends and place, most often home. Fiona said:

> The most important things are my family photographs; they're all pictures of my family getting married, my sister getting married. And that box of make-up, I love that cos me Mam gave it to me for Christmas. And that Valentine card, I got that three years ago from a fellow I went out with for six years. That's history now, nothing there. I just like the card. My video tapes of family occasions are all important too.

The artefacts in the women's rooms were important only in that they assisted the women in relationships, in reminding them of their relation to others and their place in relation to the world. According to Maalouf, identity is in the first place a matter of symbols and appearances. There is, he wrote, 'a thread of affiliation linking me to the crowd'.[7] This thread of affiliation may be thick or thin, it may be strong or weak, but it is clear and easily recognisable to all who are sensitive on the subject of identity. Imprisoned women, with their criminal and prisoner identities firmly inscribed upon them by the discourses of the media, the criminal justice and penal systems, and the prisons' structures, are very sensitive on the subject of identity.

The analysis of the data gathered during the photo-elicitation interviews with the women clearly showed that the women use their own personal prison spaces and the artefacts they arrange and display within those spaces in performances of identity recuperation. Every aspect of their prison rooms and spaces was used by them to create spaces of relation and affiliation and personal identities steeped in friendship, family and home. Home, according to Baudrillard, means a regressive attachment to domestic relationships and habits.[8] Home for the women was a place to which they escaped from prison, and the escape route to home was for each of them in their own personal prison space.

In relation to her own room in the Dóchas Centre, Anna said:

> Well I like my little room; I can't say I don't like it, cos I do. When I come in here and close the door, well I think about home. I look at my pictures and my photographs and I just get away. I'm not here, you know? I like my little room and I change it around all the time. If I get something new, if I get a new flower or a new ornament, I'll want to change the whole room around to fit in with it. I change everything. I find that if I get a new thing, I'll start; now where will I put it. It's my room, my space, and I like it. It's my own little world.

As evidenced in her testimony, Anna's personal prison space provided her with shelter and a means of retreat. Her prison room was an entire and enclosed world full of signifiers of home and belonging. Each of the artefacts in the space was a spatial incarnation of an emotional bond, each one a separate thread of affiliation linking her, in Maalouf's terms, to the crowd.

The women, through their choice of and arrangement and display of artefacts within those spaces, were signifying to prison staff and authorities, and they were signifying to other prisoners and prison visitors. They were signifying their relational ways of being. Baudrillard wrote of objects within space as symbolisations.[9] He wrote of the emotional value of objects, of their 'presence',[10] and of our retreat into objects.[11] The artefacts displayed by the women served to make personal spaces for them of their prison spaces. Both the spaces and the artefacts within the spaces provided the women with shelter and with avenues of retreat. The loneliness of prison and the tensions of prison and the mourning that is an essential part of the prison experiences described by the women were all alleviated to some degree for them in those personal prison spaces. This was accomplished by the homeliness of their personal prison spaces and by the physical evidence of identity, of humanity, of human connection and belonging, signified for each of the women by each of the artefacts displayed.

Baudrillard writes of objects serving in a regulatory capacity with regard to everyday life, dissipating many neuroses and providing an outlet for all kinds of tensions and for energies that are in mourning.[12] This, he writes, is what gives objects their soul; it is this that makes them 'ours'. The objects and artefacts depicted in the photographs that were important to the women were the artefacts that belonged to them, as opposed to the artefacts and objects that belonged to the prison. The things that belonged to them were things that were given to them by family and friends, they were the association pieces.

The women talked all the time of home, and they talked of making their rooms or cells like home or homely. Many of the objects and artefacts the women arranged and displayed within their own spaces had come from home. The women talked a great deal about those things that had come from home. Those things from home were for the most part gifts which had been brought to the women in their prisons by family members and friends. The other artefacts the women displayed were gifts they received from other women, other prisoners, within the prison. There were also some artefacts that they made for themselves in the craft classes in the prison school.

Emma said: 'My posters, my ornaments and stuff are all from home. My room is comfortable now. It reminds me of my own room at home', while Anita, speaking of her things, declared:

> I like the cotton doilies. They make the cell look fancy ... yeah, it looks homely like. The leopard print throw, my Mum gave me that. The curtains on the window, my Mum had them made for home. She had an extra one made up to give to me.

Anna spoke of her cell:

It took me a bit of time to get my bits together; my Mum passed me in stuff from home. I've got posters, my own duvet from home and my own radio from home. I've got my own cushion. I made it in the [prison] school and I've got a big Bob Marley flag. My space is lovely now.

6.5: A woman's room in the Dóchas Centre

The artefacts in the women's rooms, as stated, were important only in that they assisted the women in relationships, in reminding them of their relations with others. This helped them maintain what was for them an acceptable sense of their place in the world. The artefacts evidenced and established both visibly and visually their place within familial and friendship ties and relations. The artefacts were,

6.6: Women's cell in Limerick Prison (accommodation 2002)

as a result, fundamental to the women's identities, their sense of self. They were essential to the women's sense of belonging. Miriam said:

> This basket here, it had real flowers in it. My daughter brought it for me the first time she came. The paintings of course are my son's. The dolphins he did for my birthday. Everything here was given to me by somebody. This picture, the little round thing, Eithne gave me. All the little bits and bobs, the little piggy on the thing, Margaret gave me that. The little corn dollies, or whatever, I got those from Joanne. The little elephants up there, I got from Maria.

Lily spoke of her cell:

> The most important things to me are my family photographs and the Mass cards and that memory card; that's my nephew who died two years ago. He was only a year and six months when he died. We keep him close. The cards from my family, the videotapes of family occasions, family weddings, they're all important.

As did Bridget:

> My tapestries are the most important thing to me. I did a tapestry for my neighbours because they help my husband with minding the children and that is a big help. I made a rug for my son, a Manchester United rug. He loved it. I took it home with me to give to him the day I went home. The pictures are important too. That drawing there, Janet, my daughter, made that for me for St Patrick's Day.

For Elizabeth, her family photographs and letters were the most important things, particularly her letters and 'the thing for holding letters' her son had made for her in school.

The women spoke of body lotions and powders, all brought into the prison for them by family members: 'all my shower stuff and things, stuff my sister brings into me. She comes every week, never misses, hail, rain or shine.' Sandra spoke of the things her mother brought to the prison for her: 'beauty things ... shampoo, conditioners, face creams, perfume, make up, nail polish, deodorant, wipes for your face, all that kind of stuff'.

PERFORMING IDENTITY

The women's personal prison spaces provided them with the stage on which to perform identity plays. With their carefully crafted and artistically articulated familial relational identities, the discourses the women engaged in, the discourses they created and developed around their own identities, were discourses of family and home, of relationships and friendships. These discourses of personal identity provided the women with powerful challenges to the spoiled identities ascribed to them by those powerful and distant discourses ascribing them with criminal and prisoner identities. Within their home-like personal spaces, the women used the artefacts and their arrangement and placement within those spaces as powerful signifiers of identity, as challenges and disruptions to the identities conferred on them by criminal and penal discourses.

The women used those signifiers of identity in re-presenting or re-positioning their own personal identities. Using their personal prison spaces as stages, the women were performing preferred identities. They were performing these identities for prison authorities and for other imprisoned women. Thus the women were, in Butler's terms, performatively constituting personal identities. These enactments of self with which the women were engaged constituted powerful challenges to the criminal and prisoner identities which had been ascribed to them and inscribed upon them by their prison experiences and by Ireland's criminal justice and penological systems. These performances of identity challenged also the spoiled identities ascribed to the women in media and public discourses.

The women in performing identities within their own personal prison spaces were performing recuperative identities. They understood that, within our world, assumptions and judgements are primarily made through inference. They understood that we are all participant observers of the social world, that the other participant observers, their audiences, inferred certain understandings from the performances with which they were presented. This is Goffman's stagecraft, his stage management. It is the dramaturgy of presenting self in everyday life.[13] The dramaturgy of the women, performed in their personal prison spaces, illustrates Butler's power of acting. Through their dramatic performances, the women were invoking convention through reiteration and citation. The citational and reiterative elements of the women's performances, through the association pieces they gathered and displayed, were feminine, familial and relational.

The women, with their ascribed and spoiled prisoner identities, each take control of their individual prison space and they use that space within which to practise and perform preferred identities. They practise and perform these identities within those spaces all the days of their prison sentences. In doing this they assert their opposition to the ascribed and spoiled 'prisoner' identities with which they have been discursively conferred. In their personal prison spaces the women create and perform complex and conventional feminine identities steeped in relational and familial ways of being.

While performativity is clearly often reactive, and agentic expression is proactive, and so both are sometimes thought to be incompatible, it is possible to interpret the activities of the women in creating recuperative displays of personal identity as evidence of both performativity and agency. The women within their spaces were, through performativity, engaged in agentic expressions of self. While Bosworth found in her research that imprisoned women are able to transform or challenge power relations from their embodied positions,[14] the research carried out for this book found women in prison in Ireland to be subject

6.7: Window in a woman's room in the Dóchas Centre

to patriarchal, androcentric and, indeed, militaristic penal regimes within which they were utterly controlled. The women's agency was largely subsumed into or stifled by the dominant punitive control structures of the prisons within which they lived their day-to-day lives. This day-to-day experience of imprisonment has been detailed and explained in this book. The expression of agency that was evident was in the performative manner with which the women presented themselves within their personal prison spaces.

THE GIFT CULTURE OF THE PRISONS

The association pieces, the objects and artefacts in the women's rooms, were part of the women's gift culture. Among the women, the giving and receiving of gifts established, or re-established and reinforced for them, their relationships with family and with other women in the prison. The gifts marked the esteem and affection within which the women are held. Ricoeur wrote of the justice of exchanges of reciprocity, as dialectics of self-esteem, of action and of affection.[15] One of the women, Laura, spoke of her possessions:

6.8: Bedside locker in a woman's room in the Dóchas Centre

That light is very important to me. My sister got it specially for me and it keeps me calm. I love to watch it at night-time. Those clay models are all important to me, all the travelling girls made them for me before they got out. I love them. Then all me films and videos, they're important cos we watch them together, me and the girls.

Elaine did likewise:

This picture of my friends I made in art class, and this cloth I laid on my table, this was a gift from another prisoner who was here; she got out. And all my soft toys, they are on my bed. I love them all. We make them in the soft toys class. The heart there, I got that from the girls for my birthday.

And also Geraldine:

That little chick, that's a toy I made in the soft toys class. I gave it to Marion's daughter when she came to visit. She liked it. And that hat with the flowers, I really like that. It was a present from Julie, downstairs. It means a lot to me.

Both Mauss[16] and Douglas[17] have written about the gift. Mauss writes of the continuous flow in all directions of presents given, accepted, reciprocated, obligatorily and out of self-interest, for

6.9: Dressing table in a woman's room in the Dóchas Centre

services rendered and through challenges and pledges.[18] The system of gifting in the women's prisons is a continuous flow in all directions of gifts given, accepted and reciprocated. It is for the women an essential part of the process of establishing and consolidating both identity and belonging within prison.

In addition to the gifts the women received from friends and family, and those they exchanged among themselves, in the interviews the women discussed the prison management's gift economy. The second system of gifting within the prisons is the gift system of staff and management. Douglas holds that there are no free gifts, that gift cycles engage persons in permanent commitments which articulate the dominant institutions.[19] Certainly this is the case within the gift economy of the prison's staff and management. Within that gift economy, imprisoned women are rewarded for conformity to prison rules, regulations and standards. Gifts within the remit of prison staff include cigarettes, sweets, crisps, chocolate and biscuits; they include extra toiletries, visits in the Dóchas Centre from one yard to the other, time spent in a friend's room, extra phone calls or longer phone calls. Gifts within the remit of management include money, new clothes and shoes, such as trainers and tracksuits, a new move to progressively less secure accommodation within the prison, and temporary release, days out or weekends at home.

One of the women, Lisa, spoke of the experience of being controlled within the prison's gift economy in the Dóchas Centre:

> Yeah, in here they have a hold over you. They move you in here, into a house with less control, and then every time you look sideways you're told you're in a privileged house, and this and that and the other. D'ye know what I mean? You're in a 'ten o'clock house', so you're free inside the house to move around until ten o'clock at night when they come to lock you in your room. You're in the ten o'clock house. Big swing! It's only another room.

Gift cycles are important elements of the relationships between prison staff and management and imprisoned women. The gift cycles are designed by staff to encourage conformity among imprisoned women. In addition, however, they often serve to secure otherwise insecure women in cycles of exchange and reciprocity. This helps promote self-esteem and self-confidence in those women. The gift cycles are designed, in part, to accomplish this. The gifts exchanged within the prison and the gifts the women receive from family and friends are part of complex cycles of exchange and reciprocity, and of love and support. These gift cycles frequently do generate experiences of well-being among the women.

Occasionally, the gift cycles the women engage in among themselves and with family and friends outside the prison can be detrimental, with negative consequences for the women involved and for the prison generally. This happens when the gift-giving culture within the prison is subverted, sometimes through manipulation, harassment and threats, to serve the prison's stealthy drug culture. Women in prison are vulnerable to manipulation, to bullying and to threats of violence, and to the reality of experiences of violence. In this way they can be forced to smuggle drugs into the prison. This can be done through hiding drugs, for example, in an artefact, or through an exchange during a visit from a friend or relative. It can happen on a trip outside the prison, to the courts or to hospital, or when a woman is allowed out on temporary release. It can be difficult for a woman to withstand the pressure that can be brought to bear on her to encourage her to engage in this kind of activity. Smuggled drugs in the prisons can substantially disrupt rehabilitative efforts in terms of drug addiction. The reality of the depth and strength of many of the women's addictions was detailed in previous chapters.

That being said, in general the prisons' gift cultures secure the women within social circles of belonging and provide the women with the power to generate and direct particular discourses of identity. Within the gift cultures cycles of exchange and reciprocity, the women situate themselves within complex relationships of love and support. Within these cycles, the gifts the women receive become, in Baudrillard's terms, spatial incarnations of emotional bonds. The artefacts that are gifted become material representations of the respect, esteem and love within which the women are held. As such, they are used by the women as props in their performances of identity, within which the women position themselves very firmly within discourses of relational, familial ways of being in the world. With these discursively produced and constantly reiterated performances of identity, the women continually challenge the spoiled identities assigned to them by the criminal justice system and inscribed upon them by media, public and penal discourses.

The discourses of personal identity engaged in by women in prison in Ireland are both performative and agentic. In Ireland, imprisoned women are given personal spaces within which they spend much of their time. In expressions of agency, the women use the spaces dramaturgically for particular performative expressions of identity. Through these performances, the women affect some control over their prison environment and their experiences of it. The discourses of personal identity which they develop and perpetuate within prison are built around their connections to family and friends. They are expressive of the women's familial relational ways of being in the world.

The women's capacity to endure the controlling punitive environment of the prisons is strengthened by their locating themselves within these discourses. These performative identities function for the women in a recuperative manner. They help them challenge the prisoner identities ascribed to them. Women in prison in Ireland use their personal prison space performatively to generate and promulgate particular discourses of personal identity. These personal identities are agentic identities founded upon relational, familial ways of being.

NOTES

1. J. Butler, *Gender Trouble: Feminism and the Subversion of Identity* (New York: Routledge, 1990).
2. Ibid., p.24.
3. M. Bosworth, *Engendering Resistance: Agency and Power in the Women's Prisons* (Aldershot: Ashgate, 1999).
4. J. Collier Jr and M. Collier, *Visual Anthropology: Photography as a Research Method* (Albuquerque: University of New Mexico Press, 1986), p.45.
5. Bosworth, *Engendering Resistance*, p.3.
6. J. Baudrillard, *The System of Objects* (London: Verso, 1996), p.16.
7. A. Maalouf, *On Identity* (London: Harvill Press, 2000), p.100.
8. Baudrillard, *The System of Objects*, p.87.
9. Ibid., p.16.
10. J. Baudrillard, 'The System of Collecting', in J. Elsner and R. Cardinal (eds), *Cultures of Collecting* (London: Reaktion, 1994), pp.7–24.
11. Baudrillard, *The System of Objects*, p.19.
12. Ibid., p.90.
13. E. Goffman, *The Presentation of Self in Everday Life* (London: Penguin, 1990).
14. Bosworth, *Engendering Resistance*, p.156.
15. P. Ricoeur, *Oneself as Another* (Chicago: Chicago University Press, 1994), p.330.
16. M. Mauss, *The Gift* (London: Routledge Classics, 2002).
17. M. Douglas, *Risk and Blame: Essays in Cultural Theory* (London: Routledge, 1992).
18. Mauss, *The Gift*, p.37.
19. Douglas, *Risk and Blame*, p.157.

Chapter Seven

Conclusions: The Experiences of Women in Prison in Ireland

The book set out to explore, historically, socially and spatially, women's experiences of imprisonment in Ireland. The focus of the book, in line with the focus in recent years of studies of women in prison internationally, was on the identities and subjectivities of imprisoned women, on the subject positioning of the women within historical, social and spatial discourses. The research conducted on women in prison both in Ireland and internationally has established that women generally commit little crime in society; that women constitute a minority of prison populations; and that it is generally poverty that drives women into criminal activity and into prison.

This book examined the manner in which women experience the Irish female prison and the manner in which those experiences served to shape representations and constructions of their identities. A comprehensive critical ethnographic study of women in prison in Ireland has been presented. Through that, an understanding has been developed of the imprisoned women, of their lives and circumstances, of the crimes for which they were imprisoned, of the prison sentences imposed upon them, of the penal institutions within which they were incarcerated, of their lived experiences of those institutions, and of the identities and subjectivities they developed within that lived experience. Throughout the book different discourses have been examined, both historical and contemporary, and the manner in which, within those discourses, Ireland's imprisoned women were situated. The life experiences and prison experiences of women imprisoned in Ireland were explored. The identities ascribed to the women in the different discourses were examined. A particular concern was the manner in which the lived experience of female prison space shapes imprisoned women's identities.

Implicit in the concept of identity, as outlined in Chapter 1, are issues of power and control, the degree of control we have over who we are and who we might become and the power we have in shaping the self, the society within which we live and the wider social framework within which we act. This exploration of the women's identities is grounded in the discourses defining the women's prison experiences, and it is grounded in the women's own words – the words they used to explain their life and prison experiences, and within those, their personal identities and their senses of self.

This book, as is appropriate in ethnographic work, was concerned with developing accounts of lived experience from the perspective of those living the experience, in order to develop an understanding of people's lives from within. The book is a descriptive analysis of the everyday world of the Irish female prison. It is, to use Geertz's term, a thick description of the experiences and identities of women imprisoned in Ireland.[1] A variety of methods was used to gather information for this book. Among the sources used were archives, newspaper articles, photographs, interviews (taped and manually recorded), and objects from the field. In conducting the research there was at all times an awareness of the problems and pitfalls potentially inherent in ethnographic research and in researching vulnerable groups. The book is a feminist study; it developed from social relationships with the women studied. The essential focus is on making women's experiences visible.

MAIN FINDINGS

The Irish female prison is an institution of Irish society and its history and culture reflects the history and culture of Irish society. The class system and Victorian, Catholic, Free State, and early Irish Republican constructions of femininity have all had profound influences on women's experiences of imprisonment in Ireland. Contemporarily women in Ireland commit little crime, and that crime is generally minor. In 2008, there were in total 1,484 women committed to prison: 676 of those were imprisoned under sentence, 552 were on remand and 256 were in violation of immigration regulations and were in prison awaiting deportation.[2] Most of the women committed annually to prison come and go very quickly and, individually, make very little impact on the prison. Of the women sentenced and on remand, about 60 per cent are Irish nationals and 40 per cent foreign nationals. The Irish nationals come primarily from Dublin or from particular cities around the country, most have chronic addiction problems, many are homeless or regularly experience homelessness. The foreign nationals come from different countries. Those among them who spend any length of time in prison are serving sentences for drug trafficking. Currently there are at any time about 130 women in prison in Ireland.

This book shows that prison regime and management procedures in Ireland's women's prisons reproduce and intensify women's powerlessness and inequality, while the friendships women form in prison are among the main supports they have to sustain them through their imprisonment experiences. The Irish criminal justice and penal systems are shown in this book to be patriarchal, and there are substantial concerns regarding the manner in which women are dealt with within this system. Over half of the female committals to prison each year are committed on remand. Heidensohn, in her work, has shown that lengthy remands are imposed upon women in order to give the judiciary time to amass reports on female offenders, who they then frequently 'punished' more. Most of the women are imprisoned for stealing, and the next most commonly occurring offences are public order offences such as being drunk and disorderly, being in breach of the peace, being a danger to self, soliciting/prostitution, failure to produce identification, vagrancy and begging. In recent years the numbers of women imprisoned in Ireland on murder or manslaughter charges were very few. In fact, until the first decade of the twenty-first century, no more than three or four women were imprisoned in any year since 1928 for the offences of murder or manslaughter.

It is clear that within the Irish criminal court system men get more chances than women, and men before the courts in Ireland would not receive custodial sentences for offences for which a woman might be imprisoned for months. This gendered approach to criminal justice is frequently attributed to a culture of protectiveness towards women, associated with the chivalry concept and male paternalism. It may be, however, that it evidences quite the opposite. It is possible that it evidences a cultural disregard for extremely marginalised women, a disregard which facilitates the inappropriate imprisonment of homeless women, of women with mental illnesses, women with drug and alcohol addictions, and women suffering the effects of physical, mental and sexual abuse. Such women are regularly sentenced to imprisonment by the judiciary in Ireland because prison is the only institution in Ireland obligated to accommodate them and care for them. Such women are regularly needlessly criminalised and imprisoned in Ireland simply because there is no place else for them.

Young Irish addicts who are sent to prison tend to be imprisoned regularly for short sentences; their lives are generally chaotic, many are destitute, living lives of extreme marginality. These findings are similar to the findings of Carmody and McEvoy, who in 1996 found the population of the women's prison at Mountjoy Prison to be an extremely marginal population with chronic addiction problems. These chronically addicted women are the 'petty, persistent offenders' of the women's prisons, the women who constantly come and go, the women who place most demands on management and staff.

The non-addicted women are the 'trustees' of the prisons. They tend to be older women serving relatively long sentences and many are first-time offenders. They live relatively well-ordered, structured lives and are relatively well educated and resourced. These 'trustees', with their relatively substantial prison sentences, settle in to prison, making long-term arrangements for their lives outside. They attend the school and engage with the developmental structures of the prison. Among prison trustees are the foreign nationals who spend long periods of time in prison. These are generally international drug couriers; they have in recent years represented more than one quarter of the female prison population. These women can serve from four to six years, and these long prison sentences impact in a very pronounced way on the statistical profile of women in prison in Ireland.

The tiny minority that is the population of women in prison in Ireland has been established in this book as being representative of the type of deviance that is criminalised in Ireland, where property and drug-related crimes are seen as being allied to the public image of the typical criminal.[3] The Irish legal system was seen in this book, as Fennel found in her 1993 analysis,[4] to be partisan in nature, to be informed by stereotypical assumptions and myths regarding female roles, by myths and images of femininity which were shown to disadvantage women. The Irish criminal justice system was shown to treat women leniently when they conformed to their stereotypical roles and to treat women harshly when they deviated from those roles, when they moved beyond the boundaries of gender-appropriate behaviour. In fact, it is conventional women, women living lives deemed by patriarchal standards to be conventional who are, as was shown by Carlen,[4] treated leniently by the judiciary.

HISTORICAL CONSTRUCTIONS AND REPRESENTATIONS OF IDENTITY

Over the last 200 years women have been imprisoned in Ireland generally for offences of a petty, personal or sexual nature. This is the situation currently in the twenty-first century, as it was in the twentieth century and in the nineteenth century. In the 1850s more women were imprisoned in Ireland than in any other jurisdiction in the western world. In 1856, when the worst effects of the famine had abated (see Chapter 2), women constituted 45 per cent of the 48,446 people committed for trial. In the late twentieth century, however, fewer women were imprisoned in Ireland than in any other jurisdiction in the western world; by 1950 there were on average only 100 women being held daily in Irish prisons, and this daily average was down to twenty by 1960 and fourteen by 1970. The extremely small numbers of women imprisoned in the mid-decades of the twentieth century was a factor of mass emigration, and of the essentially theocratic nature of the Irish state. It was related to constructions of the feminine within the Catholic Church and consequently within the Irish state. The Catholic Church had a profound effect on the position of women in Irish society throughout most of the twentieth century, during which time the church controlled every aspect of Irish society and assumed the competence to comment on, guide and shape all aspects of Irish culture. The church controlled the state and through its construction of the feminine within the ideology of Mariology it controlled the family. Women within Irish Catholic culture were socialised to be private and domestic. Throughout that period women were policed by their families and their communities; deviant women were disciplined in institutions other than prisons.

Over the past two hundred years, the nature of the construction of the identities of women in prison is evidenced by the nature of the institutions within which women were imprisoned and by the manner in which, over that time period, women used those institutions. Historically in Ireland women were imprisoned in local gaols, in convict prisons and in convents. Thousands sheltered in those institutions; they sheltered intermittently and they sheltered for long periods. Some women used prison as a means of escape to another life, frequently taking their families with them from prison to the colonies. Most of the women who were imprisoned were destitute. Many behaved in ways that placed them beyond the bounds of ordinary society, women who contravened conventions of normal femininity and female sexuality. Some were destitute women imprisoned for stealing; a few, generally working-class women, were convicted of serious offences such as murder.

Women in Irish society lived restricted, vulnerable lives constructed around, formerly, Victorian and, latterly, Catholic norms of the feminine within which the feminine was constructed as private, dependent, chaste, domestic and familial. Women who stepped outside of these roles or challenged these orthodoxies risked losing the support of their society and ultimately social ostracism. The propensity of women, more so than men, to shelter in penal institutions was one of the most critical patterns identified in this book. Other critical patterns evident are the petty, personal or sexual nature of the offences of women, and the recidivism rates among them. This book has established women's engagement with criminality in Ireland to be generally trivial. The remarkable recidivism rates among imprisoned women were shown to be a feature of the repeated imprisonment of populations of extremely marginal women for public order rather than criminal offences. This feature of women's imprisonment in Ireland still holds today. This book shows how the numbers of women in prison expand with deteriorating social and economic conditions and contract when these conditions improve.

Women's imprisonment in Ireland has long been perceived as a lower-class phenomenon and it has long been shaped by religious principles. In the nineteenth century, middle-class women, under the patronage of upper-class women under the patronage of upper-class men, shaped the prison experiences of working-class and destitute women. Christian philosophies informed this work: the Quaker philosophies of the reformers, Sir Walter Crofton and Elizabeth Fry, the Protestant philosophies of the Hibernian Ladies Association, and the Catholic philosophies of the Mercy and Charity Sisters. These individuals and groups controlled the prison experiences of women and shaped those experiences to facilitate expressions of what they deemed to be appropriate feminine penality, repentance and restoration. This book demonstrates, as Luddy did in her work,[5] that within their Christian traditions, these groups constructed for imprisoned women penal experiences shaped by class principles and ideals and particular notions of femininity.

In the nineteenth century, women's imprisonment was to be entirely separate from men's imprisonment. Women in prison were to be attended by other women, who were in turn managed by men. Women within prison were easily disciplined. Separation and silence were said to work particularly well with women. Imprisoned women were said to develop when given any opportunity to do so. This contention that imprisoned women were easily disciplined contradicts assertions that imprisoned women were really wild and hard to handle. Most of the women conformed and engaged with the structures of the prison. The evidence of this book suggests that particular populations of women were difficult to manage, usually the groups of most extremely marginal women.

Through history, different voices represented imprisoned women differently. The penal reformer Mary Carpenter held that women prisoners were the most difficult to manage and their reformation far more difficult than the reformation of men. Mary Carpenter published a book on imprisoned women and her remarks have been widely quoted.[6] They are the remarks of a profoundly Christian nineteenth-century woman referring to women imprisoned at that time for prostitution. Yet they are often represented as referring to the general population of women in prison. In this way, these remarks have become fundamental to discourses of women in prison. Occasionally quoted is the 1880 comment of the then medical officer of Mountjoy Female Prison on the paroxysms of passion and violence of women in prison, which he said rendered restraint necessary. The medical officer was referring in his comments to a minority 'irresponsible class' of female prisoners rather than the general population of the female prison. Less quoted are the remarks of Delia Liddiwell, who was a superintendent of Mountjoy Female Prison in the nineteenth century, and those of the nineteenth-century inspectors general. Ms Liddiwell, commenting on the group of women she deemed most difficult to deal with, constructed their behaviour as evidence of an inclination to reckless mischievousness rather than vice. The inspectors general of prisons attributed women's criminal dispositions to extreme poverty, and they judged as trivial women's breaches of prison discipline.

It was not until the end of the twentieth century that the actual experience of imprisonment came to be deemed responsible for some if not much of the negative behaviours of imprisoned women. In recent years Carlen in her work suggested that responsibility for depressed or bizarre behaviour among imprisoned women lies perhaps in the impact of the imprisonment experience itself on the women,[7] while Sim suggests that self-injury among imprisoned women is a manifestation of the internalised anger and powerlessness the women experience in relation to their imprisonment.[8]

For 200 years women have been imprisoned in Ireland for larceny, mostly petty larceny, and for public order offences. They were and still are committed to prison as vagrants, drunkards and beggars, and were and still are divided into two classes fundamentally, good women and bad women. In the nineteenth century, a first-class of imprisoned women, dressed in a relatively fine dress, engaged in light work throughout their prison sentence. Their dress, deportment and activities all served to signify their relative sensitivity and civility. At the same time, a second-class of imprisoned women, dressed in a coarser dress, engaged in heavy work within the prisons. Their dress, deportment and activities all served to signify their relative coarseness and general lack of civility.[9]

This historical class division of women imprisoned in Ireland demonstrates how penal experiences were historically constructed around the performative, the performance of identity by imprisoned women and the manner in which they represented themselves and their identities within prison. The ultimate evidence of performativity in terms of constructions and representations of self within prison is in the manner in which imprisoned women assiduously sought on discharge from prison the shelter of the convent, and the lengths to which the women were prepared to go in terms of the selves they presented within prison in order to secure that shelter.

In the twentieth century, constructions and representations of the population of the women's prison were shaped by the imprisonment of political women, suffragettes and republican women; by the continued imprisonment and criminalisation of women for public order offences; by the establishment of the Irish state and the close connection between the Catholic Church and that state; and by the power and influence of the Catholic Church in Irish society generally. Throughout the twentieth century, the influence of Catholicism on the female prison was critical, in particular the church's normative views on gender, the church's control of sexuality, and the role of the church in maintaining patriarchy.

Over the twentieth century, up to the 1980s, the entire Irish prison population contracted. During this time there was an extraordinary reduction in the numbers of women imprisoned. Over the twentieth century as a whole there were, in fact, three notable reductions in the female prison population: the first happened in the early decades of the century when in 1914–15 only 7,773 women were committed to prison, 33 per cent of the total prison population. This reduction was attributed to developing social standards, a developing economy, and to new legislation which had been introduced to allow time for the payment of fines. The second substantial reduction in the numbers of women imprisoned occurred over the middle decades of the century. This was attributable to the control exercised over women within Ireland's theocratic state and private patriarchy and by the state's diminishing population, as people, and particularly women, emigrated. The third significant reduction was seen in the 1980s. At this time the female prison population was very small, and included a substantial number of women with HIV infection.

The trend of diminishing numbers of female prisoners began to reverse in the 1980s with the emerging impact of globalisation on the prison system. This came about through the impact of the global trade in illegal drugs, and the subsequent imposition of substantial prison sentences on female international drug traffickers.

In the 1980s the female prison population doubled, from twenty to forty. In the following decade plans were made to build a new women's prison that could accommodate seventy-nine women, twice the number the old wing in Mountjoy accommodated, and in 1999 the Dóchas Centre duly opened.

At the end of the twentieth century, as at the start of the nineteenth, imprisoned Irish women were generally destitute women imprisoned for public order offences or larceny. Over the 200 years of this study, women on the margins of Irish society used prostitution and petty larceny as survival strategies. They used alcoholism and drugs as escape strategies and used penal institutions for shelter, survival and development. Women in prison in Ireland were generally accommodated in the worst conditions available. Those conditions were so bad that they prompted, in both the nineteenth and twentieth centuries, the building of large, new dedicated women's prisons.

CONTEMPORARY CONSTRUCTIONS AND REPRESENTATIONS OF IDENTITY

Contemporarily, while there are substantial differences between the architectural and organisational dimensions of the two women's prisons, Limerick Prison and the Dóchas Centre, there are very many similarities. The staff of each prison, both discipline and civilian, receive the same quasi-militaristic training. The emphasis is on physical fitness and appropriate standards of presentation for the uniform and for the uniformed officer. Discipline is paramount in both prisons, and all considerations within them – social, developmental and personal – are secondary to the security considerations of the regimes. The regimes in operation in both prisons are hierarchical; the prisoners are in every sense subject to the staff. One of the unique features of the Irish female prison is the relationships between the staff and the imprisoned women. The population of young Irish women who come and go from the prison are frequently from two, three or more generations of prison experience, and members of staff of the prison know the women, the women's mothers, their aunts and sometimes their grandmothers and their grandaunts.

Destitute women continue to this day to shelter in the prisons. This is evident in the experience outlined in the first chapter of this book of the young woman who, when removed from the Dóchas Centre, tried in desperation to scale the walls of the prison to get back inside. She was subsequently arrested for trying to break into the prison, spent a night in a police station and was back in the prison the next day. The authorities in Ireland continue to regularly imprison destitute women, needlessly criminalising them. The structure that is the women's prison is used inappropriately. This is evident in the large numbers of women sentenced to periods of days in prison and in the problematising and criminalising of the responses of individual women to the overwhelming difficulties they experience in their lives. It is possible that the designation 'prison' is inappropriate for the institution that is the Irish female prison. The Irish female prison is currently variously used as a shelter, a hospice, a drug and alcohol treatment centre, a psychiatric hospital, a deportation centre and a women's education, training and development centre.

'Experts' on women in prison in Ireland were shown to construct notions of identity in terms of women in prison around the most marginal population in the prison – the impoverished, malnourished, uneducated, homeless, ill and addicted. The women, as shown in this book, were identified as prisoners first; they were feminine in expression and representation, and their feminine engagement with the prison, its systems and structures, was essential in terms of their securing the prison's gifts. The women's feminine representations of self facilitated their engagement with the patriarchal penal system within which they were confined. The professionals working in the women's prisons manage the women. They pity the women and they coax, cajole and ultimately coerce them into co-operating with the prisons' systems and conforming to the prisons' rules. Within expert discourses, lack of self-esteem among imprisoned women is frequently highlighted. Never highlighted are the degradations in the system within which the women are imprisoned. The structured powerlessness of imprisoned women and the ritual degradations to which the women are subjected are rarely if ever reflected in these expert discourses.

Contemporarily, imprisoned women are represented within expert discourses as ill, physically and mentally, as being in need of therapy. They are said to be lacking in discipline, control, routine and structure in their lives. Women prisoners were represented by some professionals as more difficult to work with than male prisoners, as hysterical and less in control. Foucault represented the professional gaze as fundamental to the powerful permanent petty tribunals constantly judging and punishing prisoners. Women in prison exist under a networked regime of constant surveillance. They are held in safe, controlled custody. Any negative behaviour on their part is pathologised. The women are very quickly placed on observation or they are taken to the pads to be stripped and held for observation. The healthcare provision of the Irish female prison is provided within a disciplined regime.

The media gaze is fundamental to public perceptions of women in prison. Within the popular narratives of identity and women in prison in Ireland promulgated by the Irish press, Ireland's imprisoned women were represented in a partial, hostile, indeed mythical, manner. The press represented the women as sad, mad or bad. In particular, the bad women were women who exceeded the bounds of gender-appropriate behaviour. In general the press in Ireland ignores the women's prisons and the women imprisoned within them. When it does report on them, it reports on the most extreme cases. The discourse of danger, and the sad, mad and/or bad popular narratives promulgated in the press of women in prison in Ireland have implications for the political and public perceptions of those women. The public develop their perceptions of the prisons and the women imprisoned within them from these media representations. Contemporarily, women in prison in Ireland are all held in secure prisons. This is despite the fact the majority of women imprisoned in Ireland are there for minor offences or public order offences. The conclusion that may be drawn is that the mad and bad representations of imprisoned women in the press in Ireland has produced a discourse of danger around Ireland's imprisoned women, and this discourse of danger has had the effect of generating penal policy which provides for the imprisonment of nonviolent female petty offenders behind the high walls, wire and fences of secure prisons.

CONSTRUCTIONS AND REPRESENTATIONS OF SELF

The women generally felt that their experiences of criminality and penality degraded them and their femininity. They believed that these degraded prisoner identities were socially more damaging for women than for men. Women in prison in Ireland are emphatically familially oriented. Most, although idealising heterosexuality and heterosexual relationships, are single. They are not in significant relationships. Very few expressed any interest in sex or of deriving any pleasure from sex and there was little sexual activity in the prisons. This may be related to Ireland's history of Catholic habitus and the suppression within that of female sexuality, or perhaps it is a result of the women's life experiences. Radical feminists suggest that heterosexuality is compulsory for women in patriarchal societies, and that women within heterosexual relationships emotionally, materially and sexually service men.

The women who were addicts, two thirds of those interviewed, constructed their identities around their addictions. Their addictions isolated them, rendered their lives chaotic, and rendered them vulnerable to homelessness and to physical and sexual exploitation. Nearly half of those interviewed had suffered abuse in their lives and these women were predominantly the addicts. Many of the addicted and homeless women sheltered in the prison. They regarded it as a refuge. For these women, coming into prison is a regular and fairly normal activity.

Within prison, the women constructed or re-constructed their personal identities within powerful signifying penal discourses. The women's personal identities were shaped and reshaped within these discourses. Their prisoner identities developed within powerful defining narratives and discourses of identity, the discourses of the gazes to which women in prison are subject. These discourses develop narratives of identity and constantly communicate them to imprisoned women through the structures of the prison, through the women's reiterative experiences of the prison's signs, symbols and rituals. Sooner or later imprisoned women settle into their prison neighbourhood, and sooner or later hear themselves interpellated within the discourses of the prisons. Sooner or later they each came to recognise themselves within those interpellations.

For the populations of mature, non-addicted women, the prison was a place of public shaming and punishment, a controlling and degrading environment. For them, the experience of being imprisoned was a shocking, terrifying ordeal. For all women, the process of becoming a prisoner is short and compelling. It is through this short process, a process which is, to use Finkelstein's term,[10] a degradation ritual, that the women's identities are subsumed into prisoner identities. It is in this process of induction into prison that the discourses of the prison, the rituals and signs of the prison, begin the reiterative process of ascribing prisoner identities to the women. It is in this way, through reiterated degrading prison experiences, that the identity of female prisoner is indelibly ascribed to the imprisoned women and the female prisoner is produced.

All of the women accepted the structures, signs, symbols and rituals of the prison. They became to some degree used to the punitive, psychiatrising signs and symbols of the prisons, the surveillance, the rules, the restraints, the referents for control and referents for insanity, the stripping and searching and the padded cells. The women discussed these signs in terms of their own identities as recalcitrant women, as imprisoned women, or as ill women. The women experienced prison as a male institution; they understood themselves to be deviant women, who were being disciplined within male-ordered and male-structured penal institutions. The women experienced their disciplining publicly. They felt exposed, even within their seclusion in prison, by the media. They believed the media coverage of the prisons and imprisoned women to be unfair, invasive and untrue. They believed that the general public constructs imprisoned women as dangerous, degenerate deviants and they believed the media to be responsible for this construction.

Identity is a performance. It is an ongoing or perpetual performance undertaken in response to a need to belong. It is a performance that becomes particularly critical where belonging is challenged. Challenges to belonging, in terms of identity, come from hostile defining discourses within which subjectivities are constructed. All of the women experienced the prison as a controlled and controlling environment, and all felt obliged to engage with the prison and its structures. They all felt degraded by many of the experiences they had in prison, they felt that the prison undermined their personal senses of identity. Many believed their femininity was undermined by the prison, some that the prison undermined their sense of themselves. All of the women accepted the prison's referents for control and its referents of insanity; they accepted these referents in their own constructs of their own identities as imprisoned women.

Within prison the women construct and represent themselves as caring, familial, relational and heterosexual. As with their historical counterparts, women currently imprisoned tend to have many responsibilities but few resources. This study shows that contemporary sociological theories of identity, agency, freedom, self-cultivation, self-actualisation and self-expression are far from universal. Most of the women imprisoned in Ireland are living narrow, essential, vulnerable life narratives in circumstances of desperation and/or destitution and/or addiction. Women in prison in Ireland are established in this book as being defined by class and family. They are subject to the structures of society, to the power and controls of the prison, and to the discourses and narratives that define them.

Within their personal prison spaces, the women, mindful of the identities ascribed to them by the discourses of the criminal justice and penal systems, develop their own powerful discourses of self. All of the personal prison spaces of the imprisoned women reflected the gender of the occupants. All the rooms and cells were feminine; they evidenced their occupant's engagement with feminine culture. All of the spaces were full of the personal items and bric-a-brac of the women's lives – clothes, photographs, ornaments, and beauty products. These artefacts evidenced the femininity of the women and the particular expressions of femininity the women, within their personal prison spaces, presented and performed. The women's rooms reflected their feminine and familial identities, identities steeped in relational ways of being. The centrality of familialism in the women's lives was evident in the central placing within their spaces of family photographs and mementoes. The women's rooms were full of artefacts that reminded them of home, of family, of belonging.

These personal spaces are the only spaces within the prison which each individual woman could control. The women used these spaces to represent themselves to the prison, to prison staff and prison visitors. This use by the women of the space was an expression of agency. The curtailment of agency is evident in the feminine and familial expressions of self which the women presented. The femininity of the women's personal prison spaces reflected contemporary popular feminine culture. It also reflected the expressions and representations of femininity sanctioned by the patriarchal nature of the space within which the representations were manifest, Irish female prison space. The women's presentations of self were performative. The women within their personal prison spaces presented identities that would meet with the approval of the contained, controlled and restrained patriarchal quasi-militaristic hierarchical regimes within which they were imprisoned.

DISCOURSE AND IDENTITY AND WOMEN IN PRISON IN IRELAND

The women's subjectivities are formed within discourses which transmit cultural beliefs about women, about the normal and the feminine. Within these discourses the women are disciplined into social conformity, into appropriate feminine familial and domestic roles. Women imprisoned in Ireland live their day-to-day lives immersed in ideological signs, rituals and practices that are designed to help shape them into appropriate social subjects. In their lives, the women are socialised and acculturated into particular roles. Within prison, they are further interpellated into those roles and they recognise themselves within those interpellations. It is in this manner that the Irish female prison population is produced and indeed reproduced. It is on this basis that the legitimacy of the Irish female prison can be questioned, on the basis of its reproductive capacity. This book evidences the inability of the Irish criminal justice system to distinguish between support and punishment; its inability to distinguish between poverty and crime, a feature of British criminal justice highlighted by Carlen.[11] This book also evidences within the Irish criminal justice system, the 'hidden defeat of law by order', a flaw of French criminal justice highlighted by Foucault.[12] The reproductive structures of the Irish female prison are the ideologies and hegemonic belief systems which, with their seductive interpellative powers, are thoroughly naturalised and deeply embedded in the consciousness of individuals. Within these structures, the subject is not immediately produced, but reiteratively produced.

Control over who we are, the power to shape subjectivity, identity and the self, is situated in powerful signifying ideological discourses which shape and circulate meaning and truth. The control of self and the power of shaping self for women in prison in Ireland is in fact separate from self and situated in the powerful discourses which shape identity. It is situated in the manner in which these powerful discourses create and circulate meaning and truth. In the women's prisons, power is circular but circulating only within certain circles. Meaning is circulating in all circles, but the power to create or generate meaning is vested in particular circles. This is evident in the lack of discursive struggle, in the relatively uniform representations and presentations of the identities of women in prison in Ireland of the various discourses explored. This uniformity evidences the subject positioning within dominant hegemonic ideologies of women in prison in Ireland.

FINAL WORDS

In February 2004, the minister for justice, equality and law reform announced that the new women's prison, the Dóchas Centre, was to be demolished. The site on which it stands, with the rest of Mountjoy Prison, was to be sold for development. The money raised from the sale was to fund the building of a new super-prison on a greenfield site, twenty miles from Dublin city centre. The new prison was to accommodate the three populations of Mountjoy Prison, the men, the women, and the young offenders. The Dóchas Centre represents the realisation of a vision for women in prison shared by some officials in the Prison Service, by governor John Lonergan and the management and staff of the women's prison at Mountjoy, and by two successive female ministers for justice, Nora Owen and Máire Geoghegan-Quinn. The Dóchas Centre, which opened in 1999, cost £13 million (€16.5 million) to build.

The downturn in the Irish economy, and in the global economy, interrupted the plans for the new prison, so for now the women remain in the Dóchas Centre. In April 2010, Kathleen McMahon resigned from her post as governor of the Dóchas Centre, following thirty-three years in the Irish Prison Service. In her resignation letter, which was reproduced in full in *The Irish Times*, she wrote that her role in the prison had been undermined, that there was a serious lack of consultation between the Irish Prison Service and key staff in the prisons. She added that the progressive regime which had been established in the Dóchas Centre was being destroyed through chronic overcrowding, with up to 137 women being accommodated in the prison; the prison was designed to accommodate seventy-nine women. Ms McMahon wrote that she feared that the self-mutilation, bullying and depression that had characterised women's imprisonment when the women were held on a wing of St Patrick's Institution in the 1980s and 1990s before the Dóchas Centre was built would become once again a defining feature of women's imprisonment in Ireland. In June 2010, John Lonergan retired from the Irish Prison Service after forty-two years' service; he had been governor of Mountjoy Prison for twenty-six years. On retiring, John Lonergan criticised the current penal system in Ireland and said that he shared Kathleen McMahon's concerns regarding the Dóchas Centre.

As this book goes to press there are plans to move the administrative function out of the Dóchas Centre so that the administration space can be converted into dormitories to provide accomodation for a further 70 female prisoners; this will bring the official capacity of the Dóchas Centre up to 175 imprisoned women. A further 14 places are to be provided in the women's prison in Limerick Prison, bringing the total number of women imprisoned there to 34. These plans for expansion mean that, at the end of 2010, Ireland's two women's prisons will have a capacity for 209 imprisoned women.

NOTES

1. C. Geertz, *The Interpretation of Cultures* (London: Fontana, 1993), p.9.
2. Irish Prison Service, *Irish Prison Service Annual Report 2008*, available at http://www.irishprisons.ie/Publications-Annual_Reports.htm
3. C. McCullagh, 'Getting the Criminals We Want: The Social Production of the Criminal Population', in P. Clancy, S. Drudy, K. Lynch and L. O'Dowd (eds), *Irish Society: Sociological Perspectives* (Dublin: Institute of Public Administration, 1995), pp.410–31.
4. P. Carlen, *Women, Crime and Poverty* (Milton Keynes: Open University Press, 1988), p.10.
5. M. Luddy, *Women and Philanthropy in Nineteenth-Century Ireland* (Cambridge: Cambridge University Press, 1995).
6. M. Carpenter, *Reformatory Prison Discipline: As Developed by the Rt. Hon. Sir Walter Crofton, in the Irish Convict Prisons* (London: Longman, 1872).
7. P. Carlen, 'Psychiatry in Prisons: Promises, Premises, Practices and Politics', in P. Millar and N. Rose (eds), *The Power of Psychiatry* (Cambridge: Polity, 1986), pp.249–51.
8. J. Sim, '"We Are Not Animals, We Are Human Beings": Prisons, Protests and Politics in England and Wales, 1969–1990', *Social Justice*, 18, 3 (1991), pp.107–29.
9. N. Elias, *The Civilising Process* (Oxford: Blackwell, 2000).
10. E. Finkelstein, 'Status Degradation and Organisational Succession in Prison', *British Journal of Sociology*, 47, 4 (1996), pp.671–83.
11. Carlen, *Women, Crime and Poverty*.
12. J. Faubion (ed.), *Power: The Essential Works of Michel Foucault, 1954–1984, Volume 3* (London: Penguin Books, 2001), p.xxx.

Appendix

Overview of the Research Process

This book is a description of the experiences and identities of women imprisoned in Ireland, a study of the contemporary collective processes within the everyday world of the Irish female prison. It is an account of a critical ethnographic study, concerned with developing accounts of lived experience from the perspective of those living it. The commitment was to understanding people's lives from within.

The study conducted was a feminist study. Feminist ways of knowing, of establishing knowledge, emphasise an explication of the process and context of knowledge making. Feminist research methodologies posit gender as a fundamental theoretical concept; within feminist methodology, social scientists have argued for a sociology for and by women. The term feminism came into regular use in language with a political meaning in the 1890s with feminists' concerns regarding the political and social rights of women. Feminists today are still concerned with women's political and social rights but also with the female experience, including the experience of womanhood.

The research conducted for this book examined the experiences of imprisoned women and the impact of the different discourses shaping their identities. It was conducted in an attempt to make up for the absence of research on the experiences of women imprisoned in Ireland.

Epistemologically, feminist methodology focuses on the ways we use to know what it is we know. Alienated knowledge is knowledge produced without any account of the social context of its production. Feminists struggle with issues of power and control and they are fundamentally concerned with the essential recognition of the 'subjectivity' of research participants. Feminist methodology is reflexive. It calls for a development of social relationships with the people studied, politically engaging with people and seeking their emancipation through dialogical research strategies. The focus is on making women's experiences visible.

Feminist methodology calls for a challenge to the power differential between the researcher and those researched; for the researcher to be conscious of the othering that is frequently fundamental to the research process; and conscious of the propensity of researchers to name others without consultation, to purport to somehow know others better than they know themselves.

DATA COLLECTION TECHNIQUES

The data collection techniques employed in this research encompassed quantitative and qualitative methods with visual elements. The quantitative data very quickly details and contextualises the women's prison in Ireland. It gives a general sense of the women, who they were and why they were imprisoned. It details their numbers, their crimes and their sentences, useful in developing a profile of the prison. The data cannot say very much about who these women are, about why they have been imprisoned or how they feel about their experiences of imprisonment.

While the quantitative data is very useful, it is the qualitative data that serves to elaborate the women's lives, the discourses within which they are interpellated, their prison experiences and, within those experiences, the women's subjective senses of themselves.

Observation: Formal observation was undertaken of six months of multi-disciplinary management meetings at the Dóchas Centre; twelve meetings were attended from 5 December 2000 to 22 May 2001. The meetings were a forum for the managers of the different units or areas within the prison to get together to monitor and plan the workings and the development of the Dóchas Centre. Generally in attendance at the meetings were John Lonergan, then governor of Mountjoy Prison, Kathleen McMahon, then governor of the Dóchas Centre, Catherine Comerford, then assistant governor of the Dóchas Centre, and Aileen Greally, then chief officer in the Dóchas Centre. In addition to these people, the school, trades, the kitchen, the library and the chaplaincy were represented, as were prison officers, probation and welfare representatives, the Healthcare Unit when the doctor joined the staff, and the psychology service when such a service was available within the prison.

In-depth Interviews: Three different sets of in-depth interviews were conducted for this research. In the first set, thirty interviews were carried out with experts involved with the women's prisons; the second set was conducted with women in prison, eighty-three women in total; and the final set, a series of photo elicitation interviews, was conducted with twenty women from the eighty-three originally interviewed. All of the interviews were undertaken using a judgmental sampling method, the researcher decided, based on the aims and objectives of the research and who to interview. The eighty-three interviews were undertaken from time to time using a snowball sampling technique, whereby a woman interviewed would specifically ask that one of her friends be interviewed also. Such requests were made when a woman felt that the potential participant would make a substantial contribution to the research.

The first set of interviews were conducted, as stated, with experts involved with, or working in or with, the women's prison and/or the prison service. This set of interviews gave insight into imprisoned women's experiences of management and into the manner in which experts working with them represent imprisoned women. These interviews also gave an insight into the development of policy in terms of the female prison in Ireland, into its management and staffing, and into the development of the female prison. This data provided an in-depth view of a particular perspective on the experiences of prison provided for women in Ireland, the expert and institutional discourses shaping those experiences, and ascribing identities to the imprisoned women.

The second set of interviews was conducted with eighty-three imprisoned women. The interview schedule used was constructed to facilitate a recording of the lives of the women, their personal lives and personal identities, their experiences of imprisonment and their senses of self. Within this research, the women did not engage in abstract self-refection; any early attempts made to discuss notions of identity with them were met with disinterest. They were interested in and enjoyed discussing and analysing their experiences, and this was the approach taken to these interviews. The areas explored in the interviews included the following: background information, family and home, education and training, work and employment, crime history, experiences of imprisonment, well-being in prison, experiences of addiction, experiences of being represented in the media, and hopes and fears for the future. Taken together, these areas facilitated the women in articulating their lives and their prison experiences. This articulation then allowed for the development of an analysis of the women's identities as they themselves present them.

The interviews were recorded manually because the women indicated that they were more comfortable with that method. Almost all the interviews took place in the women's private rooms/cells. During the interviews, some women lay down on their beds, some sat on a chair at their desk. Refreshments were taken, tea or coffee and biscuits, and most of the women smoked. Some moved around a lot, they went into the bathroom, they spoke from the bathroom, they put on make-up, rearranged their hair, they changed clothes, they sewed and took up hems, they got involved in conversations being carried on outside the room, they asked to go back over areas and issues. Sometimes the woman made a phone call; sometimes she took a phone call, sometimes prison officers called to the room or cell, for one reason or another. Sometimes both interviewer and interviewee went together for lunch or for supper, sometimes they went to meet and chat with other women, they called to the school, to the Healthcare Unit, to the chaplain.

The women generally commented that the interviews were interesting, that they found the process interesting, that it was one in which they could talk, confidentially confide if they wished, for as long as they wanted. The interviews lasted, on average, excluding interruptions and breaks, two and a half hours. One interview was conducted over two days, and three interviews were terminated after an hour. In general, two interviews were conducted per day in the Dóchas Centre. In Limerick Prison more interviews were conducted because the small contained nature of that prison and the level of inactivity generally facilitated this. The manual recording gave the women a sense of what was deemed to be important in the interviews. They were able to check, and they did check, on what was being recorded and why it was recorded. They frequently commented on and questioned the recording, what was recorded and why. They wanted to know why this was written down or why that was not written down and so on, and in this manner they participated in the recording of the interviews as they participated in the interviews. Particularly for women with literacy issues, this method of recording proved most useful; they could – and did – check what was being recorded.

Together, each woman and the interviewer directed the interview collaboratively, but there was an interview schedule. Every woman interviewed had a unique life experience and every one emphasised different areas of her life and experiences in different ways. The schedule used was detailed in order to ensure important issues were not lost, glossed over or forgotten. The interviews were received by those who participated as opportunities to reflect on their life and their prison experiences.

The women in Limerick Prison were interviewed over one weekend in April 2001 and eleven of the twelve women imprisoned there at that time participated in the interviews. In the Dóchas Centre, seventy-two women were interviewed over the months of July and August 2001. The courts were in summer recess at this time and so women were not being committed to the prison. Given the size of the sample of those interviewed, the capacity of the women's prison (seventy-nine) and recidivism rates in excess of 70 per cent among women prisoners in Ireland, this element of the research can be said to be representative of women imprisoned here. The interviews for the most part took place, as stated, privately in the women's rooms. In general they were conducted on a one-to-one basis. In one case, two women were interviewed together, at their request. The interview schedule used with the women in Limerick Prison was amended, given the experience of the process in Limerick, for use with the women in the Dóchas Centre.

In analysing this interview data, initially the quantitative data was inputted into SPSS (Statistical Package for Social Scientists). This facilitated a useful quantitative exploration of data that lent itself to that kind of analysis: the age range among the women, the average age, the number of women who were mothers, the social class of the women, the work they had engaged in, their levels of education, the number of convictions, the sentences imposed upon them, the number of women who smoked, who drank alcohol, who had drug habits or drug addictions, the number of women who had experienced abuse, the numbers who were or who felt vulnerable in prison, the numbers who engaged with the prison schools or who worked or had jobs in prison, the numbers who had been formally disciplined within prison, and so on. This data was used to provide background and context to the women's experiences. The process of breaking the data down into differ-ent and separate variables and categories was also useful in terms of qualitative analysis. However, the effect of the process of cat-egorising the women's responses disrupted, de-contextualised and de-territorialised the women's narratives, and so when this element of data analysis was completed, all the data was drawn together again and compiled into narratives of the women's expe-riences. Following the de-construction for analysis of the women's experiences, these narratives re-constructed the women's lives into meaningful, entire, integrated and individual experiences. Finally, the interview transcripts were divided by national and non-national status and then subdivided by age (into decades) and analysed thematically. The analysis presented in the book represents a synopsis of the quantitative data for context and an elaboration of the qualitative narrative and thematic explorations of these women's life experiences, their prison expe-riences, their personal identities and their senses of self.

Spatial Analysis: The spatial analysis of the female experience of imprisonment led to the development of a visual/photographic exploration of prison space as experienced by women prisoners. The imprisoned women's rooms or cells, areas thought of as their space, and within those spaces their dressing tables, were pho-tographed. Then a final set of interviews, photo-elicitation inter-views, were conducted with twenty women. Women from a relatively broad range of backgrounds, ethnic and cultural heritages were invited to participate. Of the twenty women inter-viewed, seventeen were in the Dóchas Centre and three were in Limerick Prison. Sixteen were Irish, three were South African and there was one woman from Switzerland. The oldest woman was 50 years of age, the youngest 20. Two of the women were serv-ing life sentences, one had effectively been serving life by instalments, seven were serving sentences of four to seven years, three were serving sentences of two to four years and the remainder were serving short sentences. One of the women interviewed was a retired company director, four were homeless, and there were two Traveller women and two black women in the group. One of the women acknowledged being HIV positive, two had been from time to time to the Central Mental Hospital and one was pregnant at the time of interview.

In the photo-elicitation interviews the women discussed the photographs taken of their rooms and they considered and/or explained the significance of the cultural artefacts depicted in the photographs. The issues explored were women's experiences of their personal prison space, the meaning of their artefacts as depicted in the photographs of that space, and their experiences of control within that space. Photo-elicitation is a method whereby the researcher uses photographs to engage the informants in verbal commentary. This involves exploring the photographs with the owners of the object or objects photographed, making full use of their expertise, and encouraging them to photograph and comment on and analyse the photographs and their expression of their identities, their culture and their space. The researcher must make it known to the subjects their taken-for-granted knowledge of the spaces and artefacts depicted in the images is not shared by the researcher and that this knowledge or understanding is the understanding the research is attempting to reach.

In the photographic element of the research the women were offered the use of disposable cameras to photograph their space, but most declined. The women were in their rooms, they were very relaxed, some lay on their beds, and they wanted to talk. They talked about themselves, their lives and their prison experiences. They were interested in the photography that was taking place, the photographing of their spaces rather than photographing the rooms themselves. This represents more an interest on their behalf in an opportunity to talk to someone in a confidential, safe space than an indication of a lack of interest in photographing their space. Their lack of engagement with the photographic project suggests perhaps that the photographic element of the research might have been undertaken separately from the in-depth interviews; however, the in-depth interviews established a rapport between the women and the interviewer, a rapport which served to neutralise, during those interviews, the overt and inherent intrusiveness of the camera. The intention was to capture visually imprisoned women's experiences of prison space and within their personal prison spaces their presentations of self. The camera was used to record a photo inventory of the women's rooms and their dressing tables, their cultural shrines. These cultural shrines provided powerful representations of the women, their creative and aesthetic individuality. While trying essentially to capture a personality, the photographic project was not relying on facial or bodily impressions or expressions to do so and was endeavouring to do it as unobtrusively as possible. In reality, photography cannot be employed as an unobtrusive, non-reactive research method, because it is neither unobtrusive nor non-reactive. It is however a substantial and data-rich research method. It can be used as a validator of other research methods whereby the evidence of the photograph, supported by the participants in the research, can represent and render visible the phenomenon under investigation. The vivid expression of personality in the lived female prison space of their rooms and their dressing tables so full of signs and representations were free from the problematic of photographing living moving individuals where fleeting expressions, mood changes, hair, face, body mass, movement, graceful or graceless, clothes and accessories, companions and props, all possibly unrepresentative in general of the underlying personality, might, through photography, be frozen forever and used falsely as permanent representations of those individuals.

The photographic element of the research required the particular consent and co-operation of the women in the prison. One woman, in the course of the time spent with her in her room interviewing her and taking photographs and inviting her to take photographs, said: 'I know what you're doing, you're trying to explain to them out there what we're really like in here', and that is of course what the researcher was trying to accomplish. The representation of this spatial element of the women's prison experience is critical, it provides a critical insight into the powerful representations of self these women created in their personal prison space. The result of this element of the research is a photo narrative of women's presentations of self within Irish prison space and a cultural inventory of Irish female prison space

Content Analysis: In an analysis of the positioning of the women in contemporary popular discourses, the representations of imprisoned women in the press were explored. Using content analysis, six Sunday newspapers, three broadsheets and three tabloids, were examined over a period of one year, and two daily newspapers, one tabloid and one broadsheet, over a period of six months; in other words, 312 Sunday newspapers and 360 daily newspapers, in total 672 newspapers. The Sunday papers were examined from 1 September 2000 to 1 September 2001 and the dailies from 1 April 2001 to 1 October 2001. This method was chosen rather than a daily analysis over one or two months as it was felt that a broader temporal spread of data collection would be likely to produce a better representation of the print media's construction of female offenders. A quantitative, qualitative and semiotic analysis of the content of the print media revealed the press's construction and representation of the identities of women prisoners and, through that, gave some indication of public and popular perceptions of the women. In all, this trawl through the newspapers yielded fifty-seven newspaper articles. Of the fifty-seven articles, twenty-one were in the tabloid *Evening Herald*, eleven were in the tabloid *Sunday World*, ten were in *The Irish Times*, there were five in the *Sunday Tribune*, four in *Ireland on Sunday* and two in each of the *News of the World*, the *Sunday Independent* and the *Sunday Business Post*. The word count of the articles ranged from 16 to 1,400, with one third of the articles being between 200 and 400 words. Between them the newspapers published forty-four photographs in thirty-five articles; the photographs were of thirteen women. Exactly half of the published photographs were of one woman, Catherine Nevin, convicted of conspiracy to murder her husband and sentenced to life imprisonment. Eight were of Deirdre Rose, convicted for her part in the murder of a young man and sentenced to life imprisonment. Deirdre Rose was released after she had served eighteen months of her life sentence. Two of the photographs were of Regina Felloni, daughter of convicted drug lord Tony Felloni. And three were of Bridie Doran, who was serving the last years of a life sentence imposed on her in the UK for the murder of her husband. Nine other women had one photograph each published in the newspapers.

Archival Analysis: The historic exploration of women's experiences of imprisonment called for the examination of a number of archives and prison records. This involved an analysis of state records and prison records, as well as some private papers and memoirs. The documents in the National Archives and in the National Library were examined, as were documents in the library at Trinity College and in the archive at Kilmainham Gaol. The records of women committed to Mountjoy Prison over a period of one year were analysed, as were those of the women imprisoned in the Dóchas Centre on one day in March 2001. Taken together with the published works on Ireland's female penal history, these documents provided the data for the historical positioning of the female prison in Ireland, for the statistical mapping of the population of the women's prison, and for the analysis of the positioning of Ireland's imprisoned women within historical discourses.

Discourse Analysis: Finally, all of the data gathered for the research came to be understood and subsequently analysed as different discourses. There is a dialectical relation between discourse and other social practices, and so discourse analysis must include analysis of the material and the structural.

In the final analysis, in this study of the discursive subject positioning of Ireland's imprisoned women, all of the discourses were analysed semiotically. Semiotics is the study of signs in society. It is a way of analysing meaning by looking at signs, while signs are the words, pictures, symbols, etc. used by people in society to communicate, to make meaning. This system of signs structures our experience of reality, and it has implications for the ways in which the self, identity, reality and society are understood. Our experience of the social world, our sense even of our own identity, is formed by the systems of communication within which we live our lives. Semiotic resources are the actions and artefacts we use to communicate. Among the obvious means of communication are language, gestures, rules, structures and hierarchies. Among the less obvious sources perhaps are the way we dress, the everyday objects that surround us, and the décor of the spaces we inhabit. These social semiotics are loaded with meaning and cultural significance, and they were studied as part of this research.

There are two components to every sign: one expresses the sign, it is the signifier; the other is that which the signifier represents, the signified. For example, the written word 'hat' is the signifier for the actual object, hat, the signified. Signs operate at different levels of signification. Signs have a function in denoting things, in referring to the *manifest* content of the sign. This is the first level of signification. As well as communicating denotatively, signs also communicate connotatively. This is the second level of signification. Connotation constitutes the *latent* content of what the sign may be said to signify. Communicating connotatively, signs trigger a range of ideas and images related to the *manifest* idea and image represented by the sign. At this second level of signification, signs connect with the ways in which society typically regards that which is being signified. Through connotation, signs, at the third level of signification, can connect with social consensus, often ideological social consensus, and this third level of signification is that of myth.

Myth is an inflexion, it is not a misrepresentation; it is the manner in which a representation is presented. Myth serves the interests of a particular group in society, those who have the means and the power to create and perpetuate the myth. Ways of representing people, institutions, societies, and so on, are structured to communicate particular messages. These messages communicate social and political messages about the world. Reading or decoding the messages in myth involves identifying the signs used and showing how they are built into messages and communications. Myths produce commonsense views of the social world; they make particular social meanings acceptable. The analysis of myth involves removing the impression of naturalness by showing how the myth is constructed and showing that it privileges one way of seeing while repressing others. Ideologies are myths; they are ways of perceiving reality and society which assume that some understandings of the social world are self-evidently true and others self-evidently untrue.

It is through the reiterative use of signs, words and phrases, symbols, rituals and behaviours that social reality is constructed. It is through the reiterative process of constructing the social that roles and identities are constructed. As these roles and identities are constructed, they are appropriated, and ascribed, and they are performed. In this book, the discursive construction and representation of women in prison in Ireland is explored. The women's identities, as they are represented in different discourses, are considered. The ideologies that inform, constrain and produce the women's identities are to some degree exposed.

Permissions: Permission at policy level to conduct the research was granted by Mr Sean Aylward, then director general of the Prison Service and now secretary general of the Department of Justice, Equality and Law Reform; John Lonergan, then governor of Mountjoy Prison, now retired; the late governor Pat Laffan of Limerick Prison; and Kathleen McMahon, former governor of the Dóchas Centre, now retired.

Select Bibliography

Annual Inspectors' General Reports on Irish Prisons, relevant years, the National Library, Kildare Street, Dublin

Annual Prison Reports, relevant years, published by the Department of Justice, Equality and Law Reform, Dublin

Bachelard, G. *The Poetics of Space* (Boston: Beacon Press, 1969)

Bacik, I., Kelly, A., O'Connell, M. and Sinclair, H. 'Crime and Poverty in Dublin: An Analysis of the Association between Community Deprivation, District Court Appearance and Sentence Severity', *Irish Criminal Law Journal*, vol. 7 (1977), pp.104–33

Bacik, I. and O'Connell, M. *Crime and Poverty in Ireland* (Dublin: Roundhall, Sweet & Maxwell, 1998)

Bacik, I. 'Women and the Criminal Justice System', in P. O'Mahony (ed.), *Criminal Justice in Ireland* (Dublin: Institute of Public Administration, 2002)

Bacik, I., Costello, C. and Drew, E. *Gender in Justice* (Dublin: Trinity College Law School, 2003)

Bartky, Lee S. *Femininity and Domination: Studies in the Phenomenology of Oppression* (New York and London: Routledge, 1990)

Baudrillard, J. 'The System of Collecting', in J. Elsner and R. Cardinal (eds), *Cultures of Collecting* (London: Reaktion, 1994), pp.7–24

Baudrillard, J. *The System of Objects* (London: Verso, 1996)

Beaumont, C. 'Gender, Citizenship and the State in Ireland, 1922–1990', in D. Alderson, F. Becket, S. Brewster and V. Crossman (eds), *Ireland in Proximity: History, Gender, Space* (London: Routledge, 1999)

Beck, U. *Risk Society* (London: Sage, 1992)

Becker, H.S. 'Photography and Sociology', *Studies in the Anthropology of Visual Communication*, 1, 1 (1974), pp.3–26

Bell, V. *Performativity and Belonging* (London: Sage, 1999)

Berger, J. *Ways of Seeing* (London: Penguin, 1972)

Berger, P. and Luckman, T. *The Social Construction of Reality: A Treatise in the Sociology of Knowledge* (London: Penguin, 1991)

Bosworth, M. 'Resistance and Compliance in Women's Prisons: Towards a Critique of Legitimacy', *Critical Criminology*, 7, 2 (1998), pp.5–19

Bosworth, M. *Engendering Resistance: Agency and Power in the Women's Prisons* (Aldershot: Ashgate, 1999)

Bourdieu, P. *Language and Symbolic Power* (Cambridge: Polity 1991)

Bourdieu, P. *Masculine Domination* (Cambridge: Polity, 2001)

Butler, J. *Gender Trouble: Feminism and the Subversion of Identity* (New York: Routledge, 1990)

Butler, J. *Bodies that Matter: On the Discursive Limits of Sex* (New York: Routledge, 1993)

Carey, T. *Mountjoy: The Story of a Prison* (Cork: The Collins Press, 2000)

Carlen, P. *Women's Imprisonment: A Study in Social Control* (London: Routledge & Kegan Paul, 1983)

Carlen, P. *Criminal Women* (Cambridge: Polity, 1985)

Carlen, P. and Worrall, A. *Gender, Crime and Justice* (Milton Keynes: Open University Press, 1987)

Carlen, P. *Women, Crime and Poverty* (Milton Keynes: Open University Press, 1988)

Carlen, P. *Sledgehammer: Women's Imprisonment at the Millennium* (London: Palgrave Macmillan, 1998)

Carlen, P. *Women and Punishment: The Struggle for Justice* (Abingdon: Willan, 2002)

Carlen, P. and Worrall, A. *Analysing Women's Imprisonment* (Abingdon: Willan, 2004)

Carmody, P. and McEvoy, M. *A Study of Irish Female Prisoners* (Dublin: Stationery Office, 1996)

Centre for Health Promotion Studies, National University of Ireland, Galway, *Healthcare Study of the Prisoner Population* (Dublin: Stationery Office, 2000)

Connelly, A. *Gender and the Law in Ireland* (Dublin: Oak Tree Press, 1993)

Cooke, P. *A History of Kilmainham Gaol* (Dublin: Stationery Office, 1995)

Cullen Owens, R. *Smashing Times: A History of the Irish Women's Suffrage Movement, 1889–1922* (Dublin: Attic Press, 1984)

Curtin, G. *The Women of Galway Gaol* (Galway: Arlen House, 2001)

Dobash, R.P., Dobash, R.E. and Gutteridge, S. *The Imprisonment of Women* (New York: Blackwell, 1986)

European Committee for the Prevention of Torture and Inhuman or Degrading Treatment or Punishment (CPT), *Report to the Government of Ireland on the Visit to Ireland*, 36 (2003)

Fairclough, N. *Critical Discourse Analysis: The Critical Study of Language* (London: Pearson, 1995)

Finkelstein, E. 'Status Degradation and Organisational Succession in Prison', *British Journal of Sociology*, 47, 4 (1996), pp.671–83

Foucault, M. *Madness and Civilization: A History of Insanity in the Age of Reason* (London: Routledge, 1971)

Foucault, M. *Discipline and Punish: The Birth of the Prison* (London: Penguin, 1977)

Garland, D. *Punishment and Modern Society: A Study in Social Theory* (Chicago: University of Chicago Press, 1990)

Garland, D. *The Culture of Control: Crime and Social Order in Contemporary Society* (Chicago: University of Chicago Press, 2002)

Geertz, C. *The Interpretation of Cultures* (London: Fontana, 1993)

Giddens, A. *Modernity and Self-Identity* (Palo Alto, CA: Stanford University Press, 1991)

Grosz, E. *Space, Time and Perversion: Essays on the Politics of Bodies* (New York: Routledge, 1995)

Hall, E.T. *The Hidden Dimension* (New York: Doubleday, 1966)

Hannah-Moffat, K. *Punishment in Disguise: Penal Governance and Canadian Women's Imprisonment* (Toronto: University of Toronto Press, 2001)

Harper, D. 'Seeing Sociology', *The American Sociologist*, 37, 3 (1996), pp.69–78

Hayes, A. and Urquhart, D. (eds), *The Irish Women's History Reader* (London: Routledge, 2001)

Heidensohn, F. *Women and Crime* (London: Macmillan, 1985)

Heidensohn, F. *Crime and Society* (London: Macmillan, 1989)

Ignatieff, M. *A Just Measure of Pain* (London: Penguin, 1978)

Inglis, T. *Lessons in Irish Sexuality* (Dublin: University College Dublin Press, 1998)

Irigaray, L, *This Sex Which is Not One* (Ithica, NY: Cornell University Press, 1985)

Irigaray, L. *An Ethics of Sexual Difference* (Ithica, NY: Cornell University Press, 1993)

Kavanagh, R. *Mamie Cadden, Backstreet Abortionist* (Cork: Mercier Press, 2005)

Kilcommins, S., O'Donnell, I., O'Sullivan, E. and Vaughan, B. *Crime, Punishment and the Search for Order in Ireland* (Dublin: Institute of Public Administration, 2004)

Lash, S. and Urry, J, *Economies of Signs and Space* (London: Sage, 1994)

Lefebvre, H, *The Production of Space* (Oxford: Blackwell, 1991)

Lombroso, C. and Ferrero, W. *The Female Offender* (New York: Wisdom Library, 1958)

Luddy, M. *Women and Philanthropy in Nineteenth-Century Ireland* (Cambridge: Cambridge University Press, 1995)

Luddy, M. *Prostitution and Irish Society, 1800–1940* (Cambridge: Cambridge University Press, 2008)

Luddy, M. *Women in Irish History from Famine to Feminism, 1850–2000* (London: Routledge, 2010)

Maalouf, A. *On Identity* (London: Harvill Press, 2000)

Massey, D. *Space, Place and Gender* (Cambridge: Polity, 1994)

Mathiesen, T. *Prison on Trial: A Critical Assessment* (London: Sage Publications, 1990)

O'Mahony, P. *Criminal Justice in Ireland* (Dublin: Institute of Public Administration, 2002)

Osborough, N. *Borstal in Ireland: Custodial Provision for the Young Adult Offender, 1906–1974* (Dublin: Institute of Public Administration, 1975)

Pollak, O. *The Criminality of Women* (New York: A.S. Barnes, 1950)

Prior, P. *Madness and Murder: Gender, Crime and Mental Disorder in Nineteenth-Century Ireland* (Dublin: Irish Academic Press, 2008)

Prior, P. 'Mad, Not Bad: Crime, Mental Disorder and Gender in Nineteenth-Century Ireland', *History of Psychiatry*, 8, 4 (1997), pp.501–16

Quinlan, C. 'The Women We Imprison', *Irish Criminal Law Journal*, 13, 1 (2003), pp.2–7

Quinlan, C. 'A Journey into the Women's Prison', *Women's Studies Review*, vol. 9 (2004), pp.59–70

Radke, H.L. and Stam, H.J. (eds), *Power/Gender: Social Relations in Theory and Practice* (London: Sage, 1994)

Raftery, M. and O'Sullivan, E. *Suffer the Little Children: The Inside Story of Ireland's Industrial Schools* (Dublin: New Island, 1999)

Rawls, J. *A Theory of Justice* (Cambridge, MA: Belknap Press, 1999)

Ricoeur, P. *Oneself as Another* (Chicago: University of Chicago Press, 1994)

Rose, G. *Feminism and Geography* (Cambridge: Polity, 1993)

Sim, J. *Medical Power in Prisons: The Prison Medical Service in England, 1774–1989* (Milton Keynes: Open University Press, 1990)

Sim, J. '"We Are Not Animals, We Are Human Beings": Prisons, Protests and Politics in England and Wales, 1969–1990', *Social Justice*, 18, 3 (1991), pp.107–29

Thomas, W.I. *The Unadjusted Girl* (New York: Harper & Row, 1967)

Van Leeuwen, T. *Introducing Social Semiotics* (London: Routledge, 2005)

Van Zoonen, L. *Feminist Media Studies* (London: Sage, 1994)

Various Prison Registers, National Archives of Ireland, Bishop Street, Dublin 8
  The Mountjoy Prison Female Convict Register (1868–75)
  The Register of Vagrants/The Register of Old Offenders
  The Register of Prisoners Committed under the Habitua Criminal Act (1869)
  The Register of Female Prisoners Committed for Further Examination
  The Register for Female Prisoners, Grangegorman
  The Register of Drunkards

Walby, S, *Theorising Patriarchy* (Oxford: Blackwell, 1990)

Ward, M. (ed.), *In Their Own Voice: Women and Irish Nationalism* (Cork: Attic Press, 1995)

Woodward, K. *Identity and Difference: Culture, Media and Identities* (London: Sage, 1997)

Woodward, K. *Understanding Identity (Understanding Media Series)* (London: Hodder Arnold, 2003)

Worrall, A. *Offending Women: Female Lawbreakers and the Criminal Justice System* (London: Routledge, 1990)

Index